D0567239

A FIRM FAITH FOR TODAY

A FIRM FAITH FOR TODAY

By

HAROLD A. BOSLEY, Ph.D.

HARPER & BROTHERS PUBLISHERS
NEW YORK

234

A FIRM FAITH FOR TODAY

FIRST EDITION

A-Z

TO

THE METHODIST PREACHERS MEETING

OF

BALTIMORE AND VICINITY

"ESTEEMED COLLEAGUES IN THE CHRISTIAN MINISTRY"

CONTENTS

PREFACE

I have always envied authors who could gaze fondly at a completed manuscript and say, "This book wrote itself." That is one thing, among many others, I cannot say about this book. Most emphatically, it did not write itself. It had to be written, initially, because a preacher in the city of Baltimore Sunday after Sunday faced a congregation that trusted him to "break the bread of life" to them. And, during the decade—1938–1948—nothing less than "the bread of life" could hope to meet the challenge of spiritual famine that was descending on mankind.

This book had to be rewritten because the Preachers Meeting of Baltimore and Vicinity was kind enough to set aside half a dozen Monday mornings in order to hear several of the discussions—and, as brethren will, lay heavy but helpful hands upon method and content. The keenness of their interest, the warmth of their encouragement elicited from me the pledge that, if ever the efforts saw the light of the printed page, they would be dedicated to them—my colleagues in the ministry.

A second rewriting of the book was demanded by the singularly searching experience of presenting much of the material in Religious Emphasis Week programs at colleges and universities and ministers' conferences in various sections of the country. Many of those long and sometimes heated forum sessions have left their imprint on the book. I stand to testify to two things about this generation of college students: first, they are keenly and deeply interested in religion; second, they will demand the intellectual passports of any and every idea, however hallowed, before they will embrace it. And, I say, "Thank God for this!" A religion that cannot survive and be enriched by their probing, anxious, earnest minds, is a mean and pathetic heir of one of the greatest traditions of rational religion known to man. The Christian faith can be presented—and in some quarters is being presented—as either antirational or suprarational: yet neither of these presentations can finally do full justice to the rational realism of our faith. Every theological effort must finally answer the terse question, "Does it make sense? If so, why, how, to whom, and in terms of what evidence?"

There are still some in the intellectual "élite" who would write off the ministry as being the final refuge of well-intentioned, good-hearted, but none too "sharp" men patterned after the bumbling rector in "Life with Father." May I suggest to all who cherish this notion, and who want to continue to hold it, that they stay a long sea mile away from ministers' conferences, pastors' schools, and theological seminaries these days? The intellectual ferment, the keen sense of responsibility, the humble awareness of the relevance of religion to the great issues of our time, so characteristic of such groups, is one of the most gratifying signs of the times. The quality and quantity of young men entering the ministry is indubitable assurance that this new interest and vision will be passed as a flaming beacon from one generation to another.

The various items of historic faith that will be studied in the succeeding pages have not been selected at random. They are the ones that have had a major influence in the development of Christian thought and ethics. Rather than spend many pages studying the historical steps by which each one grew to greatness I have usually centered attention almost exclusively on the kinds of evidence which give them contemporary validity today. In the three exceptions (Chapters X, XI, XII), it seemed wise to invoke the aid of history more copiously in order to illustrate the complex nature of the ideas.

To one who is interested in and acquainted with theological "labels," the method of studying the problems and the manner of stating the conclusions are those of liberalism. Orthodoxy in one form or other has had a great vogue over the last thirty years, and we should be grateful for the striking manner in which it has insisted upon the essential validity of the historic faith. Yet it has unnecessarily weakened its witness by a refusal to come to terms with the method and many of the conclusions of the whole range of scientific studies. It—orthodoxy—insists upon an *a priori* acceptance of the essential truthfulness of the creeds; it usually is scandalized by the demand that it "prove" them. Liberalism seeks to help orthodoxy—whether classical or neo—out of this embarrassment by accepting the validity of science and the legitimacy of the request for proof. In this book, I have refused to set science over against religion, or to place emphasis upon those religious claims, however hallowed, that do not square with the nature of reality as seen in or suggested by the conclusions of science.

To theologians who deplore this equation of the insights of science with those of religion, I can only reply that I fail to see why, in a rational universe, a reasonable statement of faith should be regarded as a scandal. A theology that emphasizes "faith" as superior to "reason" is not only irrational in method and conclusion, it seeks to affirm the fundamental irrationality of all efforts to know, to understand this divinely created universe. To me, the determination to make a rational statement of faith in terms of known facts is a humble way of saying that we believe that God knows what He is about, and that, in part, we can know it too. This book is an effort to state that faith in a more explicit manner.

Several of the chapters in this book constituted the James W. Richard Lectures in Christian Religion at the University of Virginia in the fall of 1949. Other materials presented in these lectures were drawn freely from the range of subjects here discussed.

Similarly some of the material found its way into the Swander Lectures at the Theological Seminary of the Evangelical and Reformed Church, Lancaster, Pennsylvania, in 1949.

Portions of Chapter X were used in preparing the study booklet *Our Faith in the Kingdom of God* which was published by the Methodist Church in October, 1949. The preparation of the booklet was undertaken with the understanding that the material would appear in book form at a later date.

I wish to thank the publishers of the various books and journals quoted here for their courtesy in granting permission. Obviously, a book like this would be impossible without such gracious cooperation.

I am deeply indebted to the officials of the University of Virginia and of the Theological Seminary of the Evangelical and Reformed Church both for the invitation to deliver the lectures and for the many courtesies shown me while on their campuses.

Three of these chapters were printed in the *Bulletin* of Birmingham-Southern College in December, 1948.

One word more—of a personal nature. I have emerged from the process of preparing, sharing, and writing this book a confirmed churchman. Although a "practicing parson" when I entered it, my belief in the Church (in the necessity, the practicality, the relevance, the mission, the commission of the Church, call it what you will) was none too strong. Those doubts now have their full answer in the clear-headed, warm-hearted, and free fellowship I have found not alone in individual congregations—particularly the Mount Vernon Place Church in Baltimore—but also in more general gatherings of churchmen: the Annual, Jurisdictional, and

General Conferences of the Methodist Church, the Federal Council of Churches, and the World Council of Churches. Although such gatherings are all too frequently enmeshed in trivialities and seem to move forward at a snail's pace in an age when time is of the essence, they do move, and with a sure sense of true direction and ultimate goal. In this fellowship I am proud to find my place and bear such witness as I can to Him Who is the Light of the world.

HAROLD A. BOSLEY

Divinity School
Duke University
Durham, North Carolina

A FIRM FAITH FOR TODAY

IT IS now obvious that for a number of generations we have been attempting to hold on to Christian practices without possessing Christian beliefs. But Christian behavior, which is not supported by Christian faith, is a wasting asset, as we have discovered to our great dismay.

—Arnold Toynbee

I

Why a Creed in Religion?

I

It is difficult to know how seriously to take the claim that we are witnessing a return to religion these days. " 'Tis a consummation devoutly to be wished"—if true! But how much truth is there in it?

Obviously, there is much active interest in and concern about religion just now among many who paid little or no attention to it ten years ago. But I cannot help wondering how serious and searching their interest is. Much of it reminds me of a comment made by the captain of a fishing boat when taking a party into an area of the bay where the fish were plainly breaking the surface of the water. The excited fishermen were certain they were in luck. But the captain observed, "They're breakin' but they're not bitin'." How much of the contemporary interest in religion is like this we cannot say. But we can say with confidence that interest in religion, of itself, is not a return to religion. Concern and commitment are two quite different matters. Concern about religion lacks a lot of being commitment to the religious way of life. It is the first step, to be sure—and we ought to be glad for the renewal of interest in religion—but taking the first step is just so much exercise and actually puts one in a precarious position unless it is followed by the second, third, and all remaining steps which must be taken before the stairs are climbed.

It is beginning to look tragically like this: we are interested in religion, but our interest stops short of obligation; we are concerned about it, but our concern stops short of commitment. We are "breakin' but not bitin'." We are dallying around on the first step rather than climbing the remaining ones.

You ask, "What difference does it make whether there is an actual return to religion?" I reply, "The difference it has always made! All the difference between life and death for all that we hold dear in our civilization!" Consider the desperate spiritual plight of the modern world and you will understand the dire need for a real return to religion.

It might be supposed that fifty years of unrelieved tragedy would have destroyed our conceit in our ability to find or fashion an easy way out of the enveloping doom which is threatening us all.

Among the alternatives confronting us there is no easy way. All are hard—hard to the point of despair. As we study them this simple truth comes hammering home: We must either be the best generation, morally and spiritually speaking, that this old world has ever seen, or we will be the last one. We must either rise to heights of personal and social living that heretofore men have either only dreamed of or talked about as some *summum bonum* to be reached if and when the millennium should come, or be prepared to face the very great probability that the curtain of history will drop on man and all his works in our own lifetime.

You would think that we would be about ready to re-examine with the greatest of care the principles by which and the purposes for which we live. Knowing that this world is one community; knowing that we must conduct ourselves as neighbors or perish—we nonetheless refuse to take seriously the religious ideal of brotherhood. Yet there is no other sure foundation upon which we can hope to build a world community. This being true, we need a great new ethical impulse in order to drive our thinking and living into new channels with sufficient force to remake and remold the structure of our civilization. We need a new ethical system both for our personal living and for our social policies. While much of value can be salvaged from the ethical systems that we have followed in the past, it must be made part and parcel of the building of an entirely new design—the design of one world.

Needing a new ethical system as we do, you would think that we would take seriously the fact that religion is the only force able to create and empower such a redemptive impulse. Religion alone can make ethics a living force in life. When religion is barbaric, its ethical system will foster and perpetuate injustices and tragedies of one kind and another. When religion is enlightened and humane, its ethical system will be the force for world community which we so sorely need. But the point I am making just now is this: religion and ethics go hand in hand. If we are going to have a new ethical structure for our thinking and our living today, it will be because we have a genuine return to the realities of religion.

There was a time, not long ago, when many thought and some said "Science will sire our ethics." I have not heard that mentioned since August, 1945! Evidently a good many things were destroyed by the blast of that bomb besides the lives and buildings of the unhappy people in the cities of Hiroshima and Nagasaki.

An ethic without religion is like a machine without power. To be sure, noble ethical systems have been founded on philosophical principles, but, at best, they have been able to do no more than the Ethical Culture movement in several eastern cities of this country. They gather a few choice spirits into their fellowship, but miss the masses whose corporate thought and life must be changed if we are to be saved. The great historic religions have been great precisely because they were able to appeal to the ordinary person without neglecting the intellectual and the mystic. That is why a widespread and deep-lying return to religion would be the best of good news now—if true. But is it true? How deep-seated is this movement to open the doors of our individual and collective lives to the recreative, redemptive forces of religious faith?

I confess to great disappointment as I seek the answer to inquiries like these:

Do people want to become intelligent heirs of the great rational tradition of the Christian faith?

Do they want to become sensitive participants in the Christian fellowship?

Do they want to become responsible members of a Christian church?

Do they propose to become courageous exemplars of the highest and finest ethical ideals of the Christian faith?

Are they willing to become active instruments of the God who is seeking to "make all things new" in human life?

The answers I get amount to a demurrer if not an outright denial of any such thoroughgoing intention on the part of those who want to "return to religion."

To put it bluntly and without benefit of a metaphor, this seems to be a fair over-all picture of what they want. Some want a religion without ethics. Others want a religion without creed, doctrine, or dogma. Many want a religion without a church or any clear-cut kind of social organization. Very few seem to see that they are asking the impossible and the indefensible when they seek such things. They would not think of asking science to proceed without laws, theories, laboratories, and tested experimental techniques; or education to proceed without reference to its cultural background, its ideals of good citizenship, and a definite organization for regular and systematic instruction. Yet they have no scruples about requesting that religion be considered as a thing apart from ethic, creed, and organization.

Taken all in all, what such people want is not a vital, organic religious faith but simply *a piece of one*. Instead of the full-rigged ship of great religious conviction, they want a sort of floating spar to which they can attach their shipwrecked, frightened souls while they hopefully wait for another ship flying the colors of paganism and secularism to come along and rescue them both from the dangers of the deep and the rigors of real religion. To alter the metaphor, they do not want religion to rebuild their lives; they want it to redecorate them.

But just when I am about to fall with bell, book, and candle upon people who make these incredible requests of religion, I am brought up short by two sobering facts.

First, there is a measure of truth in their request. The ethic, creed, and organization of religion are ways in which the experience of God asserts itself to and interprets itself in human life and history. Ethic, creed, and organization are the body of religion; the experience of God is its soul. While the two cannot and should not be separated by thoughtful people, the impulse to return to that which is deeper than ethic, creed, and organization is essentially sound.

This leads to the second consideration—a question which ought to probe the soul of every professing Christian: Who is primarily responsible for the widespread idea that religion is something separate and apart from ethic, creed, and organization? We churchmen stand before that question even as the stricken David stood before the striking finger of Nathan as the prophet cried, "Thou art the man!" Some of us have treated ethic, creed, and organization as practical ultimates, as ends in themselves, centering attention upon a correct pattern of words, or a proper code of conduct—almost always purely personal in nature with certain acts of charity thrown in on the side and called "the social gospel"—or the orderly organization of church life. Others of us have gone to the opposite extreme. We have treated ethic, creed, and organization as quite unimportant aspects of religion, centering attention upon the mystical and personal experience of the Divine.

The modern world is doing little more than exploiting the gap which we have made, whether intentionally or not, in the organic life of religious faith. The least we can do is to close that gap as soon as possible in our own thinking and living. To do this requires that we both think of and present religion as an organic, living whole in which the primary experience of God finds its normal and sincere expression in the intellectual, ethical, and social life of a person and society. A distinguished Christian leader, Sir Walter Moberly, warned us of our responsibility in this matter, "If the world is once again to be united to try the Christian way, the first necessity is that Christians should themselves regain some clear corporate conviction of what that way is. Here our greatest danger is that we are likely to underestimate our present intellectual bankruptcy. . . . If the Church is again to be a force in the world of affairs, it will have to rediscover its fundamental theology."[1]

What is proposed for this series of studies is that we shall seek to close the gap between creed and religious experience. Similar studies can and should be made of the relationship between the experience of God and ethics and organization. Such studies as these are but preludes to a reorientation of life under the guidance of religious insight. The actual reorientation must be worked out step by step by each person who seeks to live as becomes a servant of the Living God.

II

The first long step in the direction of appraising the worth of a creed is to be sure we understand what "creed" means.

Creed is a name for a system of beliefs held to be vital in religion. The word itself comes from the Latin word *credo* which means "I believe." Its use, historically, has been restricted quite largely to religious beliefs. However its metaphorical use to denote basic beliefs in any field is now common. A creed contains what a philosopher might call the first principles of religion, or a scientist might call the logical system of religious belief. As such it is a rock-bottom necessity in clear-headed religious faith. For a man to proceed without a creed in religion is actually to proceed without any clear sense of where he is going or why he is going there.

But it is easy to claim too much for a creed. A creed is not the whole of religious belief. Neither is the center the whole of a circle, nor the foundation the whole of a house. But the center is of fundamental importance in the being of a circle! It is essential to any circumference it may have; all diameters pass through it; all radii use it as one of their terminals. Ever since Jesus' day, the Christian faith has possessed a sure understanding of the importance of a solid foundation to a good house. While not the whole house, the whole house depends upon it in several significant ways. It determines the lines and the proportions of the walls of the house; it warns the builder what can and cannot be done if he would have the house stand. A creed is the intellectual center or foundation of a religious faith. It is a determining factor in all that religion means and hopes to mean in human life. It is a clear, concise statement of the basic ideas and aspirations of a religion.

A creed is a brief biography of religious faith. Every religious idea, doctrine, or dogma has a biography, and we will need to be acquainted with it if we would truly appreciate and understand the importance of the idea or doctrine. None of the central beliefs of Christianity—God, Christ, Salvation, and Grace, to list but a few—sprang into being in the full bloom of their maturity as Minerva sprang from the mind of Zeus. Hundreds, even thousands of years of human experience have gone into their growth and testing. They are a part of all that they have met in their long, slow journey through history.

A creed presents, in brief form, the conclusions to which the religious experience of generations has led. At this point it is especially necessary to state exactly what we mean. A creed represents *a conclusion* for the ones who reached it and put it in its form at that time. But it represents *an introduction* to anyone else—an introduction to the entire area of experience and argument which it seeks to summarize. No man can honestly claim it as a conclusion for himself unless it actually concludes something, brings to an end an argument, puts in acceptable form the lessons of experience which preceded its formulation. It is entirely fitting that one of the first great creeds of Christendom—the Nicene Creed—was part of the baptismal ceremony of one part of the early Church. That indicates the proper use and meaning of a creed. Even as baptism introduces life to new areas of divine meaning, a creed introduces us to new areas of man's experience of God and efforts to understand it.

In all humility, let us never forget that a creed is not a statement of all we ought to know, or all we want to know, or all we will ever know about the reality of God. But it is an indispensably important statement of hard-won knowledge as it has been hammered out on the anvil of human experience by the hammer of clear thinking. It is simply impossible for any man or church to pretend that it can write a Q.E.D. to the process of creed-making which has gone on apace in the Christian tradition for nearly two thousand years now. We shall make and modify creeds so long as religious experience continues to unfold in the lives of men. For "God is not dead"; He is at work in His world and in the lives of His people. Who can say that another Augustine, or Aquinas, or Luther, or Calvin cannot arise and recast our creedal formulations under the mighty impulse of a new outpouring of the Spirit of the Living God in the lives of men? It is best always to be humble in the presence of Him whose eternal nature is the subject of all our creeds!

A creed, therefore, should be regarded not as an exhaustive description of religious faith but as a finger pointing at the transcendent fact of Almighty God.

The inadequacy of language arises to haunt the creed-maker even as it troubles anyone who seeks to describe the great and eternal values in human experience. In a universe where even the simplest facts have wide margins of mystery, is it to be wondered at that in our search for proper modes of expression we apply the adage, "If at first you don't succeed, try, try again?" And that is what we have to do whether we are trying to tell someone of our love in the form of a proposal or seeking to state the essential attributes of faith in the form of a creedal confession. The confusion of the lover is an excellent illustration of the inadequacy of language, whether he uses prose or resorts to poetry. Invariably he becomes confused in his expressions for the simple reason that his feelings are so powerful that they keep blowing the fuse of his vocabulary—and his words die out precisely when he needs them most, but, fortunately, a wise listener will not mistake his confusion or silence for lack of love! The creed-maker, seeking to express his love of God, experiences a similar difficulty.

All of the great realities of life, like Mount Everest, defy every attempt to scale their mysterious heights by means of the concepts at our disposal. Someday Mount Everest itself may be scaled, but a reasonable doubt will not down that we shall ever be able to encompass the infinite meanings of God in the finite nets of our concepts. Yet, something in us will not let us give up the effort. As reasonable beings we know no other reaction to a mystery than that of attempting to understand and share it with others.

III

Why, specifically, do we need creeds in religion? Why not a creedless faith, as some of our contemporaries seem to be advocating? Among the many answers that might be given several stand out as being of primary importance.

Man is a rational being in religion as well as in every other area of life. He is not always and is never entirely rational, but one of the aims of civilized man is to be able to understand, to be able to give a reason for the faith that is in him.

The effort to be rational can be carried to ridiculous extremes. Lord Kelvin was one of England's greatest scientists. He prided himself on being thoroughly rational in every move he made. When he decided to seek a wife he listed eleven characteristics which she must have in order to be a satisfactory companion in marriage. Armed with this "yardstick" he went among the ladies, finally making his selection. Romanticists have always taken great glee in recording the fact that these rationally matched beings could not stand each other longer than a few months!

Despite the admitted hazards of trying to be rational about the great experiences of life the plain fact remains that the only alternative to a reasoned faith is an unreasoned one. Once turn our backs upon reason and we shall find ourselves screaming with Hitler, "I think with my blood!" Unless we think with our heads, by means of clearly defined terms placed in a logical relationship with each other and woven into a meaningful system of ideas and closely related to the problems of daily living, we shall be little better than animals blown hither and yon by gusts of one fierce emotion after another. A creed is a serious and sustained attempt to be rational in religion and will be accepted as essential by anyone who appreciates the role of reason in human life.

A creed is a strong binding tie to tradition. To say that we accept a creed may mean more but it never means less than to say that we propose to treat the conclusions of our fathers with the respect due any and all serious summations of experience and insight. Whoever objects to this needs to be confronted with Jowett's reminder that "None of us are infallible, not even the youngest."

An intelligent traditionalism—as distinguished from a blind conservatism—is one of the permanent needs of great religion. There are two sure ways in which religion can commit intellectual suicide: (1) cut itself off from its historic tradition; (2) bow down slavishly before it as fixed, final, and immutable truth. The only alternative to these avenues to death is a discriminating traditionalism; one that seeks to understand and dares to criticize the formulations of faith that it has inherited. Tennyson counseled his readers to:

> Love thou thy land with a love
> Far brought from out the storied past.

That is excellent advice to religionists. To follow it does not keep us from "seeing for ourselves," nor does it deny us the peril of facing an uncertain future, but it does link our life and thought with the past in such a way that we are made wiser and stronger men of faith.

A creed is the embodiment of triumphant faith. ". . . Our creeds are not only statements of belief, but paeans of triumph over defeated heretics and heathen."[2] Our creeds were written by the victors to be sure, *but their writers were victorious.* They were not written by quitters, sulkers, or spectators. Men who had borne the heat of the battle poured their life into the verbal formulations which we repeat all too easily and glibly Sunday after Sunday. Creeds are not thought out in studies; they are hammered out in life. And if it is a victorious life, the creed will be radiant with victory. That is why the great creeds of Christendom are shouts of victory and confidence; and that is one of the deepest reasons why we need to know them better these days. To accept a creed, to use it with joy and confidence, need not, should not, betray us into the perennial tragedy of dogmatism. Dogmatism is a creed with a club in its hand, willing to persuade if possible but willing to pound if necessary in order to secure conformity. An intelligent use of the creed will, as its first act, forswear dogmatism. It will make plain to all that the creed is a guarantee against incoherence and is an intelligent bridge between the experiences of yesterday and the exigencies of today and tomorrow.

A creed is indispensable to an evangelistic message and mission. It is an ironical fact that at the turn of the century, when it was the fashion for religion to give up its creeds, the nascent social and political revolutions were formulating and propagating theirs. Study the spread of socialism in Europe since the days of Karl Marx and you will be impressed with the enormous amount of time spent in defining the essentials of that faith. Whitehead points out that "The great ages of religion were the ages of rationalism," the ages when men knew what they believed and were able to defend it if need be and share it if possible with all comers. There is no point trying to take an incoherent religious faith to a thoughtful, rational people like the Chinese any more than there was any chance of early Christianity winning Greece until men like Clement of Alexandria and Origen had

A creed is an intellectual center of a religious faith.

sharpened it up for the questions that were being hurled at it from every angle.

We know now, to our sorrow, that one of the many weaknesses of modernism or the liberal movement in religion is its unwillingness or inability to state with clarity what it believes to be worthy of belief. This lack has deprived it of one of the most effective ways of transmitting a religious tradition through education. When we have ceased making sport of the wooden way in which the various kinds of catechisms have been used, or misused, in traditional religion, we shall want to take due note of the fact that it was in this manner that the vocabulary if not the ideas and ideals of the Christian faith impregnated our Western culture. A creed is essential to effective religious education—a fact we shall not want to overlook in our attempts to revitalize that portion of the church program.

IV

There have been many formulations of faith in the two millennia of Christian history. Some are ancient of origin, others recent. Some are used in a more or less serious manner by large numbers of churches; others are used by only a few. But all are serious and sustained efforts to articulate the Christian faith and, as such, demand respectful attention and treatment.

Two of the earliest creedal formulas used in the Christian movement are brief and, on their face, simple. Peter's confession "Thou art the Christ the Son of the Living God" states the heart of the message that the apostles were taking through the Greco-Roman world. An even shorter formulation is this: "Jesus is Lord." It is hard to realize that the faith symbolized in these three words carried Christianity through the period of bitter persecutions to victory over the Roman Empire. It was the center of some of the hardest choices Christians were called on to make. For the formula of civic loyalty in the empire was the willingness to stand before the idols symbolizing the empire and the emperor and place a pinch of incense on the fire, repeating the words, "Caesar is lord." When the great leaders of the Christian sect refused to do this they were regarded and treated as traitors. To them, it was a denial of Jesus Christ to say other than "Jesus is Lord."

Important as it was, this formula was much too simple to carry conviction to the cultured and educated classes of that day. When the Christian protagonists began to state their case in the forums, schools, and courts of Greece, Rome, and Egypt they ran into a literal hail of probing questions. The writings of men like Clement of Alexandria testify to the sheer necessity of careful exposition of the gospel in the face of the acute inquiries which confronted them in the cultural centers of the time. It became necessary for the Christian movement to develop "schools" for the exposition and defense of the faith in places like Alexandria, Antioch, Athens, Corinth, Rome, and many other centers of life. Under their guidance, Christian thought began to unfold and the simple creeds began to grow more complex as the leaders sought to maintain a general unity of belief throughout the Church. Persuasion was used wherever possible, but coercion left its livid scars over the intellectual formulations of the early Church.

Probably the most influential creed ever formulated is the Nicene Creed, adopted with many dissenting votes by the Council of Nicaea in the year A.D. 325. It put a formal end to the violent dispute between the Arians and the Athanasians over the relationship of Jesus to God by accepting the trinitarian formula. This proved to be the foundation for all later creedal formulations. It drew the dividing line between orthodoxy and heresy, enabling the Church to bring a measure of unity in a movement that was falling apart into many quarreling sects.

I believe in one God the Father Almighty, Maker of heaven and earth, and of all things visible and invisible:

And in one Lord Jesus Christ, the only-begotten Son of God, begotten of his Father before all worlds, God of God, Light of Light, very God of very God, begotten, not made, being of one substance with the Father, by whom all things were made; who for us men and for our salvation came down from heaven, and was incarnate by the Holy Ghost of the Virgin Mary, and was made man, and was crucified also for us under Pontius Pilate; he suffered and was buried, and the third day he rose again according to the Scriptures, and ascended into heaven, and sitteth on the right hand of the Father; and he shall come again with glory, to judge both the quick and the dead, whose kingdom shall have no end.

And I believe in the Holy Ghost, the Lord and Giver of Life, who proceedeth from the Father and the Son, who with the Father and the Son together is worshiped and glorified, who spake by the prophets. And I believe one catholic and apostolic Church. I acknowledge one baptism for the remission of sins. And I look for the resurrection of the dead, and the life of the world to come. Amen.

The Apostles' Creed is similar in form, being in fact a shorter version of the Nicene Creed. It has served as the measuring stick of doctrine and orthodoxy both for Roman Catholicism and Protestantism alike. It is undoubtedly the most widely known and used creed in Christendom:

I believe in God the Father Almighty, Maker of heaven and earth; and in Jesus Christ his only Son our Lord; who was conceived by the Holy Spirit, born of the Virgin Mary, suffered under Pontius Pilate, was crucified, dead, and buried; he descended into hell; the third day he rose from the dead; he ascended into heaven, and sitteth at the right hand of God the Father Almighty; from thence he shall come to judge the quick and the dead. I believe in the Holy Spirit, the Holy catholic Church, the communion of saints, the forgiveness of sins, the resurrection of the body, and the life everlasting. Amen.

In these latter days other formulations of faith have emerged and secured a widening circle of use in the teaching and worship program of the churches. Here are two that are winning real recognition in contemporary usage:

We believe in God the Father, infinite in wisdom, power, and love, whose mercy is over all his works, and whose will is ever directed to his children's good.

We believe in Jesus Christ, Son of God and Son of man, the gift of the Father's unfailing grace, the ground of our hope, and the promise of our deliverance from sin and death.

We believe in the Holy Spirit as the divine presence in our lives, whereby we are kept in perpetual remembrance of the truth of Christ, and find strength and help in time of need.

We believe that this faith should manifest itself in the service of love as set forth in the example of our blessed Lord, to the end that the Kingdom of God may come upon the earth. Amen.

We believe in the one God, Maker and Ruler of all things, Father of all men, the source of all goodness and beauty, all truth and love.

We believe in Jesus Christ, God manifest in the flesh, our teacher, example, and redeemer, the Saviour of the world.

We believe in the Holy Spirit, God present with us for guidance, for comfort, and for strength.

We believe in the forgiveness of sins, in the life of love and prayer, and in grace equal to every need.

We believe in the Word of God contained in the Old and New Testaments as the sufficient rule both of faith and of practice.

We believe in the Church as the fellowship for worship and for service of all who are united to the living Lord.

We believe in the Kingdom of God as the divine rule in human society, and in the brotherhood of man under the fatherhood of God.

We believe in the final triumph of righteousness, and in the life everlasting. Amen.

If none of the existing creeds seem to you to be adequate, you are under obligation to write one of your own, and secure social acceptance of it. Note that last requirement of sincere creed-making. A creed must convey a meaning to another. It is not a private affair, any more than religion is a private affair. Religion is personal, yes, but that is far from saying that it is private. Our personalities are the most intensely social creations imaginable. Physically, psychologically, socially, and spiritually we are indebted to others before us for the very form and structure of our life and thought. We are bound in one bundle of life with other persons, and one of the hallmarks of intellectual integrity is the willingness to share what we believe to be true. Creed-making is not a finished undertaking by any means, but it is getting harder and harder to improve on the penetrating, dignified affirmations of faith that come to us as the distillation of the finest thinking, and sincerest feeling of many generations of spiritually minded men and women. The only man who is entitled to reject them is one who can write a better.

THE WORKS OF GOD

"I BELIEVE in God the Father Almighty, Maker of heaven and earth." What does this mean? I believe that God has made me, and all creatures; that he has given and still preserves to me my body and soul, eyes, ears, and all my members, my reason and all my senses; also clothing and shoes, meat and drink, house and home, wife and child, land, cattle and all my goods; that he richly and daily provides me with all that I need for this body and life, protects me against all danger and guards and keeps me from all evil; and all this purely out of fatherly, divine goodness and mercy, without merit or worthiness in me; for all of which I am in duty bound to thank and praise, to serve and obey him. This is most certainly true.

—LUTHER, *Small Catechism*[1]

IN ONE GOD I BELIEVE

Sole and eternal, moving all the heaven,
Himself unmoved, with love and with desire.
For such belief not only have I proof
From physics and from metaphysics, but
'Tis also given me by the truth which flows
Through Moses and the Prophets and the Psalms,
Through the Evangel, and through you who wrote
As God's inspired guardians of the truth.

—DANTE

II

We Believe in GOD

I

The simple creedal statement, "I believe in God," is easily the greatest and the costliest conclusion ever reached by the human mind. As Job discovered in his day, and Paul in his, and we in ours, a great faith in God lies on the far side of a hard fight with every stubborn fact, every jeering demon of doubt, and every sirenlike invitation to early and easy repose in something less or something other than a sincere, intelligent belief in God.

There need be no hesitation in affirming that belief in God is the basic belief of the Christian faith. The various creeds bear eloquent testimony to this point:

I believe in God the Father Almighty, Maker of heaven and earth. . . .

I believe in one God, the Father Almighty, Maker of heaven and earth, and of all things visible and invisible. . . .

We believe in God the Father, infinite in wisdom, power, and love, whose mercy is over all his works, and whose will is ever directed to his children's good.

We believe in the one God, Maker and Ruler of all things, Father of all men, the source of all goodness and beauty, all truth and love.

Affirmations like these come first in Christian creeds because the experience of God is the primary fact upon which religion rests and out of which the creed springs. Without it there would be no creed. The purpose of the creed is to explore the fuller implications of this experience of the divine in the broad ranges of human life and history.

That is why we say that the simple statement "I believe in God" is easily the greatest formulation of the human mind. No man acquainted with the centuries of experience and thought which have gone into its making will treat it lightly. In order to be appreciated it must be approached with a high seriousness and a determination to state and understand the factual basis upon which it rests. It is no easier to validate the idea of God than it is to formulate it. Both require of man the best that he has. Emerson may have had this in mind when he asked, "What is so odious as polite bows to God?" Certainly the true worship of God must be based upon a reasoned conviction and a felt confidence in His reality and nature. Alfred North Whitehead, dean of the philosophers of this generation, master of the realms of mathematics, logic, and history of philosophy, can and sometimes does bury his ideas deep within an exceedingly difficult vocabulary, but there is no difficulty following this assertion, "The only really important question before us today is this: What do you mean by God?" Nor is he alone in raising this serious question. Dr. E. S. Brightman, another philosophical giant, has made the understanding of the nature of God and the relationship between man and God the major preoccupation of his life and writings. Canon F. R. Barry is but summing up the matter when he observes that "The utterly crucial question today is 'What God do you worship?' " If you are inclined to minimize the importance of the quest for a clearer idea of God, consider his warning as to the revolutionary social implications of the Christian idea of God, "If God is King, then there is a law higher than any national sovereign state, and to it the nation must conform or perish. . . . If God is King, then the common man is of infinite worth and preciousness in his sight, and the whole organization of society must be a means to personal fulfilment."

Those of us who either do believe in God or who want to believe in God cannot help being encouraged by the testimony of men like these. Yet we need to remind ourselves that we cannot inherit a reasoned understanding of what those words mean. That kind of understanding can be earned only if we are willing to follow the hard road of careful and courageous thinking and living.

We must never forget that the idea of God requires the best that a man has. It requires his most critical reasoning; his sincerest insight and emotion; his greatest art; his most adventurous philosophy; his truest science; and his most sacrificial ethics.

While the Christian idea of God can and should be made appealing to children, the full sweep of its intellectual and moral majesty is reserved for the mature mind. For, as Augustine observed, "God is food for the full grown." As we proceed to a careful evaluation of the Christian belief in God we shall find ourselves led to the very heart of the personal and social problems of our day. This is as it should be since the Christian faith is designed to propel men into the thick of problems, confident that they can be managed if not mastered. Better than anything else, it prepares a man for any and all of the surprise packages that life can thrust at him.

What we are trying to do in this particular study is to keep a careful eye on the facts which underlie our faith in God. We shall want to resist the temptation to overstate rather than understate the meaning of these facts. What I am trying to formulate now might be called a "minimum conception of God." By that I mean simply that while you may and undoubtedly will want to mean more by the word "God" than what I shall be saying, you cannot mean less than that and be true to the facts. To put the matter in a somewhat different manner, you cannot ignore the facts upon which the idea of God rests without meeting the charge that you are deliberately refusing to face facts, that for some reason you are guilty of self-deception, wishful thinking, and reality dodging. Not many of us will want to be guilty of that sort of tactics.

What, you ask, are these facts which must be faced and which, when faced, will yield a firm foundation for the Christian faith in God? In answer, I should like to call your attention to three principles or types of order plainly discernible in known facts about the universe in general and life in particular. Upon these the Christian faith rests its belief in the reality and relevance of God.

II

First, there is *the principle of order in the world.* We live in a cosmos, not a chaos. This is very ancient as well as ultramodern knowledge. Primitive man in his stumbling efforts to learn how to live in a most precarious world and a modern scientist working in the most adequate laboratory—each in his own way discovers the fact that orderliness is one of the most dependable characteristics of our world.

Of course, the principle of order, plainly found in the universe, is nothing like as simple as we once thought it was. Up to and including the Middle Ages man was sure that he lived in an orderly world. But order to him was a kind of "animal, mineral, and vegetable" affair in which each part of reality was quite separate and distinct from the rest. They existed side by side, to be sure, but were quite independent of each other for their status and meaning in the total scheme of things. Each one was thought to have been created by a separate and distinct act of God in conformity with His holy will. It was a neat little world, fully deserving the title once given it: "bandbox universe."

Now, thanks to the discoveries of astronomy and physics, we know that we live in a quite different kind of world. To be sure, the principle of order still prevails, but our explorations have uncovered mysterious heights and depths in reality. Within the last fifty to one hundred years we have witnessed the development of a whole series of various sciences that aim to explore and discover the nature of underlying principles of order on the various levels of reality. Any college curriculum in the sciences will illustrate this point. Physics, botany, biology, zoology, anthropology, sociology—all these are ways of studying various levels of reality which while separate and distinct from one another in many definite ways are still deeply interdependent with one another. Now as never before we are keenly aware of the fact that there is more that we do not know than we do know about this universe in which we live. But, even so, we have every reason to be confident that a fundamental and reliable orderliness stretches from atom to galaxy, from ameba to man.

The scientist, then, better than anyone else knows that we live in a cosmos, not a chaos. Were this not true, he would be unable to conduct any of the experiments or to make any of the explorations which are meat and drink to modern science. Standing firmly on what he knows and believing that it is truly related to what he does not know, he moves with confidence into the unknown. But without complete confidence that an orderliness pervades the universe, and that this order stretches from what he knows to what he does not know, even the most astute scientist would be as helpless as a baby.

Religion affirms that the proper name for the principle of order that is clearly a part of the universe is God. A long line of eminent scientists gladly testify to the fitness of this term. Each sees God through the window of his own field of research and reflection, to be sure, but together they tell a single story of the orderly, if only half-understood, processes of this universe. Some of these scientists shy away from the intensely personal meaning of the word God, preferring to speak of Intelligence, or Design, or Pattern, or System. Even so—and we will want to respect the humility and caution which prompt their hesitation in this matter—all bear witness to the reality of order in the universe. Recently the National Conference of Christians and Jews circulated a pamphlet entitled *My Faith*. It contains the religious views of six of the most prominent scientists in this country. Each one grounds his statement in his life's work as a scientist. Dr. Kirtley F. Mather, of Harvard, says flatly, "We live in a universe, not of chance or caprice, but of Law and Order." And when Dr. Albert Einstein writes, "Certain it is that a conviction, akin to religious feeling, of the rationality or intelligibility of the world lies behind all scientific work of a higher order," his colleagues lift a chorus of reverent "Amens."

Religion, then, stands squarely upon known fact when it affirms that there is a principle of Order in the world, and it is well within the limits of logical discretion when it cites this fact as evidence for the reality and rationality of belief in God.

III

Another well-authenticated fact steps forward to take its place at the side of order: *The principle of growth*. The evidence for its reality constitutes an actual embarrassment of riches. The astronomer speaks of the evolution of our own planetary system from that far-off day when, due to invasion or explosion or something else, what had been a fairly stable star suddenly shot a whole brood of fiery children into space. As if regretting her initial impulse to hurl them forever from her sight she tied them to her long gravitational apron strings and kept them under an ever watchful eye. Then, "It came to pass" over immeasurably long periods of time that one of the smallest of these children became the scene of strange doings. Certain basic conditions having been met, life forms began to emerge. How, when, and in precisely what form we do not now and may never know. But the staggering fact is that it did happen, and when it happened those life forms were off on the long pilgrimage from ameba to man. This pilgrimage did not proceed in escalator fashion, smoothly and irresistibly from simpler to more complex forms. It was a long, costly, and essentially tragic process—like most pilgrimages are. Scientists, poets, and moralists alike have cried aloud in protest at the enormous cost in pain and failure which was paid all along the way. Yet all accept the fact that in man the whole developmental thrust of life reaches a new level of complexity in organization and possibility in adjustment.

Nor is this principle of growth something to be studied from afar. Every parent can view it in the growth of a child. Certainly all of us who are blessed with children have marveled at the principle of growth as it manifests itself in the conception, formation, birth, and growth of a child. Beginning with the union of two minute cells—the spermatozoon and the ovum—the embryo takes form, gathers actual and potential characteristics from both parents. With birth, a tiny organism is projected into the world, needing food and care of every kind. As these needs are supplied the organism grows, and with its growth other specific needs such as companionship in play and responsibility in work and other relationships emerge. As each new set of needs emerge and are met, the child passes on to a new level of growth—he is "growing up," we say! The maturing of body must be paralleled by maturing of mind and spirit if a well-balanced personality is to be the end product of these first twenty years of growth.

Now all this comes close to being a miracle—if ever that word is to be used with any specific factual content. Organism plus oatmeal and care equals not just the same organism, but the unfoldment of latent capacities within the organism. Every mother will sympathize with one who, looking at her husky fifteen-year-old boy, wondered how many tons of food she had prepared for him over those years!

In still another area we feel the strong power of the principle of growth: *the growth of values.* By any manner of reckoning, friendship and love are essential values to life, underlying as they do the kind of relationships that every man needs for normal living. Yet if you will separate out any particular friendship and trace its career in your life, you will feel the pulse of growth throbbing through it. Ordinarily, friendships and love begin with the simple fact of geographical proximity *improved upon!* Two persons are close enough together to see and hear each other. They begin to get acquainted—which is to say, they begin to throw bridges of communication across the chasm between them. Not many at first and not strong either, but numerous and strong enough for ideas and meanings to begin to be exchanged. As each feels more confident, more at home, in the presence of the other, new bridges are built and a strong friendship or love is under way. Talking together, doing things together, facing problems together, disagreeing with each other, learning to depend upon each other—these are the ways in which the great values and the great relationships of life become *real.*

There is nothing optional about our need for such relationships; they are obligatory. To have them is to have life unfold in a new and definite manner; not to have them is to be deprived of the kind of enrichment which only they can bring. And it is as necessary to the normal development of self for us to have them as oatmeal is necessary to the normal growth of the infant organism!

Wherever we touch life—whether on the level of physiological processes or that of values, that is, value-relationships—it is animated by desire, will, purpose. It is not content with where, whether, or what it is; a principle of growth, of development, of further unfoldment is one of the fundamental facts about it and factors in its health.

Actually, of course, the principle of growth is not something separate and distinct from the principle of order. Growth is the principle of order in and for life. The order or structure of life is indicated by the word "growth." To live is to grow; to grow is to live. When the principle of growth departs from life so also does the principle of order—then life is at an end.

So when religious faith calls the principle of growth to witness to its right to proclaim its belief in God as the basic fact and factor in life, it is but asking each one of us to bear witness to the process by virtue of which his own life has come into existence and to the values by which he lives from day to day.

IV

There is one other fact to which all faith calls attention as it indicates the factual foundation of its belief in God: *The principle of judgment.* This, with the principles of order and growth, constitutes the main areas of fact which are both indubitable aspects of reality and essential constituents of the Christian conception of God. The principle of judgment is so closely related to order and growth that we might consider it a part of them, as indeed it is in life. The only justification for considering it separately is that by so doing we are able with greater clarity to see it for the decisive power and fact it is in human life. If the principles of order and growth were optional rather than obligatory aspects of life, if we could pick them up or lay them down at will—*and with impunity!*—then the principle of judgment would have little or no factual foundation on which to stand. But, so far from being incidental footnotes to the process of living, order and growth constitute the text. In so far as and to the extent that a life conforms to their meanings, it is strong, creative, good. In so far as and to the extent that a life defies their meanings it is destructive, confused, and evil.

Which is to say that there is no way life can ignore or be neutral on these principles. It must come to terms with them, consciously or not, willingly or not. To alter the figure, it is weighed in the balance—and no man can escape the measurement. That, in minimal terms, is the factual foundation of the principle of judgment as it operates in life.

Manifestly, when you study order and growth through the lens of judgment, living becomes serious business! And the effort to live the good life becomes the major objective of any rational person! For hovering over any and everyone who ignores this moral ultimatum of life is the grim warning: "Be sure your sins will find you out." With all the good will and generosity in the world, we have found no way to evade or lighten this judgment.

We trifle with the law of gravitation at our own grave risk. We ignore or neglect the laws of health, and illness invariably strikes. The laws of mental health require that we learn how to manage our defeats and enmities—if we do not, we become unstable, and mentally ill persons. The same sort of vigorous sanction attends the great values and relationships of friendship, love, and family. We do not determine their nature; we discover and conform to it. The crowning error of moral and ethical relationships is the idea that what I think is right is right for me, and what you think is right is right for you. This is simply not true. Underlying every enduring and creative relationship are the great values of truth, respect, and a willingness to share. I do not know exactly why I cannot lie, steal, and misuse a person yet have him for a firm friend. I only know I cannot. Every counselor these days knows how much stark tragedy grows out of an unwillingness on the part of our married couples honestly to search for and find the moral laws which underlie a happy marriage.

Here is a couple who was dismayed when their marriage drifted into boredom. Being disciples of Bertrand Russell in spirit if not in name, they decided to engage each in his own way in extramarital affairs, thinking thereby to get a "rest" from each other, and to enjoy the thrill of new experiences. Shortly, they discovered that they were no longer in love with each other—they could not stand the sight of each other! And what was even more tragic, they felt cheapened beyond calculation in their own sight. Resisting the temptation to brazen it through, they determined to find out what had gone wrong with their marriage and why their solution had not worked. Like so many others, they had learned the hard way that a principle of judgment is coupled with every value and relationship in life, and that he who breaks with the essential nature of the relationship cannot escape the crushing stroke of judgment which will descend upon him.

Wherever the principle of order goes or seeks to go the principle of judgment goes also. We are trying to build "one world," we say. We know we must do so or perish. But the world we are working on keeps falling apart. We want to blame someone else for this but, in truth, the reason lies deep within every nation. We want order in the world, yes; but we want order at the point of our own maximum advantage. We will lower our standard of living to win a war, but not to avert the ravages of hunger which will lead to the kind of instabilities that perpetrate another war. We know that we must, by an act of faith no harder for one than another, learn to trust each other and to try honestly to live with each other's peculiarities and differences. Yet we cultivate and nourish mistrust; we listen with our fears, not with our faith—and then wonder why we are veering toward another war!

We can have one world, a world of security and peace for all—of that we can be certain. But we cannot dictate its nature; we can only discover it and conform to it. If we are not willing to do this we will be inviting that final stroke of judgment upon our civilization that most students are sure we cannot survive.

V

These, then, are some of the unshakably valid and unquestionably valuable facts that underlie belief in God: order, growth, and judgment. The Christian faith studies their meaning and draws a reasonable inference from them when it arrives at the best definition of God we know: *God is love.*

Dr. Charles A. Hartshorne prefaces his exacting logical study of the meaning of the idea of God with this assertion: "The ground . . . for this book is the conviction that a magnificent intellectual content—far surpassing that of such systems as Thomism, Spinozism, German Idealism, positivism (old or new)—is implicit in the religious faith most briefly expressed in the three words, God is love."[2] As we examine at closer range "the magnificent intellectual content" of this hallowed conception of deity we shall find that it is a well-warranted inference from such facts as we have been considering.

Students of the New Testament have made it clear that the Greeks had two words for love: *eros* and *agape.* The former, *eros,* denotes erotic personal affection and emotion;[3] the latter, *agape,* denotes a feeling of oneness, community, mutuality, togetherness, brotherhood. When New Testament writers speak of *love* either as a Christian virtue or an attribute of God they use *agape.* Important as it is to note this singular usage, it is possible to press the distinction between *eros* and *agape,* as they relate to deity, too far, so far as their Greek usage is concerned. For the Greek mind, *eros* was a form of divinity, not only in mythology but as the all-pervasive, all-powerful amalgam and power in life whereby individuals become parts of a larger whole. The early Christian rejection of *eros* as a manifestation of deity is better understood as an inescapable corollary of the current notion that the body is the stronghold of iniquity and that all bodily passions are sensual and evil. With the modification or outright rejection of this underlying conception of the nature of the body comes a consequent rethinking of the place of *eros* in any factually grounded concept of life and of God. Without slighting or slurring the very real difference in emphasis upon the meanings of *agape* and *eros,* it is of paramount importance that they be seen as separate yet related instances or manifestations of the same creative power or spirit in the universe.

The claim that God is love draws attention to three specific meanings of the idea of love, including the two already mentioned—personal affection and social mutuality. The third one—and basic to the other two—can and should be stated in terms of a universal principle.

Love denotes the principle of progressive integration or development in the universe which manifests itself on the human level in the growth of values and those creative relationships through which life unfolds. God, so conceived, is a concrete principle or power, giving stability, definiteness, and creativity to the universe. This "vision" of the meaning of God is affecting the greatest philosophic minds of our time as the "vision" of the Copernican universe affected Bruno. The foremost impressive metaphysical systems of our time (Bowne-Brightman, S. Alexander, John Eloof Boodin, Whitehead-Hartshorne) are efforts to explore its fuller meaning in terms of the problems it raises. God, for them, is no projection of impotent man; He is the foundation of reality. He is not a mechanical structure or order: for He is the source, the sustainer, and the recreator of life. Even though He is the One in whose will the stars find their way He is also and as truly the One in whose will men find their way. To call God "the Wholly Other" is a form of metaphysical nonsense reserved for those theologians who refuse to examine the plain as well as possible implications of known facts. God is no more "wholly other" than life is "wholly other" or we are "wholly other." God is more than life and infinitely more than we are, but He is the formative principle underlying and never abandoning both. The idea of denying the existence and relevance of God was possible when He was regarded as a tribal war god enthroned on Mount Sinai, or limited to the boundaries of a race or a country. But when the principle of integration and development in the universe becomes the fact indicated by the word "God," He is the fundamental fact about the universe, including, of course, life and history. He is the difference between a cosmos and a chaos. This, then, is the primary factual meaning of the great declaration, "God is Love!"

The second meaning of the assertion that "God is Love" is found in the sheer necessity, the dynamic strength of the intimate human relationships of friendship and love. The seemingly individual, unattached, human person is, in reality, the most social being imaginable. His very being is the result of the sharing of life with life in and through his parents. Intimate affectional relationships are the environment in which life grows, unfolds most normally. That is the deepest reason why every man needs and most men seek that kind of relationship. When we have finished our fun at the expense of the sickly sentimentalism of Tin Pan Alley and Hollywood we cannot help asking why men respond to them so eagerly and, at least for a moment, seem to find in them a fleeting experience of warm security and personal richness. Whether consciously or not, these media of wide public appeal lay their hands on the simple and finally undeniable fact that we need each other, that man neither lives by bread alone nor by himself alone, that we are "bound in one bundle of life" whether we will it or not—and that the life we have demands for its completeness intimate, creative, dependable affectional relationships with others. Friendship and love, then, are necessities not luxuries of life.

All this must seem obvious, yet one of its implications drives its taproot in the heart of the universe itself. Men need one another because God in His wisdom made life that way. Friendship and love are His will for our life, His mandatory way toward the full life, His way of revealing the hidden depths of meaning in our common life. The couple at the marriage altar; parents studying with incredulous and insatiable curiosity their first-born; the father waiting for his son's return and the son's ultimate discovery of where "home" is; the long, desperate vigil at the bedside or the bier of a loved one; the overpowering sense of shame in the presence of a friendship or love betrayed; the agonizing process of accepting the fact of the breakup of a marriage or a home and the long struggle back to an inner sense of social acceptability on the part of all involved in the breakup—all these are instances of the human meaning of the love of God as a tremendous power in human relationships.

The third meaning of the historic affirmation "God is Love" is enclosed in the idea of brotherhood, community, mutuality, or oneness. The factual content was indicated earlier when attention was called to the social nature of man.[4] Men do not decide to be social; they are made that way, and that way they must live, or perish. The clear realism of the social nature of man, as visualized by Christianity, has been blurred in the past by two widely separated movements, one strangely yet essentially religious in origin and intent, the other secular and social.

The former was an exaggerated emphasis upon the soul of the individual person. The two Catholic traditions as well as classical Protestantism built their views of life and history on the reality of the individual soul and the necessity of shepherding it safely into eternal bliss. The world was denoted as "this vale of soul-making" and the ultimate meaning of history was stated in terms of the wrestle between God and the Devil for the possession of each immortal soul. Personal salvation was the only kind so much as thought of for centuries. The world was written off as evil; society was fled by truly religious souls as the abode of the Devil himself, and the earnest man sought as the supreme end of life to be personally "right with God."

No criticism of the elements of lasting worth in this extreme emphasis is intended by saying that *it is exaggerated,* leaving out, in sober fact, almost as many salient facts about life as it sought to include. Now we know that it is simply impossible to draw a sharp line between person and group, between soul and personality, between men and man. Whatever life we have here and whatever destiny we may have beyond death are, so far as available facts and legitimate inferences are concerned, not so much "flights of the alone to the Alone"[5] as they are journeys and ventures shared with others each step of the way.

The secular slight of the social nature of man has found many expressions, the most eloquent being the Social Contract theory of society.[6] According to this view, men found living alone so precarious an enterprise that they decided to form groups of various degrees of complexity, culminating in the state. Such groups, of course, restricted the unfettered functioning of the individual but, in return, gave him a full-orbed security. It was a good exchange for man.

On the face of it this theory of society stands condemned by the now known facts about human life and society. There is no record of individual men deciding to form basic social groups; they have had them as far back as the records go. To the best of our knowledge they, in some form, are coextensive with men. The existence of such groups as family, tribe, race (whether a real or fancied group), and in these latter days, nations, has posed the gravest problems for human history. For from the beginning intergroup relations have proceeded sometimes by co-operation, but usually by collision. Rivalry, conflict, and warfare have been the bane of man's existence. Every effort to treat them as normal and accept them accordingly has finally come under the adverse judgment not alone of the dreams of men but of the utterances of their consciences as well. Springing from the depths of our social nature is the desire for community, the yearning for a real sense of belonging to all men everywhere, the vision of the day when brotherhood will prevail throughout human affairs.

Out of this dream came the positive impulses which have supported our Leagues of Nations, World Courts, and United Nations. Fear, of itself, can no more explain the almost pathetic hope with which each such effort is greeted by mankind than it can explain the origin of religion itself. If successive failures could discourage a hope, this one would have long since died. But the vision of world brotherhood rests on a more substantial foundation than a prudence born of an accurate tally of successes and failures of human efforts to realize it.

It is the contention of those who believe that God is love that His will for human life is at once the real foundation in fact of the vision and the deepest reason why every effort to stabilize the world on any other basis is doomed to fail. It is the will of God that the men who are brothers one of another should not rest until they bring into being a condition of mutuality and oneness in the human family.

At the risk of laboring the obvious, it should be noted and never forgotten that you do not take God, so conceived, by an act of blind or irrational faith. God, so conceived, is not a religious postulate flung into the unknown by men standing on the edge of the known. Belief in God, so conceived, is not an effort to find a basic and ultimate friendliness in an otherwise alien if not hostile universe. It is not the final posture of a fear-driven and despair-laden humanity to feel that, somehow, it "belongs," is at home in this world.

God, as we have been describing Him, is a demonstrably rational inference not so much permitted as required by the very structure of human facts. He is a personally experienced power and reality in human life and history. He is the unifying, the cohesive, the integrative character or nature or thrust clearly discernible and experienced in reality. This is not to say that you can either "find" God in a test tube or encompass His meaning is a syllogism. But the order of fact found in a test tube or statable in terms of a syllogism is an integral aspect of a much larger order of fact and, therefore, a valid clue to its nature. The ancient query, "Can man by searching find out God?" was clearly rhetorical in nature, the answer, by common consent, being "No!" It is still a good question—one of the most important in life—but to most thoughtful men it is no longer rhetorical and, for an increasing number of them, the answer is "Yes!"

God not only can be, God is known: known to be a fact; known to be a distinctive kind of fact; known to be the only truly fundamental fact in life and history; known not only as an essential aspect of reality, abstractly conceived, but also as the very heart of the life process of the universe; known because experienced, both as sustainer of the values which when chosen and followed underlie the creative relationships of life and as judge in the disvalues which, when chosen and followed, impoverish and finally destroy the very meaning of life; known as the One in whom we live and move and have our being.

God can be loved: loved as the one on whom we are dependent for life, and for the possibility of the good life; loved as the source and sustainer of all creative relationships—colleagues, friends, loved ones; loved as the One in whose eternal nature and will the great and the good facts of life have their final validation and ultimate strength; loved as the One whose will for our good is eternal and untiring; loved as the One whose will for man as seen in the life and teachings of Jesus Christ is so filled with understanding, compassion, tenderness, and mercy as to require the highest and holiest word we know, even "Love"; loved as the One in whom life finds its origin, meaning, and ultimate destination beyond reach of the fact of death; loved with all our heart, with all our soul, with all our mind, and with all our strength.

God can be served: served not as a slave serves the master or a prisoner the jailer or a subject the tyrant, but as a dutiful son serves a wise and good father—with love, joy, understanding, and trust; served with our mind in order that we may be able to give a reason for the hope that is within us; served with our will that we may earnestly seek to do His will for our life and time; served with our entire life knowing that, finally, the only effective token of belief is life itself—a life made radiant and purposive by the love and the will of God; served with an awareness of real freedom and responsibility because He has chosen to extend to us the high privilege and calling of being co-workers together with Him in the creation of His Kingdom in human life and history; served because His will is ultimate and as eternal as the heavens and in it we find both our way and our peace or miss both—and the meaning of life—forever; served with singleness of mind and spirit not alone because every road away from or in defiance of His will is a road away from the great value-relationships which give meaning to life, but, even more importantly, because the roads which lead toward Him lead to the most abundant life dreamed of by man; served because the probing truth that "Thou hast made us for Thyself, we are Thine," requires of us a responsible reaction—and that can be no less (and no more) than humble service.

Say, then, that you believe in God, and be prepared both to say what you mean and mean what you say.

God is this deep and abiding meaningfulness of life; God is this essential togetherness of values; God is this unalterable definiteness in life in terms of which life finds purpose and meaning; God is love; God is the peace that passeth all understanding.

To say that we believe in God, then, is to say that we believe it is possible for us to find the purpose of our life in His Purpose for life, to find the strength for fulfilling that purpose in His strong Presence within us yet always beyond us. To believe in God is to seek to lose our life in His that we may find it again—redeemed, renewed, and made radiant with His love.

ONE SOLITARY LIFE

HERE IS a man who was born in an obscure village, the child of a peasant woman. He grew up in another obscure village. He worked in a carpenter shop until He was thirty, and then for three years He was an itinerant preacher. He never wrote a book. He never held an office.

He never owned a home. He never set foot inside a big city. He never traveled two hundred miles from the place where He was born. He had no credentials but Himself.

He had nothing to do with this world except the naked power of His divine manhood. While still a young man, the tide of popular opinion turned against Him. His friends ran away. One of them denied Him. He was turned over to His enemies. He went through the mockery of a trial. He was nailed upon a cross between two thieves.

His executioners gambled for the only piece of property He had on earth while He was dying—and that was His coat. When He was dead He was taken down and laid in a borrowed grave through the pity of a friend.

Nineteen wide centuries have come and gone and today He is the centerpiece of the human race and the leader of progress. I am far within the mark when I say that all the armies that ever marched, and all the navies that ever were built, and all the parliaments that ever sat, and all the kings that ever reigned, put together have not affected the life of man upon this earth as powerfully as that One Solitary Life.

—Author Unknown

III

We Believe in JESUS CHRIST

I

One of the tokens of maturity in religion as in every other important area of life is the determination and the ability to give a reason for the faith we cherish, the cause we serve, and the goals we seek. We have a right, nay, we have a duty to be profoundly suspicious of any person or institution that asks us to take anything on faith or tradition alone. What is more, we ought to be profoundly suspicious of ourselves when we are tempted to accede to that request. For people who are willing to borrow and seek to use as their own the uncriticized and the untested beliefs of someone else, whether church or government, whether teacher or preacher, are both a weakness and a menace to every worthy institution and good cause they seek to serve.

Let it be known, therefore, and widely known, that the Christian religion is prepared to present her intellectual passport to any man or to any generation of men. That is what we are trying to do in this series of studies of the fundamentals of our faith. We are trying to state the facts upon which they rest. We are trying to list the reasons which have woven these facts into the Christian way of thought and life. We began by considering the necessity of a creed, regarding it not as something which binds our mind but as something which indicates the way pointed out by previous experience. Then, we inquired into the factual basis of our belief in God. Now we are going to continue the study and examine that simple phrase: *We believe in Jesus Christ.*

Simple though it seems to be, it differentiates Christianity from all other religions. For other religions believe in God (though with a wide variety of meaning) but the Christian religion alone makes, and consciously makes, Jesus Christ the central fact in faith and life. This difference has not been lost upon other religions. I well remember what one of our long-time missionaries to China said upon his return to this country when he was recounting certain memorable experiences he had had there. One such was a period of prolonged study with the head of a Buddhist monastery, during which they, in an effort to understand the deep devotional springs of each other's faith, placed the fundamental ideas, institutions, and practices of their faiths side by side. When the Christian missionary presented Jesus Christ for consideration, the priest shook his head and said, almost sadly, "We have no one who can compare with him in spiritual insight or moral grandeur."

Add to this the testimony of Dr. Aldrich, an American philosopher, who once posed this query: if Jesus and Plato should return to earth for just one hour and were scheduled to lecture on the same campus at the same time, which one would I go hear? After wrestling with the problem for a while, he concludes that it is really no problem, for who would go to hear even so great a one as Plato talk on the Truth when he might listen to One who was the Truth?

The historic creeds of Christendom are most explicit about the centrality of Jesus Christ in the Christian faith. I quote excerpts from four of them:

I believe . . . in Jesus Christ his only Son our Lord; who was conceived by the Holy Spirit, born of the Virgin Mary, Suffered under Pontius Pilate, was crucified, dead, and buried; he descended into hell; the third day he rose from the dead; he ascended into heaven, and sitteth at the right hand of God the Father Almighty; from hence he shall come to judge the quick and the dead.

I believe . . . in one Lord Jesus Christ, the only-begotten Son of God, begotten of his Father before all worlds, God of God, Light of Light, very God of very God, begotten, not made, being of one substance with the Father, by whom all things were made; who for us men and for our salvation came down from heaven, and was incarnate by the Holy Ghost of the Virgin Mary, and was made man, and was crucified also for us under Pontius Pilate; he suffered and was buried, and the third day he rose again according to the Scriptures, and ascended into heaven, and sitteth at the right hand of the Father; and he shall come again with glory, to judge both the quick and the dead, whose kingdom shall have no end.

We believe in Jesus Christ, Son of God and Son of man, the gift of the Father's unfailing grace, the ground of our hope, and the promise of our deliverance from sin and death.

We believe in Jesus Christ, God manifest in the flesh, our teacher, example, and redeemer, the Saviour of the world.

It is probably unnecessary to point out that the first two statements are ancient in origin, coming from that early period in Christian theology when the doctrine of Christ was the subject of hot debate and, frequently, bloody fights. Each one of their assertions about the life and meaning of Christ was intended to still certain controversies that had been raging about him. They were intended to bring unity in the sadly divided Christian group, to distinguish orthodoxy from heresy, thus enabling the temporal powers of the Church to enforce sanctions against unbelievers.

One need not subscribe to the latter and very practical aim in order to appreciate the fact that the creed-makers were sure that Jesus Christ combined God and man, the here and the hereafter, in a great new way. They cast this faith in the thought-patterns of their day. And according to the dominant metaphysics of that time, each thing or kind of reality had its own peculiar essence. God was composed of divine nature and man of human nature, and the two were utterly dissimilar. God was eternal; man, temporal. God was infinite, man finite. God was immortal, man mortal. God was good, man evil. Thus ran the thought of the ancients about this sharp division in the realms of reality. All religions sought to bridge that gap, and most of them succeeded only in falling into it. Christianity bridged it with the difficult concept of the dual nature of Christ; he was both God and man, "very God of very God, very man of very man" in the sonorous words of the Nicene Creed. This fact about him enabled the eternal, infinite, immortal, good nature of God to enter into depraved human nature as a great new saving fact. Without it, man was lost beyond redemption; with it, man was saved, becoming "a new creature in Christ."

The later formulations of faith came into being under a different metaphysical star and do not state their faith in Jesus Christ in terms of the Greek dualism between divine and human nature. Nor is there any good reason why they should. This does not make them any the less concerned with him as the saviour of mankind. He continues to be "Son of God and Son of man," the one in whom we have our clearest revelation of God's will for man, the one in whom we see God's will for human life exalted and glorified.

These are great answers to the question he himself once put to his disciples, "Who do you say that I am?" But, great as they are, they cannot be our answers until we have earned them. They are conclusions—conclusions to a long and desperate intellectual struggle on the part of the men who made them, but until and unless we too have proved them in the struggle with facts we have no right to use them as conclusions by which we seek to live.

You would soon discover, even though I were not to confess it as I now do, that it is far from easy for me to write with objectivity and restraint about One who has meant and means so much to me. The quiet confidence which I myself have found in him for more than twenty years might be better expressed if I were to launch into an old-fashioned "testimonial" to him in and through whose life and teachings I have found God most clearly and convincingly. Yet I must set my face steadily against the temptation to do that. We are here on a different mission—one with which we must not break faith. That mission is to discover the salient facts about his life and teachings and to determine what beliefs about him can and must be based on these facts. We are not asking, "What would we like to believe about him?" We are raising the more fundamental inquiry, "What must be believed about him in order to be true to well-established facts regarding his life and teachings?" The kind of facts I am talking about now are not the peculiar property of the "insider"—one who is a confessing Christian. They are public property in the exact sense that they can be found by anyone who is willing to look. Once having found them a conscientious thinker must come to terms with them, and, as he does, he will find that he, like the lawyer, "is not far from the Kingdom."

II

The first thing we mean when we say "We believe in Jesus Christ" is this: *We believe that he was a historical figure.* This will come as a surprise to those who take it for granted. But if you are acquainted with Christian history you will know that this is one of the things which has never been taken for granted. For two hundred years the early Christian community was split on the proposition as to whether or not he was a man, whether or not he had actually lived on this earth as a human being. A strong contingent held that he only appeared to live; that he was a phantasm; that he was a god all the time who had put on the appearance of humanity, without ever really being human. At the end of about two hundred years Christian leaders saw that they would have to make up their mind on this matter or be forever divided about it. They discussed it from every conceivable angle and reached the conclusion which is found in the earthiest section of the Apostles' Creed: "I believe in Jesus Christ . . . born of the Virgin Mary, suffered under Pontius Pilate, was crucified, dead, and buried." And just to make it really explicit these telling words were written into the Nicene Creed: "And was made man. . . ." To all intents and purposes that conclusion settled the controversy and it remained settled for many centuries.

Near the middle of the nineteenth century the conclusion was challenged again and the conflict broke out into the open. The active factors in the conflict were the judgments of certain scholars who, looking at the Gospels, pronounced them unreliable historical records. It was charged that the Gospels are partisan documents; that they make no pretense of being objective, even though they contain all we know about Jesus' life; that there are no supplementary records coming from any other source to bolster them; that they contradict one another in many fundamental ways being, obviously, the handiwork of men. One of the immediate conclusions drawn from these challenging observations was that Jesus Christ, the central figure in the Gospels, is not necessarily a bona fide person; that he may be more readily regarded as a creature of the imagination of the authors than a historical person.

This challenge took the Church by surprise, to say the least, and religious people of that time reacted as they usually do when criticized. First, they looked around for a suitable club with which to pound the critics. But sober students saw that the critics had a point, that the Gospels are partisan documents, that they do contain 99 and 9/10 per cent of all that we know about Jesus Christ's life and teachings. "But," the defenders of the faith asked, "do these facts add up to the conclusion that he never lived?" In answer to that question some of the best books in the field of Biblical research were written—some in Germany, some in France, some in England, and one of the most effective in the United States by Dr. Shirley Jackson Case bearing the title of *The Historicity of Jesus.* And the answer they gave to the question: "Was Jesus a historical figure?" is an unequivocal "Yes!" And, to the best of my knowledge, these scholars answered the question so decisively that it has not been raised within the last twenty-five years.

Once more we may regard that matter as settled. We may accept with confidence the conclusion that Jesus was a historical figure and sum up his life in some such fashion as this:

Jesus lived in Palestine, and the span of his life according to our calendar was approximately from 4 B.C. to A.D. 29. Most of his life was spent as an artisan in Nazareth of Galilee. His public ministry was very brief, lasting from a year and one-half to three years. During this time he got a mixed reception: in the early stages of his ministry he received a large hearing, but in the latter stages, only the most devout disciples were with him. When he died, he left as his legacy to his disciples the commission to take his gospel to the ends of the earth. The third day after his death the disciples were convinced that he had risen from the dead. Inspired by this conviction, which they shared without any reservation recorded in our Scripture, they went on their mission to preach his gospel to the ends of the earth. That is the common historical heritage of the Christian faith today.

III

A second fact undergirds the statement "We believe in Jesus Christ": *He is one of the greatest, if not the greatest, teacher of ethical religion the world has ever known.*

Any fair evaluation of Jesus as teacher will begin by noting these three characteristics of his teaching: he knew God; he knew man; he knew the proper relationship between them.

Like every good Jew brought up as he undoubtedly was in the synagogue school, Jesus was intimately acquainted with the faith of his fathers. Important as that was and is in any understanding of his message then and now, the real clue to his greatness is to be found in deeper levels of fact. It is hard to improve upon the almost extravagent statement of this matter made by Professor J. H. Robinson:[1] "He knew his Bible, especially Deuteronomy and the Prophets. But he knew more than these things: he knew God. . . . We know God, but imperfectly and intermittently: Jesus knew Him fully and permanently . . . And the impression made by his teaching was not a matter of detail. It was the whole taken together with his amazing personality that so affected men with his sureness of touch and his certainty of truth. He never guessed, and never qualified his statements. He saw universal truth as God sees it, and *knew* that he had the mind of his Father. That was the source of his authority—he knew God."

God, to him, is the supreme object of religious thinking and living. God alone is good; God alone is perfect; God alone is truly merciful. Our best efforts, our sincerest desire to understand, while inspired by God, are always answerable to Him by reason of their incompleteness and inadequacy. God is the central sun in the universe of Jesus' thought and life. All else revolves around Him, getting meaning from Him.

Faith in God, for Jesus, is more than formal religious belief. It is purposive living; a way of life, as we say. Looking squarely at the fact of God, Jesus drew the only conclusion that rational men can possibly draw: *This is the most important fact in life.* He felt and taught that the perception and acceptance of this truth at face value ought to make a marked, even a revolutionary, difference in a man's life. Not that he counseled a demonstration of piety! That sort of hypocrisy felt the lash of his criticism upon many occasions. But he said that Zaccheus, for example, reacted wisely to his discovery of God. No sooner had this happened than Zaccheus sought to right the wrongs he had committed and to guard against their repetition in the future. He also sought that unity of life with God which would make his efforts at ethical living normal, rational, and enjoyable. Wherever Jesus went, men seem to have been stirred by his matter-of-factness on the point that belief in God, being the most important thing in life, ought completely to transform the life of one accepting it.

Add to this knowledge of God his knowledge of man; in Biblical language: "He knew what was in man." He had a clear picture of what man is as well as of what he ought to be. No Pollyanna, he was more keenly aware of the evil in man than the most confirmed pessimist and cynic who ever lived. With almost pitiless clarity he centers attention upon the evil progeny sheltered in the human heart: greed, lust, pride, passion, hypocrisy, cowardice. No teacher of ethics had a better right to ask the one question Jesus never asked: Can any good thing come out of the human heart? When that question was put to Augustine and Calvin their answer was an immediate "No!" And that, better than anything else, indicates the difference between their and his stature as a teacher. He was certain that good was not only in the human heart but also could be augmented by faith and life in God until man could stand upright as a child of God.

Besieged as we are today by sermons and sustained theological efforts to breathe new life into Calvinistic versions of the classical idea of moral depravity, we need to remind ourselves that Jesus knew the good in man. Nor is it hard to understand the source of his knowledge. He was surrounded by love in his home; he had a deep affection for and long-range confidence in his disciples; he had experienced the adoration of Mary and the busy tenderness of Martha; he had experienced the recreative power of understanding love in Zaccheus, Mary Magdalene, Matthew, and many others; he said to an alert, earnest lawyer, "Thou art not far from the Kingdom of God"; whereas Jonathan Edwards took his four-year-old daughter on his knee and explained the doctrine of original sin to her, Jesus said to his disciples, "Suffer the little children to come unto me and forbid them not for of such is the kingdom of heaven."

Jesus knew, further, that the evil and the good are locked in mortal combat in the soul of every living man, and he sought to awaken men to this fact. He tried to help them find that relationship with God which would undergird and multiply the good and break the control if not the actual strength of evil. To this end, as teacher, he lifted up the most glorious ideal of the good life men have ever seen: citizenship in the Kingdom of God. In the Sermon on the Mount in Matthew and a succession of matchless parables in Luke he details the meaning of that citizenship.

What, you rightly ask, are some of his world-stirring teachings that stamp him one of the greatest, if not the greatest, of our teachers? Obviously, it is possible to list only a few of them at this time, though many others undergird other chapters in this book. All of them deserve study and continuous attempts at better understanding. But some appear to have done more than others to redraw the ethical and religious map of the human spirit.

Consider this invitation to disciplined living: "Anyone who wishes to be my disciple will practice self-denial and take up a cross and follow me." Dating from that utterance, sober men have realized that Christian living is a special vocation requiring our staunchest courage and our most earnest humility to keep life pointed in the right direction. Christian living begins as internal redirection of one's whole self. It is facing upward and outward with the total energies of one's life. Now this is not an easy achievement, as Paul, and everyone else who has tried it, discovered. Sometimes it is a "living death" with the sole source of peace and strength being the conviction of the all-sufficiency of Jesus Christ. Christian living undoubtedly encounters grave difficulties when the aspiring Christian encounters other people, but its earliest and severest test lies within the mysterious abode of the spirit of the believer himself.

How do we, citizens of an age that is given to boastful and arrogant utterance, react to this invitation to humility: "Anyone who exalts himself will be humbled, but one who humbles himself will be exalted"? Or how many of us in this world which cries for self-expression will accept this definition of self-realization: "Anyone who aims to preserve his own self will lose his soul, but anyone who loses himself in the cause of the Gospel will find himself"? Here, manifestly, is a radical view of what constitutes success and self-realization! To say that these are hard sayings is to put it mildly. They counsel the impossible to the point of being incredible, most of us feel. Yet, somehow, we cannot dispel the haunting realization that success attained and self realized according to popular notions are usually cheap and tawdry prizes. There is something almost pathetic in the way we keep going back to his principles in this matter, only to turn away with a wistful shake of the head.

Dr. Karen Horney has referred to "the neurotic personality character of our civilization." She and many other students of human emotions are certain that we must learn the secret of spiritual peace if we are to survive. The late Dr. Alexis Carrel once said, "Men cannot follow modern civilization along the present course because they are degenerating." While the doctors disagree, as doctors will, among themselves as to the precise nature and cause of the emotional chaos in which we live, they are in complete agreement that it must be restored to some sort of order at once in the interests of sanity. Dr. Brock Chisolm, an eminent Canadian psychiatrist, has mounted all the fervor of a frontier revivalist behind his "sermons" to psychiatrists to "save the world." Let a book promise "peace of mind" or a way to "confident living" and our neurotic age seizes it with trembling hands.

It comes as a shock to realize that a most penetrating formula for the management and conquest of worry was given by Jesus Christ. The teachings of Jesus on worry may be briefly summarized thus: "Worry is unnecessary, because God knows and cares. He gave the life; it is only reasonable to expect him to sustain it. . . . In the second place, worry is futile; it can achieve nothing and escape nothing. In the third place, it is dangerous; it will inevitably conflict with that single-hearted concentration which the quest of the Kingdom demands."[2] Although all possible skill of the counselor is needed to help a disorganized person into this view of life and worth, once achieved it will give real balance to life.

A good many Christians today, and not a few Christian leaders, have told us that Jesus did not really mean to be taken seriously when he said, "Bless those who curse you and pray for those who despitefully use you." They find all sorts of rubbery ways of distorting the obvious meaning of this very clear description of how we should deal with enemies. Some of them tell us that it is the counsel of perfection and has no immediate application in this relative and imperfect world. Then why did Jesus say it? Why was it treasured by his disciples? How did it get into our Gospel records? Why does it constitute a literal hairshirt for the Christian conscience in this and every other day of conflict? We have been told that for our enemies' own good we must first smite them hip and thigh in order to bring them to their senses sufficiently for them to appreciate the magnanimity of our forgiving spirit! Like Festus, Christians who reason this way await a "more convenient season" in which to face up to the ethical realism of Jesus' thought on this matter.

Why is it that such teachings of Jesus catch us so off our guard? Why is it they penetrate to the heart of all, leaving us profoundly dissatisfied with all that we have been able to do, even in his name? Is it not because he sets life in the perspective of God's intention for man? We live by the horizontal view of things pretty much from day to day. We do not see very far. We see ourselves in relationship to a few persons, a limited responsibility, and some degree of achievement. But Jesus looked at life from the perpendicular angle as well. He saw it not only as we see it, but in its total context. When we look at it through his eyes, we see what we do in relation to that vast and immeasurable range of God's meaning for us. Hence the breath-taking sureness which pervades his teaching. Hence the eternal truths that irradiate them, and both condemn yet encourage us. None other than the greatest of teachers could so join time and eternity, man and God.

IV

The fourth fact supporting our belief in Jesus Christ can be put this way: *We can believe that he is our clearest revelation of the will of God for the life of men.*

In saying this, we take another stride toward a deeper appreciation of him. One of the most reliable scholars of our day writes, "Jesus Christ is 'final' in this sense—that the nearer we get to Him, and the more we know Him, the more truth and reality we find in His yet unexhausted revelation." This statement, I believe, can be translated into everyday vernacular in some such way as this: Jesus Christ faced in principle every problem that human beings have to face and his suggested answers are truer than any other answers we know anything about. After we make due allowance for the fact that all such statements about Jesus Christ come from men who are already his followers, I do not see how we can avoid the conclusion that those who follow him find him to be the peerless leader of the human spirit as it keeps pushing beyond the frontiers of what we think and know. The very unity and power of the Christian witness on this point is as complete a demonstration of truth as we can ever hope to get outside the area of mathematical proof itself. For, wherever we turn in the Christian tradition, we find men aware of the fact that Jesus Christ has set before us certain "open doors" into more abundant living; doors which, being opened by God through Jesus Christ, cannot be closed by man; doors through which none can force us against our will and choice; doors beyond which we glimpse a portion of "the house not made with hands, eternal in the heavens."

One such "open door" is the right way to regard all men: We are brothers one of another. We are bound in one bundle of life by the creative will of God, by His dealings with us in history, by His love for us which desires that all shall find fulfillment in Him.

This basic attitude toward men is Christianity's enduring contribution to ethics and morality. It repudiates the Hebrew conception of "Chosen People" and the division of men into Jews and Gentiles. It repudiates the Greek belief that men can be divided into two groups, Greeks and Barbarians. It condemns, as superficial, the Roman division of men into Romans and non-Romans. It is equally severe in its judgment on the contemporary craze to reduce man to the level of being "merely another animal." It condemns our color line for the vicious, sinful, unchristian thing it is. When Paul stepped through this "open door" he discovered that he was in a spiritual dwelling place "where there is neither Greek nor Jew, circumcision nor uncircumcision, Barbarian, Scythian, bond nor free: but Christ is all, and in all." And, when John Oxenham entered by that door, he found himself in the same room:

> In Christ there is no east nor west
> In Him no south nor north;
> But one great fellowship of love
> Throughout the whole wide earth.[3]

Another "open door" which we see in the life and teachings of Jesus Christ is this: forgiving love is the only proper way to deal with enmity, ill-will, and hatred.[4] Insults, injuries, and indignities abound in human life. And we have developed certain impulsive ways, supported by pat rationalizations, of meeting them. They all reduce to one grim formula: The same to you, only more of it! I take it that we who live in these fearful days will not require an elaborate historical documentation of two obvious points: (1) that we have followed this formula faithfully; and (2) that the condition of the world today is the direct result of its effective application.

To Jesus, injury, injustice, and indignity were problems to be seen, understood, and solved. Any solution that aggravates or perpetuates them is no solution at all. The only true solution is one which both removes these evils and wins the one who practices them from the status of enemy to that of friend. And he nowhere indicates that this is an easy answer to find, yet he everywhere indicates that it can be found and must be sought. It must be sought because it is the only real answer, God being what He is. It can be found, as he knew, and when found, it literally indicates a new way of life—life as God intended it to be.

The first and all important step, determining as it does the direction to be taken toward redeeming enemies, is to master the spirit of forgiving love. At this point we are sure to hear the challenge from non-Christian critics: "There you go getting sentimental about the evil-doer and ignoring the fact that he must bear full responsibility for his vicious ways." One implication of the challenge is that the whole notion of forgiving love is an amorphous mass of undisciplined sentimentalism. And another is that forgiving love, if not actually immoral, is certainly amoral because, in its concern for perfection, it ignores the relative, the limited character of all moral judgments in life. These are serious charges whether directly leveled by critics or suggested by innuendoes from friends of the faith. And they are as false as they are serious.

Whatever else forgiving love may be, it is not a gush of emotion. It is composed of an unswerving loyalty to a definite relationship among men, the one found in God's love. The first test of this loyalty comes when we realize the great distance which separates most of our actual relationships from this potential and desirable one. The second test comes when we prepare to "push off" in the necessary direction. So far from being a substitute for wisdom, insight, and courage, forgiving love depends upon them for the achievement of its goal; namely, the mending of broken human relationship and their progressive enrichment in all ways.

Forgiving love is no leap into ethical darkness. It cherishes the good, the right, the true, and the beautiful wherever they appear in human living. What is more, it recognizes their partial, incomplete, and wholly inadequate nature in any given instance of their expression. It alone has the courage to survey the best that we do and acknowledge, "All have sinned and come short of the glory of God." This prevents an easy division of men into good and bad, enemy and friend. It confronts us with the unquestionable fact that the ones who injure, insult, and otherwise harass us are doing things that we ourselves have been and are guilty of in spirit if not in actual deed. It affirms that the more we hurt another the worse we wound ourselves. It affirms the reality of external as well as internal enemies of the good life. William James was close to the ethical realism of forgiving love when he said that we have our deepest dealings with reality in the moment of moral choice. But, and this is why men reject it, it insists that its means must be congruent with its goal rather than be the weapons thrust into our hands by hatred. This is a hard saying for creatures like us, moved as we are by furious impulse and almost incurably addicted to self-righteousness. But, hard or not, it is an open door which the life and teachings of Jesus Christ set before us. We shall not be wholly lost so long as we keep stepping to that door, seeking a glimpse of what lies beyond.

Such open doors as these are always before one who seeks to understand him whom we honor as our Leader. As teacher he taught them, as man he himself walked through them. Thus he is the symbol of what life ought to be like for us all. He stirs to life the best that is within us. He is the highest moral ideal we know —and as such he deserves to be understood and appreciated. The more persistently we seek to understand and follow him the easier it is for us to understand why his disciples hailed him as the Son of God, and why, through the centuries, he has been the fountainhead of new movements and new men. In short, we find ourselves saying that when we see him we see God's will for human life.

V

A fifth fact which underlies our belief in Jesus Christ can be stated in this manner: *he is God's supreme effort to save the world.* Which is to say that in and through Jesus Christ the power of God was inserting itself in history in a special way. We must be clear on this: the point of contact through which this power enters history is the individual person. In Jesus Christ, God addresses all men as His sons and calls them to a new life. In so far as His call is heard and heeded, history, in the large, takes a new turn. When God spoke to Paul through Jesus Christ, He was making His supreme effort to save Paul. And through this remarkable transformation a tremendous force for the creation of the Church and the regeneration of the world was let loose in human history. Repeatedly, to men like Augustine, Luther, and Wesley, God has spoken His mighty word of salvation in Jesus Christ, and each in his own way became, like Paul, a channel through which a powerful spiritual impulse flowed into history.

The least we can say about his influence on history is this: it is easily the most important aspect of the heritage of Western civilization. His followers have lived in various cultures: Hebrew, Greek, Roman, Feudal, and Modern. For nineteen hundred years the turgid stream of history has swung through these and other influences. But always he has emerged from each one as Lord and Master. The best of each has been rallied to his cause. And he has survived the collapse of those cultures that have now gone, and he will survive the collapse, if collapse it is to be, of ours today. Those faint-hearted ones among us today who counsel us to believe that Christianity and democracy stand or fall together would do well to take new courage from these facts. Dr. John Baillie has given an accurate sketch of the extent of his influence in these words: "In these Western lands the Christian gospel has not only reached every ear but left some mark on every heart. . . . There are many who live as if Christ had never come, but are there any who do so with complete peace of mind?"

Of him alone can it be truly said that he is *in* history yet not *of* it. He is an essential fact and factor in our art, literature, and philosophy, yet he is not exhausted by any or all of them. Their final act toward him is one of respect, awe, or reverence as befits one "the hem of whose garment we are not worthy to touch." The reality of his historical and suprahistorical character is especially apparent in these days when the world seeks a new spiritual foundation and the Christian churches a new sense of unity in him. If the ecumenical movement becomes the power we are praying and working for, it will be because the various churches find in him their common ground. In so far as the ideal of world brotherhood has any rootage in reality today, it is among those who look to him as the light of the world. G. B. Shaw was writing either the epitaph for the old world which persisted in its folly or the preface to a new and fairer world than men have known when he penned these sober words: "I see no way out of the world's misery but the way which would have been found by Christ's will if he had undertaken the work of a modern practical statesman."[5]

All this is contemporary evidence to the truth of the ancient and unwavering Christian belief that in Jesus Christ, God was working a mighty work of redemption in the affairs of men. Those highly controversial stories about his birth, the incisive and indispensable doctrine of the Incarnation, Paul's notion that he is the "fulfillment" of history, Dr. John MacMurry's assertion that Jesus is "the intention of God"—all these are ways of making the same point, namely, that God, in and through Jesus Christ, was making a supreme effort to bring men to their senses about themselves, their world, and God Himself.

Jesus Christ is God's supreme effort to awaken us to our utter and complete dependence upon His will for us and for all mankind. He is God's supreme effort to sting us into realizing the true extent of the poverty of our lives apart from God. He is God's supreme effort to save us from ourselves, from the evil of undisciplined and insubordinate passion and pride; from the evil of ignorant and brutal ways; from callous indifference to the needs and rights of our brothers; and from the horror of their inexorable vengeance. He is God's supreme effort to bring to pass that transformation of life which comes when men see life as a trust and living as a disciplined stewardship of that trust. In short, Christ is God addressing us about all that really matters in life.

And God's supreme effort was successful! A new spirit, a new standard of values, a new appraisal of life, ability and opportunity have been working like leaven in the habits, thoughts, and aspirations of men. Slowly but surely the name of this Man of Nazareth has been taken to the ends of the earth. His influence has been growing through nineteen hundred years now, and will continue to grow. When it will command the loyalties of men more perfectly, we do not know. We only know that our hope is in God, in whose endless patience "a thousand years are but as yesterday when it is passed, and as a watch in the night," whose unfailing love for us is seen in Jesus Christ, whose bountiful mercy welcomes us to become "new creatures in Christ," and whose confidence in us comes in the great commission to "preach this gospel to all nations."

Let us, therefore, confront Jesus Christ ourselves, and present him to the world as a historical figure, as one of mankind's greatest teachers of ethical religion, as our clearest revelation of the will of God for the lives of men, as God's supreme effort to save the world—one through whom God was and is seeking to redeem, to recreate human life and history, as one in whom life finds purpose and death meaning. Less than this, we dare not do, more we cannot do; the issue rests with God.

A CANTICLE OF PENTECOST

THE GRACE of the Holy Spirit be present with us and make our hearts his dwelling.

Merciful Spirit, illuminator of mankind, purge all fear and darkness from our mind.

Holy lover of thoughts that are wise, pour forth thine anointing on our understanding.

Thou purifier of all iniquities, Holy Spirit, cleanse our hearts from secret faults:

That the Father of all things may be beheld by us, whom the eyes of none save the pure in heart can see.

Thou didst inspire the prophets to chant aforetime their glorious heralding of Christ and didst confirm the apostles to bear Christ's trophy throughout the world.

When by his word God made the heavens, the earth, and the sea, thou didst stretch out thy Godhead over the waters, and didst cherish them, O Spirit.

By thine inspiration thou grantest men to be spiritual; thou didst unite the world, divided both in tongue and faith, O Lord.

Best of teachers, thou recallest idolaters to the worship of God; wherefore by thy mercy, hear us who call upon thee, Holy Spirit.

Without thee all our prayers are vain and unworthy of the ears of God.

Thou, O Spirit, who by embracing the saints of all ages, dost teach them by the impulse of thy divinity.

By bestowing upon the apostles a gift immortal thou hast made this day forever glorious.

Glory be to the Father, and to the Son, and to the Holy Ghost; as it was in the beginning, is now, and ever shall be, world without end. Amen.[1]

IV

We Believe in THE HOLY SPIRIT

I

Words have a way of getting detached from the experiences that gave them birth and meaning. When this happens they are like a ship that has slipped her moorings and begins to drift. Once useful and dependable, she is now the plaything of tide, current, and wind—a menace to everyone, whether aboard her or some other ship. Capturing and making her fast to her moorings once more becomes the first order of business of every responsible man in the port. Drifting words are as great, though not as dramatic, a menace as drifting ships. And words detached from the experiences that made them useful and dependable are drifting words. They are a menace to everyone who uses them or lives with others who use them. Capturing and making them fast to their moorings of meaning is a primary obligation of all who seek to live as responsible persons.

The tragedy of becoming separated from the experiences that produced them haunts the central concepts in every important area of life. The reason, I believe, is quite simple: we can inherit the words but not the experiences—these we must win for ourselves. Unless we can recapture, in imagination, the essential structure of the experiences which produce the words we inherit, we shall not know what they meant to the ones who coined them. Furthermore, unless we can relate these inherited words to experiences of our own, they are bound to seem hopelessly vague and actually unimportant, because irrelevant to the business of living.

Two of the great words we in the Western world have inherited are *democracy* and *Christianity*. But for many of us they are drifting words—they have slipped the moorings of their meanings in human experience and are the playthings of desire, impulse, and momentary need. As a matter of cold fact, they are menaces to everyone and everything until we are able to identify the experiences which produced them and commit ourselves to the kinds of experiences which continue to give them meaning and validity.

We have found it easy enough to inherit the word "democracy." We know in a general way that it indicates a form of society. Certain treasured documents give us some insight into the experiences which produced the word and made it important in contemporary civilization: documents like the Magna Carta, the Declaration of Independence, the Constitution, and Lincoln's Second Inaugural Address come to mind. The word "democracy" also indicates legal and political patterns of life. We have certain "rights" as citizens and before the law, we say. Democracy in history has produced certain kinds of educational and humanitarian institutions which seek to minister to the "general welfare" of all men. A generation like our own can inherit the word "democracy" and these great documents and the institutions which are based upon them. We can even exalt the fathers who produced the documents and honor the ones who have given their lives to the creation and preservation of the institutions which we inherit. But unless we are convinced by our own experiences that democracy is the best form of society, we have signed its death warrant so far as we and our children are concerned.

The same thing is true of the *Christian faith.* We can inherit the great creeds that have sought to bring system into its basic beliefs. Anyone who has even a speaking acquaintance with the Christian faith knows that it exalts great ideas and words like God, Christ, Holy Spirit, Church, and the Forgiveness of Sins. And, as a matter of course, we repeat the creeds in public worship services, feeling that they must have been very important to Christian people once upon a time. But until and unless we can see these creeds and great words as expressions of vital experiences and basic relationships between man and man, and man and God, we shall never sense their true importance. And as we use them we shall be like they "who having eyes see not, and having ears hear not." Their vitality depends upon our seeing not only what they meant in the long ago but also what they mean in the here and now. For in simple truth, if they are not vital, they are not important; if they are vital, they are all-important. Every responsible Christian will accept as a primary responsibility the task of trying to relate these great concepts firmly to the experiences and meanings which gave them birth and which give them relevance in contemporary living. When this is done, we shall find them to be as useful and dependable for us as they were for our fathers who coined and preserved them.

Our study of the idea of God as outlined in the great creeds—both ancient and modern—must be carried one step further. To our consideration of God as Father and as Son there remains to be studied the claim that He is Holy Spirit. For lying at the foundation of Christian theology is the notion of the triune nature of God—"God in three persons, blessed Trinity." This concept of the multiple nature of God has proved to be a stumbling block for many a thinker. In truth, every serious effort to grasp and articulate its meaning has emerged with head unbowed—but obviously bloody! There is real comfort in the fact that so disciplined a philosopher of religion as Thomas Aquinas was content to leave the matter in some such way as this: "The Trinity is a holy mystery."

The key to many if not most of our difficulties lies in the word "person"—which meant one thing to the Latin fathers who coined it and inserted it in Christian creeds and means quite another to us who approach it from the angle of the human individual. For the theologians of the second and third centuries, the word "person" meant "mask." It comes from the Latin word *persona* which was widely used in the theater of classical Greece and Rome. *Persona* indicated the masks that were the standard equipment of the theater of that day. One actor could put on a whole show if he had the proper assortment of them. They differed from each other in color and general design: white for purity, black for evil, red for anger or lust. The same actor would appear in different masks. Although the same man, he had a different meaning, and the mask indicated the basic meaning of his activity at any given moment. The word "persona" was a ready-made and powerful metaphor for the theologians who wanted to express the different kinds of activity of God which seemed to be clearly evident in His works in nature and in history. He was one and the same God in every case, differing only in meaning and activity. Yet both His unity and the diversity of His manifestations were real. This, then, suggests the ancestry of the word "person" as we find it in our creeds and hymns. Unfortunately, its usage in Christian thought has been far more complex and difficult to understand than its use in the classical theater.

It is undoubtedly fair to observe that the idea of the Holy Spirit has not received anything like the same amount of theological attention that has been given other members of the Trinitarian formula despite a plethora of eulogistic references to it and a few solid works expounding it. Yet, as we are discovering, this is proving to be an omission of major magnitude. We need to know what is meant by the work of the Holy Spirit if we want to know what the Christian idea of God means in its fullness.

II

Most contemporary Christians will sympathize with the twelve Ephesian Christians who had been converted, they thought, to the Christian faith by the teaching of Apollos, an early and famous preacher. But when Paul came on them in one of his journeys, he began checking up on their faith. He asked, "Have ye received the Holy Ghost since ye believed?" Astonished, they replied, "We have not so much as heard whether there be any Holy Ghost." We may count on it that Paul filled in this gap in their knowledge without loss of time!

Yet these Ephesian Christians were exceptions to the rule because most early Christians spoke familiarly of the Holy Spirit since it was an ever-present reality in their personal and communal experience. William Newton Clarke describes it this way: "What it [the New Testament] contains is not so much a doctrine as a consciousness, and a consciousness of indescribable richness and power."[2] Professor C. K. Barrett's study of *The Holy Spirit and the Gospel Tradition* finds New Testament Christians relying steadily upon the Holy Spirit though they make few references to it. Understandably then, if we are to get at the meaning of the doctrine, we must begin with this experience of richness and power upon which it rests. For when the writers of Acts, the first history of the early Christian movement, speak of "receiving the Holy Ghost," and of being "baptized with the Holy Ghost" they are referring to an experience of such crucial importance that later theologians felt impelled to weave it into the Christian doctrine of God. The place for us to begin, then, is with a study of the outstanding experiences of the Holy Spirit as recorded in the New Testament. This is not to say that, for early Christianity, the experiences stopped with New Testament times and persons. Actually, such experiences have been the touchstone of vital Christian faith from that day to this.

The record of experiences centering specifically in the work of the Holy Spirit is confined almost entirely to the New Testament so far as the Bible is concerned. True enough, Isaiah makes two references to the "Holy Spirit of God" and the Psalmist prays God, "Take not thy Holy Spirit from me." There are many references to the activity of the Spirit of God, the spirit of prophecy, the spirit of truth, the spirit of wisdom, the voice of God, and the hand of God—and the meaning these phrases carried for the faithful cannot be sharply separated from the later conception of the Holy Spirit as developed by Christian thinkers. Professor Barrett builds up an impressive witness to this point (without always intending to do so) as he studies in detail every reference to the activity of the Holy Spirit in the New Testament. Couple this fact of the Hebraic awareness of the reality of Divine activity in human life and history with a strong similar emphasis by the theologians and religious philosophers of Greece, and the stage is set for the development of the idea of the Trinity among Christianity and other latter-day arrivals in the Greco-Roman world.

But the simple fact that Judaism takes no special theological note of this particular manifestation of Divine activity is all the evidence we need that the theologians of Israel felt that the meaning of such experiences could better be explained otherwise. For God, to their way of thinking, is by no means a passive agent in the life of the world. He is its soul, its moral purpose and will, its true foundation. They felt they were able to do full justice to the meaning of Divine activity without creating a special theological category to describe it. In this they have been seconded by all unitarian theologians of the Christian tradition—and there have been many who were not dismayed by the designation of heretic! What we need to keep in mind at this point is the fact that without the New Testament experiences and emphasis there is little reason to think that the idea of the Holy Spirit would have developed to the status of a formal religious doctrine.

Pentecost is the most important manifestation of the power of the Holy Spirit in the New Testament. It is, in fact, the turning point in the history of the Christian movement. Due to it, the group of disciples were galvanized into vigorous action. "There is . . . no disputing [the] statement that the church of the first century believed that the Holy Spirit had been poured out upon it in a quite exceptional manner."[3]

The story of what happened at Pentecost is well known. The disciples (meaning many more faithful followers of Jesus than just the eleven remaining disciples) were gathered in prayer when the Holy Spirit, promised by Jesus, descended upon them. It endowed them with the courage, power, and confidence to come out of hiding and take their faith to the streets, the market places, and even the sacred precincts of the Temple itself. Due to this "in-dwelling of the Holy Spirit," the very men who had fled in fear when Jesus was arrested and who had remained in seclusion while he was being executed were empowered to face the forces that had put him to death. Their gloom and indecision gave way to a radiant faith and driving purpose. Pentecost projected the Christian movement squarely into the main current of human history.

The fact that Professor Barrett is able to devote an entire book to a study of all references to the Holy Spirit in the New Testament suggests that we limit ourselves to noting but a few of the more important ones here. The traditions of the Virgin Birth attribute the conception of Jesus to the activity of the Holy Ghost; a claim to which the historic creeds call attention since it helped establish the reality of a unique relationship between God and Jesus Christ. (Yet it is instructive to note Luke's attribution of the conception of John the Baptist to the activity of the Holy Ghost.) Luke, principal author of the Gospel that bears his name and the Book of Acts, relates how the Holy Spirit was present at Jesus' baptism and how it led him into the wilderness following that event. "The declaration that Jesus is the servant of God is inevitably accompanied by the gift of the Spirit, since the Servant must be equipped with the Spirit for the performance of his service."[4] Later, after Pentecost, Peter in his preaching to the Greeks points out how God anointed Jesus of Nazareth with the Holy Ghost and with power: "Who went about doing good, and healing all that were oppressed of the Devil: for God was with him." The Gospels literally abound with traditions of miracles attributed to the activity of the Holy Spirit working through either Jesus or the disciples themselves.

Experiences and claims like these make it easy to understand why, in the early Church, the proof of conversion was whether the Holy Spirit had invaded and taken possession of one's life. Paul articulates this when he declares, "as many as are led by the Spirit of God they are the sons of God."

As used in the New Testament, then, the Holy Spirit means a special manifestation of God's presence and power in men who accept Jesus Christ as their Lord. So far from being a form of words or a vague mystical experience, the visitation of the Holy Spirit was demonstrated by certain fruits in life which Paul outlines for the Galatians with some care: ". . . the fruit of the Spirit is love, joy, peace, long suffering, gentleness, goodness, faith, meekness, temperance. . . . If we live by the Spirit, let us also walk in the Spirit." Thomas Aquinas quotes Gregory to the effect that "the Holy Spirit gives wisdom against folly, understanding against dullness, counsel against rashness, fortitude against fear, knowledge against ignorance, piety against hardness of heart, and fear against pride."[5] If Paul and Gregory are anywhere near the truth in their analyses of the meaning of the Holy Spirit in life, then its presence is the basis of the Christian ethic.

III

Certainly four great qualities have been associated with men who have felt the hand of God laid on them in these experiences we have been studying:

(1) *Power*—the power of God which makes courageous men of cowards, enabling a vacillating Peter to face those before whom he had so recently fled and say, "We must obey God rather than men." What our fathers called by that expressive term "holy boldness" is one of the qualities with which experience of the Holy Spirit arms the faith of man. Empowered by the Holy Spirit, Luther was able to face the entrenched powers of his day and say, "Here stand I! God helping me, I can do no other!" Empowered by the same spirit, John Wesley was able to face the taunt that he was a priest without a parish with the reply, "The world is my parish!" Wherever the Holy Spirit has invaded the life of a man, it has come clothed with the kind of power that men can neither give nor take away.

(2) *Truth*—the truth of God's will for man, of His love of man, of His presence in life and history is another such quality of the Holy Spirit. Strengthened with this confidence, the early Christians went into a world saturated with the decadent philosophies of the day. Each city had its "disputers," "questioners," and "men of wisdom." For the most part, they were such cheap imitations of their great forbearers—Socrates, Plato, Aristotle—as to be un-

worthy of the same title, but they were much in evidence and widely if not highly regarded as truth-seekers and philosophers. The Christian missionaries took "a dim view" of them and met their questions unafraid because of their confidence in the Truth as revealed in Christ and witnessed to their spirit by the Holy Spirit itself. This, better than anything else, explains that remarkable advice and still more remarkable assurance which Jesus gives to the twelve disciples as he dispatches them on a missionary journey: "When they deliver you up, do not be anxious how you are to speak or what you are to say: for what you are to say will be given you in that hour; for it is not you who speaks but the spirit of your Father speaking through you" (Matthew 10:15-20).

(3) *Righteousness*—the righteousness of God bursts upon the vision of a spirit-filled man like a towering peak sometimes emerges suddenly above the cloudline. God's righteousness so far transcends all human righteousness that "all we have sinned and come short of the glory of God." It remained for later generations of Christians to depreciate all morality as "filthy rags." Fortunately, the "mind of Christ" as well as the main mind-set of the New Testament afford no basis for this extreme view of righteousness. While the vision of the righteousness of God keeps us humble about our moral ideals and codes, judging them to be inadequate, it at no time discards them as worthless. The experience of the Holy Spirit did not pull men away from an ethical and moral relationship among men; it did deepen and enlarge their notions of what constituted God's will for that relationship.

(4) *Love*—the love of God is the crowning gift of the Spirit. St. Augustine saw this in his discussion of the Trinity when he wrote, "If therefore any one of these three is especially to be called Love, what is more fitting than that this should be the Holy Spirit? In the simplicity of the divine nature the Substance

is not one thing and the Love another, but the Substance is itself the Love and the Love is itself the Substance, in the Father and in the Son and in the Holy Spirit—and yet the Holy Spirit is called Love especially." Apart from the concept of Divine Love, there is no adequate explanation of the life and teachings of Jesus Christ. These make sense only on the assumption that "God so loved the world that he gave his only begotten son. . . ." Apart from love, there is no explanation of the experience of redemption which is a well-attested fact in the Christian community from the very beginning of the Christian tradition. Then, too, the notion that love is power, the power of God, explains as nothing else could the amazing growth of the Christian fellowship through the centuries. The Love which came through the Holy Spirit was the Divine Assistant of all who sought to live as Sons of God. It demanded that they grapple with anger, hatred, and injustice, and enabled them to do so with confidence and patience. It is the New Testament experience of Emmanuel—"God with us."

IV

This experience of the presence of the power of God in the lives of the faithful was a potent factor both in the creation of the Church and in its maintenance through succeeding centuries. For the mainspring of the Christian mission is the call to testify to the present power of God in human life and history. The Church bears witness not alone to the mighty deeds of God in the past but also to the "even greater things" which Jesus said his followers would do. This makes the Christian gospel a contemporary in any age. It is the messenger of the living God. The high moments in Christian history have occurred when the hand of God was laid, with special emphasis it seems, upon the lives of certain great spirits who, like Matthew, "left all and followed Him." It is their unanimous testimony that they were "called of God," "set apart by God," or "led forth by Him"—sometimes on a Damascus road, sometimes in a moment of mighty moral revulsion at the prevalence of idolatry and superstition in the established church, sometimes through a "heart-warming" experience. The history of the Christian movement is the record of this recurrent irruption of new spiritual life from the depths of God's will which underlies and irradiates that movement. Small wonder Christians treasure the belief in the power of the Holy Spirit.

As a matter of fact, the inclusion of the doctrine of the Holy Spirit in the creedal formulations has had one effect that would have made some of the more dogmatic formulators pause if they had foreseen it. It has proved to be "an enemy within the gates" of intolerant theology and bigoted orthodoxy. For if there is one manifestation of God's activity that simply, on the face of it, cannot be limited by or to human categories or formulations, it is the activity of the Holy Spirit. As Jesus said, "The spirit bloweth where it listeth," inferring that man could neither anticipate nor alter it. Man could only be prepared to accept and co-operate with it if he were wise, or oppose and ignore it if he were foolish. New movements, particularly reform movements, could and have appealed their right to live to the reality of just that Spirit of God. The very presence of the idea in the creeds both testifies to its prevalence in Christian experience and has provided a source of hope for new life and light in the dark days of blind ecclesiasticism and stark paganism. It is significant that both Luther and Calvin had no hesitation in quoting the Nicene Creed in support of their revolt from the Roman Catholic Church. They did not regard themselves as heretics from the great tradition of the Faith; they felt that the power of God was manifesting itself in and through their reforms. Believing as they did in the Holy Spirit, this seemed only natural.

In humbler and equally important ways, the idea of the Holy

Spirit has ministered to the needs of the Christian fellowship. It has been standing assurance of the omnipresence of God "where two or three are gathered together" or in the "great congregations." It has been the Spirit of God that comforts the lonely, consoles the sorrowing, and reassures the fearful. It has been "God present with us for guidance, for comfort, and for strength."

V

It is fair to say that we can find incontrovertible evidence in human experience, both individual and social, both historical and contemporary, for at least three eternally important meanings which, hitherto, have been carried explicitly or implicitly in the conception of the Holy Spirit.

The first is intensely personal in nature, being in fact this: God is always at work in the life of a person, seeking to redeem it from sin and shoddiness, seeking to lift it onto new levels of light and meaning. The evidence that this is so rushes in upon us like a tidal wave, gathering force not alone from the experiences of men in Biblical times but also from our own.

It is a matter of historical record that when Paul accepted the meaning of God which he found in Jesus Christ he became a new man. His life acquired a new center, his life a new foundation, his future a new and almost pitiless purpose. Whoever he touched was aware of this difference; he sought tirelessly to interpret it to others and to persuade them that the same thing could and would happen to them if they would but turn their lives toward God in Christ. Who can correctly estimate the indebtedness of the Christian tradition to Paul? At least this is true: second only to his Master, he is the most influential person in Christian history. No one can question Adolph Deissmann's appraisal: "Compare Paul with the others [apostles]. Then Paul is spiritually the Great Power of the Apostolic Age: he labored more, and not only labored more, but created more than all the others. Therefore the others recede behind him, and therefore the historian, as he surveys the beginnings of Christianity, sees Paul as first after Jesus . . . but what Paul is, he is in Christ."[6]

Further, it is a matter of historical record that when men like Francis of Assissi, John Hus, Martin Luther, and John Calvin accepted the leading of God for their life not only were they changed men themselves, but the impact of their change registered itself deeply in the affairs of men. They along with Paul give evidence of the fact that when God wants to change society He summons a man to be His messenger and begins by recreating that man. This miracle of the transforming touch of God continues to work its mighty work in human life today. E. Stanley Jones, Georgia Harkness, Thomas Kelly, and Pierre Van Paassen are among the many contemporaries who have born eloquent testimony to it. Dr. Elton Trueblood in his book, *The Knowledge of God,* calls it, "the primary datum of religion" and gives this statement of it: "Millions of men and women, throughout several thousand years, representing various races and nations, and including all levels of education or cultural opportunity, have reported an experience of God as the spiritual companion of their souls. In prayer and worship, whether at stated times or in the midst of everyday duties, they have been acutely conscious of Another who has sustained them in life's darkest as well as life's brightest moments."[7] The modern creeds are doing little more than taking this tremendous fact at face value when they say: "We believe in the Holy Spirit as the divine presence in our lives, whereby we are kept in perpetual remembrance of the truth of Christ, and find strength and help in time of need"; or, "We believe in the Holy Spirit, God present with us for guidance, for comfort, and for strength."

The second permanent meaning of the Holy Spirit is this: God is always at work in the world. He is the Supreme Fact in the world. He is no absentee Deity such as that visualized by the Epicureans or the Deists; He is an active, concerned Factor in all that is or is to be. The Christian belief in God the Creator, the Father, makes this abundantly clear. He is at work all through reality from atom to galaxy, from ameba to world community. He is not limited to any one period or people or faith or segment of history. Evidence of His work as creator, sustainer, and redeemer is found everywhere.

One immediate corollary of this fact is or should be a spirit of tolerance toward other religions and cultures. As Paul assured his pagan hearers in Lystra, God "did not leave himself without witness," anywhere on earth. Read the holy books of other religions and you will sense the same earnestness in the presence of ultimate questions that characterizes the Jewish-Christian tradition. To write all this off as "idolatry" and "paganism" is both intolerant and blasphemous. God has said certain things about *brotherhood* through Buddhism that Christianity can well afford to study. He has said certain things about *order* through Confucianism (calling it a religion for the moment) that Christianity and the rest of the world needs now. He has said certain things about *humility* and *obedience* through Islam that are essentials of vital religion in all ages and places. There is no reason to blunt the point of this evidence by inferring or saying that "Christianity has all these things and therefore has nothing to learn from the other religions." The point is clear: God has been trying to get men to understand that their world is basically His world and that they basically are His children. The purpose of all religions is to help men find the home of their spirit in the mighty will of God which is the foundation of all reality.

Against this background, the missionary movement becomes not so much a "taking" as a "sharing," not so much a dispensary as a communion table. We need not fear the outcome of this change in emphasis which is already standard practice in the mission field. Many nonessentials of the religious life as lived today will drop off each great religious tradition through the ages to come. Many so-called fundamentals will become details and finally be discarded as worthless. But the result will be the achievement of a spiritual foundation for world community.

Actually, the idea of the Holy Spirit confronts the provincialism of religion with the challenge of universalism. Where in it is there any room for the idea of "a chosen people" or "special privilege" or "privileged nations"? One of the strongest incentives to believe that work for one world can and will succeed is the presence of the Holy Spirit of God throughout creation, seeking to make all things one.

The third meaning of the Holy Spirit is that God is at work in the life of the Christian community. This is no compromise of the idea of universalism about which we have been thinking. It is a simple statement that the Christian community, from the beginning of its historic career, has felt the Holy Spirit in its life. We have seen what this meant in the early Church life. Without it as a vital fact, the New Testament would never have been written nor the creeds formulated. The Holy Spirit is no more a peculiar property of the Christian fellowship than the Christian faith is the peculiar property of that fellowship. The Christian faith belongs to all men who are willing to accept it as the light and leading of the will of God for the life of man. It is an open door through which any man can enter. When a man enters that door and stands in the room beyond it he finds himself a universe where certain convictions regarding the nature of life and history prevail. And as he accepts them as binding upon his thinking and living, he finds released within himself a certain quality of life characterized by power, truth, righteousness, and love which effectively recreate and redesign his thinking and living. Carefully scrutinized and tested evidence drawn from the life of the Christian fellowship makes it abundantly plain that this special redemptive activity of God has worked with great freedom and power within the Christian community. This is what we mean and all that we mean when we say that the Holy Spirit means that God is at work in the life of the Christian community. In so far as Christian people have been more keenly aware of the activity of the Holy Spirit and, ideally at least, have been more willing to co-operate with it, it has found in and through them specially effective instruments for expressing itself in the life of mankind. God alone knows how far short Christians have fallen of being anything like adequate expressions of the will of God, but at least they have been made aware of their shortcomings by the presence of the power of God in their lives.

We see then that the permanent meanings of the Holy Spirit, indicating as they do God at work in the life of the person, of the world, and especially in and through the Christian community, make it important for us to have an affirmation of the Holy Spirit in our concept of God. Almost from the beginning of Christian thought, thinkers have seen this and insisted upon the inclusion in the creeds of the phrase "We believe in the Holy Spirit." If today, in a fit of theological absentmindedness, we should drop out this affirmation, we should not only be the poorer for it, but the amazing expansive and assimilative power of the Christian tradition would be deprived of its most coherent and plausible explanation. To believe in the Holy Spirit is to believe that the hand of God is always on your shoulder seeking to lead you in the direction of His full will for you and your life. To believe in the Holy Spirit is to believe that God is seeking to bring order, His order, out of the confusion and chaos of our history. To believe in the Holy Spirit is to believe that the God of the past and present is the God of the future as well. Constituting as they do the very stuff of intellectual integrity and spiritual courage and hope, these affirmations, grounded in evidence, will cause any thoughtful man to say, "I believe in the Holy Spirit."

THE BIBLE

THIS BOOK contains the mind of God, the state of man, the way of salvation, the doom of sinners, and the happiness of believers. Its doctrines are holy, its precepts are binding, its histories are true, and its decisions are immutable. Read it to be wise, believe in it to be safe, and practice it to be holy. It contains light to direct you, food to support you, and comfort to cheer you. It is the traveler's map, the pilgrim's staff, the pilot's compass, the soldier's sword, and the Christian's character. Here paradise is restored, heaven opened, and the gates of hell disclosed. Christ is its grand object, our good its design, and the glory of God its end. It should fill the memory, rule the heart, and guide the feet. It is a mine of wealth, a paradise of glory, and a river of pleasure. It is given you in life, will be opened in the judgment, and will be remembered forever. It involves the highest responsibilities, will reward the greatest labor, and will condemn all who trifle with its sacred contents.

—AUTHOR UNKNOWN

V

We Believe in THE BIBLE

I

The chancellor of the university in which I did my undergraduate work had a motto so placed in his waiting room that everyone sitting there saw it and could hardly avoid reconsidering the matter he was about to discuss with the chancellor! "What are the facts?" the motto demanded. It is not hard to see why it was displayed in that particular place. The persons who saw it were usually waiting for a conference on some problem or other. Human nature being what it is, it is difficult for most of us to be even reasonably objective about something which concerns us deeply. Yet, if we are ever to get the right answer, we must come to terms with the facts about even such matters. The motto was both a warning and an invitation: a warning that the chancellor intended to be objective, and an invitation for us to be prepared to co-operate.

We are trying to be guided by the spirit of that motto in this series of studies in Christian fundamentals. We are seeking nothing more and will be satisfied with nothing less than some knowledge of the factual foundations of our faith. To try to do this should be regarded as the most natural thing in the world.

For the great affirmations of our faith sprang up and out of the world of fact and can be tested in that selfsame world of fact. So far from being creatures of ignorance, superstition, and fear (as is sometimes claimed), they rest solidly on the kind of experiences which a reasonable person can approach and find to be reasonable. You don't need to check your intelligence as you enter the household of faith. In fact, you'd better not, for if you do you will never get beyond the front hall: the great rooms where men live and keep their treasures will be closed to you forever. These great affirmations are not exhibits in the museum of the intellectual history of the Western world. They are either valid insights into the nature of human life and history or they are rank impostors. They are either trustworthy spiritual and ethical guides to the good life, or they are pious deceivers and ought to be rejected forthwith. They are trustworthy guides, we say—yet in saying it we assume the responsibility of giving reason for our confidence.

The urgency of making some such factual study of our faith grows out of the fact that religion must get down to fighting weight at once. She is facing the severest test of her long career, and the future of civilization is at stake. If we are able to give a persuasive reason for the faith we cherish, if we have a firm foothold in fact, our spiritual strength may mount to the point where, in the grace of God, we can help tip the balance away from annihilation.

II

Our immediate purpose is to describe, understand, and appreciate some of the facts which make the Bible both a basic book in our religion and one of the most valuable books in the world. William Lyon Phelps contributes this vivid evaluation of the Bible:[1]

Everyone who has a thorough knowledge of the Bible may truly be called educated; and no other learning or culture, no matter how extensive or elegant, can, among Europeans and Americans, form a proper substitute. Western civilization is founded upon the Bible; our ideas, our wisdom, our philosophy, our literature, our art, our ideals come more from the Bible than from all other books put together. It is a revelation of divinity and of humanity; it contains the loftiest religious aspiration along with a candid representation of all that is earthly, sensual, and devilish. I thoroughly believe in a university education for both men and women; but I believe a knowledge of the Bible without a college course is more valuable than a college course without the Bible. For in the Bible we have profound thought beautifully expressed; we have the nature of boys and girls, of men and women, more accurately charted than in the works of any modern novelist or playwright. You can learn more about human nature by reading the Bible than by living in New York City.

This high praise ought to assure us in advance of the wisdom of getting better acquainted with the Bible and of understanding what we mean when we say we believe in it. As a first step, we need to be sure of the facts which help us answer the question: What is the Bible?

Someone has truly said, "The Bible is not so much a book as a library." It is a collection of sixty-six books written over a space of fifteen hundred years by an unknown number of authors, some of whose names we know but most of whom are and will remain anonymous. These sixty-six books are but a fraction of the total number of religious documents written by Jewish and Christian writers over that long period. We have fragments of many other such documents and reasonably complete copies of a few. All these writings were not of equal value: some stood the test of time while others slipped into disuse and finally disappeared in whole or in part. Those that survived soon gathered a great and growing authority in the lives of faithful people. They came to be regarded as "inspired," i.e., animated by the breath of God, and were both treasured and thought to be inviolable. They were gathered into a "canon" or body of writings held to be too sacred either to alter or to criticize. As such they became holy writings or scripture as differentiated from other forms of writing.

The process by which such documents got into the canon can be summed up in this manner: they were found to be valuable, they were voted to be valid revelations of God's will. The Old Testament is the creation of Judaism; the New Testament of Christianity.

I wish I could report that there was no difference of opinion among Christians on what the Bible means, or how it should be used in our own thinking and living. But, unfortunately, that is not the case. Two widely divergent interpretations of it have grown up in the two thousand years of Christian history. On the one hand, there is the Roman Catholic interpretation which says that the Bible, as interpreted by the Church, is the authority for faith and practice. On the other hand, the traditional Protestant position affirms that the Bible is the authority for faith and practice. The difference between these two interpretations is immediately apparent. The real seat of authority in the former is in the Roman Catholic Church. The Protestant churches have held the Bible to be self-evident authority, not needing the interpretation of the Church. This divergence in views has not been a matter of academic distinction. The Roman Catholic Church did not take kindly to the idea of a general distribution of the Bible among the faithful. It interpreted the Bible to them, and always made the interpretations agree with the essential positions of the Roman Church. The Protestants translated the Bible into the vernacular and made it widely available, believing that it had its own divine word to speak to the needs of men.

Both interpretations have had trouble maintaining themselves in actual practice. The Roman Catholic position is logically untenable: First it seeks to justify its claim that it is "the only Church" by quotation from scripture—which would seem to place the seat of authority in scripture itself; then it reserves the right to interpret the scripture—which moves the seat of authority from the Book to the Church. No amount of logical refinement has been able to remove this basic dilemma from the Roman Catholic interpretation of the authority of the scriptures. Consequently, since the days of the Reformation various groups have arisen from within the Roman Catholic Church which quote the scripture against the tenets and practices of the Church. Without exception they have been given the choice to recant and accept the authority of the Church or get out.

The interpretation advanced by historic Protestantism has not had much easier sledding. The old clash between fundamentalism and modernism bears eloquent testimony to this fact.

Fundamentalism holds the Bible to be the inspired, infallible, inerrant Word of God. It claims to "believe" the Bible from cover to cover. In its more belligerent moods it is likely to insist upon the validity of punctuation marks and the paragraph and verse divisions of the King James version. And this in the face of the fact that neither the original Greek nor Hebrew had any kind of punctuation marks! All that needs to be said about fundamentalism for the thoughtful person is this: its basic claim runs counter to two hundred years of careful scholarship; it is no longer possible to accept both the basic tenets of fundamentalism and the results of Biblical scholarship. Only a completely anesthetized intelligence can accept this interpretation of the meaning of the Bible today.

Modernism, briefly, accepts the results of Biblical scholarship and on that basis makes four towering claims about the meaning of the Bible: First, the Bible is the central book in the Christian faith and ought therefore to be a part of the common knowledge of Christian people; second, the Bible is the source of our deepest and truest insights into the nature of God and man, and anyone who desires to live deeply and truly in this world will want to know what those insights are; third, the Bible is our best guide to the Good Life—it exalts those facts and virtues in terms of which the richest potentialities of human life, individually and collectively, can be realized in human history; fourth, the Bible is our only source of knowledge about the life and teachings of Jesus Christ—as such, it is of imperishable worth to the Christian faith and the common good of mankind.

III

Looking back, as we can, from the vantage point of time on the fifteen hundred years of human experience which went into the writing of the Bible and the nearly two thousand years which have gone into living with it as a guide to religious living, what can we mean when we say that we believe in the Bible? Among the many answers that could be given to this question, three impress me as being of indispensable worth.

We believe the Bible to be the most creative Book in the world. Its influence upon literature is well known and widely acknowledged. Dr. MacArthur, a contemporary Biblical scholar, gives it as his considered judgment that the Bible is "the fundamental factor" in Western literature. When you consider the prodigious contributions which have been made to Western literature from many other sources, like the folk literature of many peoples, and by so many powerful writers such as Dante, Shakespeare, and Milton, this is high praise.

The influence of the King James version of the Bible on our literature is second to no other factor. No student of Shakespeare feels that this great dramatist is slighted or undervalued when such a statement is made. What a coincidence it was that these two tremendous literary influences were originating side by side in early seventeenth-century England! Both belong in the category of "literature of power," with the King James version of the Bible exerting an unparalleled breadth of influence on the lives of common people. Wherever the English language has gone this translation of the Bible will be found in the use of men who desire to think clearly and speak or write powerfully.

Another way to measure the creative influence of the Bible can be put negatively: take Biblical themes and motivations out of classical art and, while all would not be lost, some of our richest treasures would be gone. Michelangelo, Raphael, and Leonardo da Vinci are among the masters who fed their spirits on the bread of Biblical imagery and ideas. The whole and richly varied tradition of ecclesiastical architecture and liturgy becomes quite meaningless apart from Biblically rooted and nurtured religious aspirations. From the first rude flat stone altars laid on high hilltops to the Cathedral of St. Peter's in Rome, men have sought to build an adequate temple of worship. Churches are the "House of God"—that is their essential character. Apart from it these leaping lines, these qualities of color, sight, and sound, these liturgies, songs, prayers, and sermons—all are without ultimate point and purpose. So far as art in our culture is concerned, its dependence upon the Bible can be stated in some such way as this: Biblically grounded aspirations and principles are to art what the heart is to the body. Still the heart, and the pallor of death spreads swifty over the whole. So long as the heart keeps going some measure of health and life is in existence.

Turn now for a moment to one of the most vigorous parts of our culture—natural science—and ask what influence the Bible has exerted on it. To say that the modern world has a confused picture of the interrelations between the Bible and science is to put it mildly! It is quite clear to any student of the Bible that whatever ideas it may seem to have or suggest on the various sciences were formulated in prescientific days. This being true—and it cannot be denied—these ideas frequently and understandably are at variance with tested knowledge. Therefore, to defend the Bible as a reliable book of science is to defend an absurdity. And this we are not called upon to do!

But the Bible has made a tremendous indirect contribution to the growth and spread of modern science. Dr. A. N. Whitehead, one of our greatest theoretical scientists, asks, "Whence was it that the western world has derived the conviction, on which all scientific research depends, that the universe is a system, not a chaos, that it responds to the demands of reason, and that what the mind sees to be true and necessary will be found to hold good in the natural order?" And this is his answer: "It is the faith, derived from the Jewish and Christian Bible, in one living God of truth and righteousness, sovereign and creator of the universe, upholding all things by the word of His power." Let those who think that somehow or other modern science supplants the Bible ponder that judgment! If it is true, science can no more supplant the Bible than the superstructure of a building can supplant its foundation, or a plant get along without its seedbed. To be sure, the Bible is obviously no textbook for any kind of science, as we understand that term, nor does it claim to be, but it does provide the sure foundation of faith in the reliability of the universe apart from which no textbook in science would ever be written. Which, to my mind, is creative influence of the highest order.

A second fact comes to mind when we affirm our faith in the Bible: *The Bible exalts God as no other book does.*

No one idea of God dominates the Bible from beginning to end. Rather, it exhibits several ideas put together like a staircase, which in its totality is a tremendous faith in God. Each step in a staircase can be studied separately since it has its own individual place to be and work to do. But the actual importance of what each step does is determined by where the bottom step begins and the top step ends.

The first and lowest step described in the Bible is really on the level of a form of life so primitive as to be indistinguishable from barbarism. Naturally the idea of God in vogue then fits in with such surroundings. God is regarded as being a tribal war god living in splendid and awful solitariness on Mount Sinai. And there He stayed until and unless His tribal kinsmen got in such a plight that, in order to save them (and His face!) He would have to leave His sacred habitat and lead them to victory in battle, or work some other miraculous deliverance from evil.

The second step finds God as the unifying deity of the twelve Hebrew tribes. By means of a common covenant—the Decalogue—He knits them together in a semblance of social unity. The agreement is simple and far-reaching: If they will keep His miraculously revealed Law, He will take care of them. He will be their God if they will be His people.

The third step finds an expansion of God's power. He it is who permits the enemies of the Hebrews to punish them. This He does in order to chastise the Hebrews for their infidelity, and not because He loves their enemies. He loves only the Hebrews, and merely uses other peoples as implements in His dealings with His chosen people.

The fourth step finds God more generously disposed toward all peoples. He rules all nations in righteousness even though He has singled out the Hebrews for a special mission and duty in the total life of mankind. Slowly but surely the idea of God is dropping off the garments of a tribal deity and is taking on the vestments of a universal Father.

The fifth step carries the logic of this development still further and portrays God as the Father of all peoples, the spiritual Ground of all existence, the One toward whom all prayers are directed under whatever name He may be called. God becomes truly universal and omnipotent.

The topmost step comes when it is said that, "God so loved the world that he gave his only begotten Son that whosoever believeth on him shall not perish but have everlasting life." I say this is the top step because it reveals One whose truth and justice are rooted and grounded in an all-consuming, all-conquering love for all mankind.

This staircase of ideas describes the way in which the Biblical idea of God grew up, ethically speaking. Grew up from wrath and vengeance to love and forgiveness, from One who dwelt alone on a mountain to One in whom all men live and move and have their being. Different though each step is from all the others, they nonetheless join together to form an unbroken exaltation of God as Creator, Sustainer, and Redeemer—at first of a tiny tribe, later of the whole world. The Bible is one long chronicle of the necessity of faith in God even though ideas of God should differ from age to age. In the Bible, God is no idea; He is a Doer, Actor, Creator.

The Bible is pregnant with *the deeds of God.* It begins with God the Creator and ends with God the Re-creator. It begins with the creation of the world and ends with the redemption of the world in the new Jerusalem, the abode in which "God shall wipe away all tears." In between the recital of these mighty acts of creation and redemption, the Bible dwells on the themes of God's search for man and man's response to that search. What a search it was! God left no stone unturned in His efforts to lead man aright; He literally tried everything. He sought man's conscious and loving loyalty through the laws of nature and history, ordering events for human welfare, *if man would but see, under-*

stand, and obey. He sought man's unforced obedience through the conventions, rituals, customs, and traditions of religion, revealing the majesty of His power, the integrity of His purpose, the steadfastness of His love, *if man would but see, understand, and obey.* And it is to the everlasting credit of mankind that at least a few men did see, understand, and obey. The Bible celebrates the succession of great souls like Moses and Jeremiah who had some inkling of what God was trying to do. But, by and large, mankind continued, or so they thought, to elude "the hound of heaven." Finally—and it is God's supreme effort—He sought man in the sheer act of pure love which is Jesus Christ. When we hail him as "the only begotten Son of the Father" we may mean many things, some controversial and some conventional, but they must all add up to this, finally: the love of God for man is revealed supremely in the life and teachings of Jesus Christ.

One thing more deserves to be noted in the Bible's exaltation of God. No easygoing optimistic faith in God can be Biblically rooted. Not if you know and pay due regard to your Job and Romans! The authors of these moral epics emerge from their battle with bitter facts with neither adolescent queries nor immature convictions, but feeling more like the Pilgrim in Matthew Arnold's *Rugby Chapel,* who reported thus to God at the end of his perilous journey:

> We bring
> Only ourselves; we lost
> Sight of the rest in the storm.
> Hardly ourselves we fought through,
> Stripped, without friends, as we are.
> Friends, companions, and train
> The Avalanche swept from our side.

Yet, in that mood and moment of desperate triumph, the writers of Job and Romans discovered to their amazed joy, like Elijah, before them, that God was with them and had been with them all the time striking the blinders from their eyes, spurring their flagging spirits when all seemed lost, opening up passageways through blank walls, leading them through tempests as well as in green pastures and beside still waters.

This Bible that we cherish is a Book about God; a Book that takes God seriously, a Book that stands or falls with faith in the God whom it exalts.

We believe that the Bible is the most morally earnest Book in the world. This, I suspect, is the deepest reason why we of the modern world and this Book of books have parted company. Like one of O. Henry's heroines, we want "to wear life like a rose on her bosom." The Bible makes short work of such superficiality.

The Bible is founded upon the reality of right and wrong, of good and evil—which is the prerequisite of any morality. It introduces us to a morally rigorous universe and says, "This is your home. Live in it." It jolts us out of the easygoing attitude of compromise summed up in the words: "What I think is right is right for me; what you think is right is right for you." The Bible has none of this oh-so-convenient attitude. Why not? Because this view of truth weakens us morally for facing the great issues of life even when it seems to ease the way in smaller things and ways. Put the spirit of moral compromise in another way and this is about what it adds up to: "Where nothing is forbidden everything is permitted." The Bible knows that we do not live in that kind of world. God alone knows how many more times our moral vacillations must collapse in a flaming day of terror, tragedy, and ruins before we know it, too, and begin to build upon other and deeper foundations. The Bible introduces us to a world which is founded upon the solid rock of God's will as the foundation of truth, justice, and righteousness. It asks us to build on that foundation and upon no other, on penalty of ghastly failure.

Dwight L. Moody wrote these words on the flyleaf of a young man's Bible: "This Book will keep you from your sins, or your sins will keep you from this Book." If this is an overstatement, and I am inclined to think it is, it at least overstates a truth which can more safely be overstated than understated. The Bible is not a simple description of how life is lived; it is an almost terrifyingly plain statement that life ought to be lived with the clear realization that there is both a right and wrong way to live it, the rightness and wrongness of which are rooted in the reality of God's will for our welfare. Wherever we turn in it, the Bible keeps confronting us with God as the Contemporary Fact, outweighing and outranking all other facts in stark importance for human living.

Early in the nineteenth century an observing Frenchman, de Tocqueville by name, paid a lengthy visit to the United States. He says of the pioneer: "He was equipped with a Bible, an ax and a newspaper. He was acquainted with the past, curious about the future, and always ready to argue about the present."[2] H. L. Mencken and his kind have had a good deal of fun over the phrase "the Bible belt." They have made it synonymous with ignorance, superstition, and bigotry. But, I ask you, are these to be regarded as the enduring products of Bible reading and study? Anyone equipped with any amount of historical data knows better. Arthur Holt asks:[3]

If we, as American people, tell Bible stories to our children, what will be the effect upon their mental furnishings? [And his answer is:] They will recognize the supremacy of God over the conscience of men. They will know that this God has sought spiritual maturity on the part of his children, that he is ever seeking to keep alive in them the principle of consent. They will know that there are no preferred classes or races in the community of the spirit. They will demand a social order of which this is also true. They will hold their property for the glory of God and not for personal glory, and will demand that the gains of a commonwealth shall be shared gains. They will see that they have received through Jesus Christ a "calling" and not a command to obey a law, and to that extent they will demand that they be left free to accept a vocation, not from the state but from a source superior to the state. They will demand the right to criticize the state and will grow up to understand that freedom of worship and freedom of discussion are necessary thereto.

Laugh that off, you sophisticates who ridicule the Bible belt! Do you know of any better way to recapture the essentially humanitarian and even-handed idealism so essential to democracy than by a renewed study of this Book which meant so much in terms of the coin of courage, hope, and understanding to the men and women who planted and nurtured this country?

There is no substitute for and no parallel to the moral earnestness of the Bible. I cannot but be disturbed by the obvious deterioration in Bible reading and study among churchmen of our day. We of all people should know and prize this Book above all other books. The fact that we give it lip service signifies our good intentions, but the further fact that we give it little else bodes ill for the strength of Christianity at precisely the historic hour when her strength should be at its peak. Few things are more discouraging than the large number of churchmen who want and expect the Church to be a mighty factor in world reconstruction while they themselves neglect the great resource of religious strength to be found in the Bible. We must either conquer this contradiction between what we want and what we do, or be conquered by it. To us, as to earlier generations, comes the ancient cry of division: "Choose ye this day whom ye will serve!" "Well," you ask, "aren't you overdrawing the picture a bit when you say we neglect the Bible? Isn't it the best seller today as always?" I must answer yes to the latter, but without too much conviction as to its worth. We should remember that the Bible makes a most attractive gift to graduates! And many a Bible, so given, should bear this inscription, "From me who hasn't read it to another who will do likewise!"

Enshrined in this Book is the word of God, not as enunciated by fiat but as hewn out in personal life and human history. We shall be a generation of ingrates if we let the Bible gather dust on our shelves when it could be bearing fruit in our lives. *It isn't enough to own it; we need to be owned by it.* It isn't enough to read it or even to study it; we must read and study ourselves in the light of it. Like men of old, we need to search the scriptures because they are the words of eternal life, pointing out the way of God to our way-lost generation.

A CANTICLE OF THE CHURCH

ARISE, shine; for thy light is come, and the glory of the Lord is risen upon thee.

For behold, darkness shall cover the earth, and gross darkness the people.

But the Lord shall arise upon thee, and his glory shall be seen upon thee.

And the nations shall come to thy light, and kings to the brightness of thy rising.

The abundance of the sea shall be turned unto thee; the wealth of the nations shall come unto thee.

Thy gates shall stand always open; they shall not be shut day or night.

That men may bring unto thee the wealth of the nations, and their kings led with them.

For the nation and kingdom that will not serve thee shall perish; yea, it shall be utterly wasted.

Violence shall no more be heard in thy land, wasting nor destruction within thy borders.

But thou shalt call thy walls Salvation, and thy gates thou shalt call Praise.

The sun shall be no more thy light by day; neither for brightness shall the moon give light unto thee.

But the Lord shall be unto thee an everlasting light, and thy God thy glory.

Thy sun shall no more go down; neither shall thy moon withdraw itself.

For the Lord shall be thine everlasting light, and the days of thy mourning shall be ended.

Glory be to the Father, and to the Son, and to the Holy Ghost; as it was in the beginning, is now, and ever shall be, world without end. Amen.[1]

VI

We Believe in THE CHURCH

I

How many times have you heard people say that they believe in religion but not in the Church? Most people who make this assertion, I dare say, would be insulted if you were to point out that that is like saying they believe in love but not in marriage and the home. But without intending any insult at all, the plain fact should be pointed out that one basic, ethical principle underlies both assertions. Here is the principle: they believe in all of the privileges implicit in the emotion but in none of the responsibilities implicit in its fulfillment. It is one of the results of the intense individualism of the nineteenth and the early part of the twentieth centuries that so many of us today are in this anomalous and decidedly dangerous moral situation. We as a generation believe in love. We mouth the word and maul the emotion it connotes in a manner seldom equaled and never surpassed by any other age in the long history of man. And by love we usually mean an emotional attachment whose deepest meanings not only culminate but actually terminate in the sexual act itself. People who hold this view of the meaning of love are candidates for the unenviable description of being exciting lovers, poor husbands or wives, and worse fathers or mothers. They believe in love, they want to drink deep of its privileges, but they are impatient of the restraints and responsibilities of marriage and the home.

Likewise, we believe in religion in a vague sort of way. We want to enjoy its assurance of the essential worthfulness of human life, the essential goodness of what we in our highest moments try to do. We want to believe that there is a far-off divine event toward which the whole creation moves. We want to believe that our limited, fleeting, and nondescript lives can somehow count for good. We want to face the anxieties and the tragedies of life, strengthened not alone by the assurance of the reality of God, but also by the belief that He is concerned about us and our welfare. Wanting and needing these fruits of vital religion, we simply take them from the Christian tradition which has brought them to us. Without so much as a "thank you" we take them from the life of the Church which has nurtured them for two thousand years and apart from whose ministry they would not be available for us in our hour of need. You would think, would you not, that courtesy alone would prompt us to be sincerely grateful to those who through the years have made this possible? And that we would be properly humbled by the realization that unless we invest our lives in the perpetuation of this tradition, our children will have far less spiritual food than we have had. The Church can well say with saddened King Lear, "How sharper than a serpent's tooth it is to have a thankless child." For people who depend, consciously or not, upon the Church yet upon whom the Church cannot depend, constitute one of her greatest problems today.

If you are acquainted with the religious census of this country, you will know how real a problem it is. One-half of the people of this country have no connection with and make no recorded contribution to the support of or the attendance upon a church or a synagogue. Nor are we alone in this grim situation. A British clergyman visited this country recently and reported that there is a wall of indifference to religion in his country that will come close to breaking the heart of any minister who must find his way through it. Identical reports come to us from every country in Europe and in the Americas. Therefore it is no little, no isolated problem that we talk about when we inquire into the meaning and the future of the Christian Church today. It ought to be clear that unless this apathy toward the Church can be transformed into active interest the values of religion are going to mean less and less instead of more and more in the dark days through which we must live the remainder of our lives.

The first step toward combating this apathy is not to scold those who are apathetic. We who are active in religion are probably as much to blame as they for their lack of interest in the Church. And it certainly would be beside the point to scold those who obviously are not apathetic to the meaning of religion and not unresponsive to the claim of the Church. But there does rest upon those of us who believe in the Church the necessity of rekindling the fires of our own conviction in the Church as an indispensable expression of the Christian religion. We must know whereof we speak when we say that you cannot have a Christian religion without a Christian Church. The Christian religion has not perpetuated itself without an institution; it has always perpetuated itself in and through an institution of some kind or other. There is no reason to believe that the Christian religion can or will continue to exist without some kind of an institution. We need to take this simple fact seriously, so seriously that our lives, beginning with our thinking, will become ablaze with the conviction of the irreplaceable importance of the Church. Then and only then may we expect others to light their lives from ours. To this end, then, let us review some of the more important facts which underlie our belief in the Church. We are not now seeking to praise the Church; we are trying to understand it.

II

The first fact is this: *some kind of religious organization is an essential of vital religion.* Study the history of mankind with care and you will discover this to be true: vital religion always expresses itself in and through some kind of institutional and historical tradition. But for the institution the insight of faith would have perished rather than been perpetuated in a tradition and thereby made available to subsequent generations. There doubtless have been many noble insights here, there, and yonder in the human scene over these tens of thousands of years that have blazed up like candles in the dark only to go out because they were not perpetuated by some institution. No one knows how much squandering of spiritual capital there has been in the long range of human history because of this oft-repeated and always tragic fact. It is a good thing to acknowledge our debt of gratitude to the schools of disciples who gathered around men like Jeremiah, Isaiah, and Amos. But for them we might not know so much as the names of these spiritual giants. But thanks to these "schools" of earnest followers, we know their names and much of what they thought and said in their day and generation. We are not so fortunate as regards many other prophetic figures. We know only their names because they were hermits, living alone, separating themselves from any kind of institution or social group through which their insights might be passed on to subsequent generations.

It is no accident that we find a social group, an institution, in every vital historical religion. For religion is as social as life itself. Not many of us will claim to be "self-made" men—even though we may act that way upon occasion. We are inseparately related to the lives of others, physically, socially, psychologically, and spiritually. Speaking, as religion does, to the whole of life it must speak in social as well as personal terms, to a social as well as to an individual being. That is why vital religion is and must always be as truly social as personal in its outlook and organization.

Religion is intensely personal—let there be no mistake about that!—but it is not therefore private—let that be understood too! It is concerned with our relationships with other people and with Almighty God. Everything that has been important in art, or science, or literature has expressed itself in schools, or traditions, or institutions. By any manner of reckoning, one of the tokens of the importance of religion—though not the only one—is this determination and ability to insert itself as a social and institutional fact in the unfolding historical life of man.

The Christian faith has expressed itself through not one but many different forms of social organization. In fact, I am of the opinion that, over the nineteen hundred years of Christian history, we have seen every conceivable pattern of social organization tried within the Christian Church. We have churches with and without stated liturgies, with and without bishops, with and without preachers, with and without sacraments, with and without centralized institutional government.

It is easy—far too easy—to dismiss the Church as being hopelessly divided because of these broad differences which do exist. Not a few critics would challenge our right even to speak of "the Christian Church" as though it were a unitary fact. Yet such critics overlook the unity in purpose which binds all branches of the Christian Church into a church. Dean Willard Sperry has stated this central purpose in these words: "It is the business of the Church to make God real to every generation." A stickler for theological exactness might wish to amend this to read: "It is the business of the Christian Church to make the will of God as revealed in the life and teachings of Jesus Christ real to every generation."

It is a matter of historical record and achievement that the Church has accomplished this purpose with some measure of real success. Its growth and spread constitutes one of the most amazing facts in human history. Beginning with a handful of persons living in a relatively small area of the eastern part of the Greco-Roman world, it has spread to the corners of the earth in less than two thousand years. It has crossed all known borders and barriers that usually separate men: clan, race, nation, culture. Though it has taken on (and cast off) many different social forms, the purpose of and in each was the ancient goal of the disciples: to preach Christ to all men. The true marvel of the Church is not the existence of so many different social forms of expression, but the continuing fidelity of each form to the single purpose of the Christian faith.

I repeat, this social organization has been and is the "carrier" of religious faith from one generation to another as well as from one culture to another. Were it not for some such "carrier" there is no reason to doubt that the Christian faith would not have survived the first generation of Christians. But it not only survived; it grew swiftly and began to bear fruit everywhere. And the end is not yet.

When various forms of the Church trumpet abroad the claim to be "the only true form" it is well to listen quietly, even respectfully, without forgetting the multiple forms through which the Christian faith has asserted itself in the lives of men. Whether, in our creeds, we say we believe in the "one catholic and apostolic Church," or in the "holy catholic Church," or in "the Church as the fellowship for worship and for service of all who are united to the living Lord," we are pointing a steady finger at the fact that a social organization has been and is the actual carrier or bearer or interpreter of the Christian faith through the ages.

This, then, is the first fact which gives realistic content and actual body to the assertion, common to all forms of historic Christianity, "We believe in the Church."

III

But having emphasized the fact that the Church is a social organization, sharing many characteristics with other social organizations, we must now pay proper attention to the fact which differentiates it from all other social groups, namely, *its purpose.* This is to present the will of God as revealed in the life and teachings of Jesus Christ to every generation. In a word, *the Church is a religious communion.*

To say that the Church is a communion distinguishes it at once from other institutions. For the central fact about the Church is not a particular kind of organization, or a special set of sacraments, or a creed, or a liturgy, or even the Bible—important as all these are in the total life of the historic church. The Church, essentially, is an assembly of people in rapt adoration of a Vision: "And we beheld His glory as the only begotten Son of God." The Church, then, is the disciples listening to the Sermon on the Mount, or following Him along the roadways of Palestine, or breaking bread with Him. It is the disciples waiting for the visitation of the Holy Spirit on Pentecost. It is Peter and his comrades eying the leaders of Judaism and saying, "We must obey God rather than men!" It is Martin Niemöller and his brethren in the Confessional Church defying Hitler through the wire of the concentration camps. It is Kagawa keeping the spirit of the Christian group in Japan alive during the desperate days of the war. It is the mother who, reflecting on the death of her only son in the war, said, "I don't hate anybody for this. I don't want the man killed who killed him because I don't want anyone else to suffer as we have." Wherever men's lives are made luminous by the light of God as seen in Jesus Christ, there is the Church.

This vision created the Church in New Testament times, and sustained it through succeeding centuries. It has been the dynamic experience which set off and sustained some of the most creative developments in the history of Christianity. If we are to judge an experience by its fruits in life, then this vision of God in Christ is one of the most fruitful of all known experiences. It has translated itself into social, institutional and historic terms as effectively and more consistently than almost any other experience.

The Church, then, in principle is a communion, a fellowship of persons who share a common vision of God in Christ. This is the only really fundamental fact about it; others are important, to be sure, but important relative to it. They must never set themselves before it, or impede it in any way.

At the risk of laboring an obvious point, attention must be called to the ways in which the Church as a religious communion proceeds to try to make God real to every generation. She presents her claims through four distinct yet inseparable ministries within her own life and program. They constitute the Church at work, or, in the fine phrase of our fathers, "the Church militant."

First, there is the ministry of worship. The Church must both practice and cultivate the practice of the worship of God. This is the true foundation of her purpose, the true meaning of her life. She is not an end in herself, she is the means to the end of the will of God. She is not God! She is a finger pointing at the fact of God. Formal worship services are little more than solemn and, I'm afraid, rather dull spectacles if they do not somehow enable the participant to glimpse anew the glory of God which is trying to burst through the hymns, scripture, prayer, and sermon. The first and fundamental movement in the life of the Church is this mood of worship—a sincere worship of the living God.

The God approached in and apprehended through the movement of worship is and must be a living God. He must not be simply Someone who was real to Moses and Isaiah: He must be Someone who is trying to be as real to us and to all men as He was to them. It is this vital sense of the presence of the living God that gives a worship service its soul, its reason for being. Without this awareness of God, it is little more than a parade of archaic forms; with it, worship can be lips cleansed and consecrated by divine fire, a life recalled from aimlessness and redeemed in Divine Purpose.

The forms used in worship are important but decidedly secondary to the aim of worship. Elijah heard the voice of God in the stillness which followed the storms of fire and wind; Isaiah heard it beating through the moving ritual of the Temple; John Woolman heard it in the period of quiet of the early Quaker societies—but whatever the differences in the circumstances of its coming, it produced a single effect upon them: it galvanized them into action in the name and in the service of God. Worship is man earnestly endeavoring to confront God; it is man humbly but courageously trying to think God's thoughts after Him; it is man trying to get some clear insight into the will of God in order that he may make God's will the will of his life. As such, worship humbles the pride and indicts the self-righteousness of men for in the sight of God "all have sinned and come short of the glory of God." Having stripped man of the tinsel trappings of feigned virtue and false pride, worship reveals the true glory of a life dedicated to, lost in, the will of God.

Second, and as a consequence of the first, *the Church has a ministry of education.* This is a necessary work for an institution which tries to bring nearly three millennia of human experiences to bear on our problems today. The Bible is the central document in our religious tradition—and only one who has never studied it seriously can think it a simple, easily understood, and quite teachable book. One need not be a pedant to appreciate the complexity of the task of Biblical translation and interpretation. There is no one final translation of the Bible. Each of the several fine translations now in existence has its own peculiar advantages and is, therefore, useful.

It is no easy task to establish the relevance of Biblical teachings to many of the problems we face today, yet, if the Bible is not to be treated as irrelevant, it must be brought into a vital relationship with everyday perplexities. To do this requires not only a knowledge of the Bible but an acute understanding of the problems that are breaking the minds and spirits of men today.

Then, too, the rich store of human experience that comprises the Christian tradition and Christian history demands interpretation if for no other reason than the desire to avoid making the same mistakes twice. One source of the richness of the Christian faith is the wide variety of significant movements which have arisen within it. Take, as an example, the Reformation, about which we Protestants are hearing and ought to hear a good deal of talk these days. To understand the Reformation with any adequacy demands careful excursions into the cultural, economic, social, and political areas of that day. I do not mean that you cannot grasp some notion of the greatness of Martin Luther without specializing in all these fields! God forbid! But I do mean to say that a careful understanding and presentation of the meaning of the Reformation requires a carefully constructed ministry of education on the part of school and church.

It is safe to say that in no area of the Christian program today is there so much heart-searching both as to principles and program as in religious education. This unrest is inescapable: and for several good reasons.

(1) The Church must pursue her mission in an increasingly literate world. "Educate or perish" is the law of survival for social institutions today as never before. Education is big business in this country. It involves the expenditure of billions of dollars, the life energies of millions of people, and is the lifeblood of many industries. Laws require children to go to school for a longer period of their life than ever before. With all the sentiment for lower taxes, no seasoned political leader would think of decreasing the amount of public moneys which flow into the school systems. It is much safer to present himself as one who wants *better schools.* I have lived through the heat of many municipal elections without seeing one exception to this rule. The rule holds because people want a good educational system. They may be confused about what constitutes "good"; they may want it without being willing to pay for it—but the all-important point for us just now is *that they want it.*

The newspaper, radio, and motion picture are powerful media for driving home ideas, suggesting attitudes, cultivating tastes, formulating opinion on matters of morals, manners and practices. Indeed, they are so powerful that they come to us bearing a blessing or a curse, depending upon the use to which they are put.

(2) The Church has been paying increasing attention to religious education as a major part of her program. The problem of training converts and children must be faced by any group that seeks to perpetuate itself. Historically speaking, there is no single form or pattern of religious education in the Christian tradition. Of course, the Church has always had some type of educational procedure, the form of which has varied from age to age and from one kind of civilization to another. Here in America we have

passed or are passing from one dominant type to another within our generation. The actual architecture of a certain city church illustrates the change. When it was built seventy-five years ago, the prevalent form of religious education was to undergo the experience of conversion and then share in the class meetings. Architecturally, the religious educational plant of that church consisted of the sanctuary, the altar, and four large rooms, each capable of holding a class of one hundred or more persons. The program of the church consisted of revival services once a year, weekly class meetings, and Sunday-school classes which were distributed throughout the church. That this setup—with all of its strong points—was inadequate is a simple historical fact. Changes were forced upon it because the church was growing weaker instead of stronger under its continued operation. Finally, over the years, these needed changes are articulating themselves in a new type of program which calls for a new type of building plan. Now, one of the classrooms is being divided into several church-school rooms, each of which aims to serve a particular age group. Another large room is a social hall for games, parties, motion pictures, and other forms of entertainment. Still another large room is being divided into a chapel, the social parlors, the library, and the waiting room of the church. The fourth large room is unchanged in size but a stage has been added for plays, pageants, and musical programs.

The old camp meeting idea has undergone a similar evolution. All of its grosser emotionalism has either passed away or is under sentence to do so. Yet the Church is making extensive use of special conferences and assemblies, of retreats and study groups, which divide their efforts between inspiration and information, as they say. Nor are mass meetings forsaken, even though they are no longer the emotional orgies they once were. They represent powerful ways of persuading men to think, plan, and act as responsible social beings.

I cite these facts to illustrate the changes in the religious educational programs which have come about in less than a century in our church life. They, better than anything else, demonstrate the vitality of the ministry of education which is an essential part of the ministry of the Christian Church.

(3) *The Church must be a ministry of fellowship.* Dr. George A. Buttrick has wisely described the Church as "a nucleus of brotherhood." Historically, the Church began in the homes of the faithful. Too few to need and too poor to build a separate sanctuary, they gathered in the largest of their homes at the close of day for an evening meal and a service of worship. The letters of Paul are eloquent with incidents that must have given the early groups lively concern. The problem of any one of the brotherhood was the problem of all. Paul makes it clear that there was something downright disgraceful in two Christians pressing a quarrel between themselves to the point that they were haled before a heathen judge for trial! He discusses any and all of the problems that agitated the lives of his flock. His lash always fell on those practices and attitudes which tended to separate or destroy the unity of the Church. To him as to every great Christian spirit in subsequent generations, unity and community are to be the tokens of Christian fellowship. "By this shall all men know that ye are my disciples, that ye love one another."

The ministry of fellowship is an indispensable part of the work of the Church. For man is a social being. He was not meant to live alone, but in communion with others. When, for any reason, the bonds that bind a man to a given group are severed, instead of being freed thereby he is more frequently lost.

Some years ago a man sought out the pastor of a city church at the conclusion of a Christmas carol service. He said, "I would give $25,000 for a Christmas card." As his story unfolded, his home was broken, largely through his own fault, and he was separated from his wife and two grown children for the first time at Christmas. The freedom he had sought and found was bringing him little joy—so little that he longed for some symbol of continuing concern and care on their part. When none was forthcoming his life literally trembled on the brink of suicide. At the suggestion of the minister, he agreed to try to build a new life, beginning within the church. Through four long years—before his business took him elsewhere—he was a faithful and creative member of that church. For four years the ministry of fellowship (extended all unaware of his special need) of that congregation enfolded him, drained the poisons off his wounds, healed him, and set him on his feet and way again. As he took leave of the minister he said, "I have found my way again!"

The Church, to be true to her vision, must extend the mantel of fellowship to all men evenly. A class church, or a race church, or a national church are contradictions in terms, since they attempt to include some and exclude others of the human family from the fellowship of the Church. In so far as the Church permits herself to become identified with some part or fragment or segment of mankind, she ceases to speak a universal message. The rapid growth of the ecumenical church in our time is evidence of the desire of churches to center attention upon their points of unity rather than of disunity.

(4) *The Church must fashion a ministry of social conscience* if she would be true to her commission. In the memorable words of the Encyclical Letter which conveyed the results of the Lambeth Conference of 1948 to the Protestant Episcopal Church of the World: "The Church is the champion of man against all that cheapens and degrades him; for the Gospel is the charter of man's

dignity. The mission of the Church, now as always, is to proclaim and live out the Gospel by which alone men can be saved from sin and judgment, and the world from despair and self-destruction. . . . We must bring the teaching and example of Christ into our everyday lives. . . . Nothing that is good in the sight of God should be outside the Church's interest." Theoretically, the Church has seldom taken any other position than this, but, actually, she has been most reluctant to take this one seriously. Now, with the sands of time about run out from the hourglass of our civilization, she is getting down to business, so to speak.

The growth of social creeds among churches is a phenomenon of almost the last forty years. Beginning with a few tentative statements about the outstanding social problems of the times, they now encompass the entire range of evils which weaken our common life.

The Church has no choice but to accept as her own any and every sincere concern and problem of her people. To do less is to admit her irrelevance at precisely those points where she has or ought to have the most to contribute. That the acceptance of this strategy will bring every controversial issue of the day before the Church for consideration and judgment goes without saying. This need not and should not transform the Church into either a forum on public affairs or a debating society. But it does clearly mean that the Church will create ways and means of giving controversial issues a most careful and conscientious hearing. Some churches have social action committees that are charged with the responsibility of keeping the church informed on all such issues. In others, the minister in his preaching strives to interpret the implications of the faith for the issues at hand. The ecumenical conferences of 1937 and 1948 spent considerable time seeking and clarifying the Church's responsibility on social issues.

IV

Consider again these facts about the Church: some sort of social organization is not only found in but is actually necessary to the survival and transmission of vital religious insights from one generation to another; the purpose of the Christian Church is to make the will of God as seen in the life and teachings of Jesus Christ real to our generation; the Church is a religious communion working through the fourfold ministry of worship, education, fellowship, and social conscience.

Intellectual integrity requires that we accept these facts at something like the face value of their meaning. And moral integrity goes one step further, requiring that we ask where we fit into the life and work of the Church. I do not mean that you are to play a role of docile acquiescence in the Church as she is. In fact, I most sincerely hope you will not do that. For the Church is far from perfect; she needs critics to help her understand the nature of her shortcomings. But remember the saying current in Occupied France during the war: "He who speaks across the border speaks with a hollow voice." This is doubly true of the Church and criticism. She has never been seriously affected by outside critics, but she has repeatedly been transformed by "inside" critics. Critics who stand outside the Church remind me of a dog who operates, shall we say, on a road just outside the city in which we live. He crouches by the roadside and springs up barking fiercely and chasing each passing car for a small distance. Then he returns to his crouch waiting for the next car, undoubtedly congratulating himself upon saving the house from invasion!

The Church is not touchy about criticism when it comes from within. She has raised up her own most searching critics all through the centuries. And the end of this process is not yet.

If you feel for some reason you cannot step inside any one of the existing churches, then you have still another choice forced upon you by your moral integrity: *You must start a new church!* It has been done before, so do not shrink back from it if it seems the only honorable thing to do. But see to it that you get others to go into it with you in order to give it—and you—the social buttressing you need. There is no other way in which you can take seriously your religious insight. To do less is to play around with it as though it were your own peculiar private possession, to let live and die as you please. But if your religious insight means something to you, it will mean something to your children and to your children's children. You must find some way of carrying it to them. Either that, or you cancel out your moral integrity. To say you believe something without seeking to be guided by it and to share it with others, is to admit of moral bankruptcy.

The great insights of the Christian religion as to the dignity and worth of man, the ultimate aim and hope of human history, the continuing care and strength of the living God—these are needed if we are to pull contemporary civilization out of the descending spiral of catastrophe in which it now is. No less an authority on contemporary affairs than Mr. Walter Lippmann has said that the foundations of Western civilization lie in the moral and spiritual ideals which have been cherished by the Christian Church. He is not alone in this judgment. But what worries me is the way in which Mr. Lippmann and many others who will make this judgment stand outside the Christian fellowship, seemingly expecting someone else to carry on the institution which has cherished and strengthened the moral and spiritual ideals upon which they are dependent.

People who, a few brief years ago under the terrible crisis of World War II, were willing to own the religious ancestry of the great values for which they said they were striving in the war, seem to have forgotten all that now. Once they were willing to exalt these religious values as ends worth living and dying for, if necessary, but now that, for a moment, the crisis seems to have passed, they want to become objective, they want someone else to carry on these erstwhile supreme values. This, it appears to me, is the very height of irresponsible living. People like that remind me of little boys running through someone else's apple orchard. They take off the best apple they see and run right on, without ever asking the man who has raised the apple tree, whether they may share in his crop. If you were to confront them with the situation, they would admit that apples are not going to grow forever unless somebody takes care of the tree. The intent of the metaphor is quite plain: if there is to be any spiritual food for the next generation, if we are to recover a consciousness of dignity and worth in human life, it will be because people like us take seriously our responsibility for understanding and perpetuating the Christian tradition which has come to us through the Christian Church. If you mean it when you say you believe in the Church, you will take your stand in the Church.

WHAT IS MAN?

WHEN I consider thy heavens, the work of thy fingers, the moon and the stars, which thou hast ordained;

What is man, that thou art mindful of him? and the son of man, that thou visitest him?

For thou hast made him a little lower than the angels, and hast crowned him with glory and honour.

Thou madest him to have dominion over the works of thy hands; thou hast put all things under his feet:

All sheep and oxen, yea, and the beasts of the field;

The fowl of the air, and the fish of the sea, and whatsoever passeth through the paths of the seas.

O Lord our Lord, how excellent is thy name in all the earth!

—Psalm 8:3-9

VII

We Believe in MAN

I

I cannot discuss this theme without recalling an experience on the campus of a girls' college in the South. I was giving a series of lectures and, on the way to the convocation one morning, found myself in a long line of students. This fragment of a conversation came floating back. One girl asked, "What's he talking about this morning?" The answer was, "What Is Man?" The first replied, "This I gotta hear!"

It would have been far easier to have discussed this theme—"We Believe in Man"—a hundred, or even fifty, years ago than it is today. Fifty years ago men were singing with Swinburne, "Glory to man in the highest, for man is the master of things." And a hundred years ago man was even more optimistic about his chances to master the earth. To borrow a crude figure from farm life, he thought he had the world by the tail on a downhill pull. A movement called the Religion of Humanity, which deified man and displaced God, was widely influential in European thought and life. Buffon, a French philosopher of the period, exclaims, "What enthusiasm is nobler than believing man capable of knowing all the forces and discovering by his labors all the secrets of nature?" Shakespeare's famous eulogy of man was one of the favorites: "What a piece of work is a man! How noble in reason! How infinite in faculty! In form and moving, how express and admirable! In action, how like an angel! In apprehension, how like a God!" Laplace, one of the leading French scientists of the day, was interpreting the scientific world view to Napoleon, who finally asked, "But where in that is there room for God?" Laplace replied, "Sire, I have no need of that hypothesis." This famous reply is a fit symbol of man's supreme confidence in himself—a hundred or more years ago!

"Oh, what a falling off there has been" since then! A series of hard blows has shaken man's confidence in himself to its very foundation.

The first jolt to his conceit was the announcement by Darwin and Wallace of man's interrelatedness with other forms of animal life. It was bad enough for them to announce it—but when they proved it—that really hurt. After living as king of a universe that had been created for his special benefit, it was a comedown to realize that he was a relatively late arrival in the scheme of things, that the earth had been peopled by many forms of life in the millions of years which preceded his coming, and that his hold on life was probably as tenuous as it was brief. This was a bitter pill for man to swallow, and he did so most reluctantly.

Then, as if that were not enough, man was confronted by an increasing amount of social and economic confusion—the very area where he thought everything was under control. The modern industrial era not only wrecked the remnants of feudalism all over Europe, it also brought havoc into the life of agrarian countries like England. But it promised to work the wonders of production for the benefit of all—when as a matter of cold fact it soon demonstrated that its vices were almost if not equally as strong as its virtues. Poverty—the kind of grinding poverty known only to people huddled so closely together around mines and factories that they have neither room nor time for gardens and crops—began to follow as a nemesis the spread of the industrial system. Poverty bred discontent and revolutionary movements, which, of course, challenged the illusion of man's self-sufficiency.

Another disturbing blow was the increasing intensity and frequency of wars. What began as "the sport of kings" has become the destroyer of civilizations. War began as an affair between professional armies, but a hundred years ago mass armies of highly trained civilians were beginning to take the field, and whole provinces were utterly destroyed in the conflicts which raged all over Europe and the Americas. Finally, in our time, a mushroom cloud, presaging the early and imminent end of civilization, if we should become involved again in a major conflict, has dispelled the last elements of the golden haze through which man once viewed himself.

Looking back on this descent of man (rather, the deflation of man's ego), Professor Irwin Edman has wisely said, "The tragedy of the nineteenth century was its inability to believe in God; the tragedy of the twentieth century is its inability to believe in man." He has the support of Dr. William Urban of Yale who writes, "For some time now man has been trying to make up his mind whether he is a high-grade simian or the Son of God." In view of all that we have done, are doing, and are planning to do to each other, it takes a brave man to say that he believes in man, much less to hail him as a Son of God. Yet that is what the Christian faith does both implicitly and explicitly. Our immediate task is to discover what facts underlie this faith.

The problem we face is slightly different from that encountered in the earlier discussions of Christian beliefs. For then we had to give answer to questions like these: "Is God real?" and "Is Jesus Christ a fact or a fancy?" Such questions will not be raised about man! We know we are real! We know we are in great trouble. We are wondering whether there is a way out. We need to get convincing answers to such questions as these: What is man? What is his essential nature? What is his destiny? Is he capable of achieving anything which remotely corresponds to the ideal of a Good Life and a Good Society?

So far from being purely theological questions, these go to the roots of a host of educational, economic, and other social questions. In fact, if they were not important elsewhere, they would not be important in theology. But they are important everywhere. Our educational system turns on the answers, right or wrong, which we give them. When an economic or social order is in confusion, as ours is now, we may be sure that it has tried to build itself on a mistaken notion of what man is. Scientists tell us that earthquakes originate thirty miles below the earth's crust. This, surely, is a profound parable for interpreting the confusion which has overtaken us today. Its origin lies in the deep and disturbing problem of what man is. I cannot think of a more realistic or practical concern than that of getting the right answer to this basic question.

II

Strange as it may seem, none of the creeds of Christendom, whether ancient or modern, have an affirmation of faith in man. This omission calls for explanation.

The first and most obvious reason is that there was no real dispute about the nature of man during those centuries when the early creeds were in formation. That, of course, is true. The classical conception of man held the field unchallenged by any other so far as the large part of the Church was concerned. This being the case, a creedal statement about it would have been a statement about the obvious. We have previously called attention to the fact that if you listen to the creeds you can hear the echoes of the conflicts which the various affirmations were supposed to conclude. Every statement in the Nicene and Apostles' Creeds is the end result of a bitter controversy and, ideally at least, was supposed to settle it. The real dispute over the nature of man did not occur until the Renaissance had conjured up the ancients' notion that man was essentially good, whereas both Catholic and Protestant orthodoxy believed him to be evil. The great debate was joined with both disputants overstating their case with increasing vigor. Scientific discoveries about the nature of life injected a new note in the controversy since neither of the older antagonists was actually prepared to embrace them. Thus the matter has stood until now, laying upon the Church the great necessity of trying to make some kind of definite statement about it.

A second reason why the historic creeds make no mention of belief in man is that they were preoccupied with the transcendental aspects of religious faith. God, Christ, the Holy Spirit—these great realities of Christian experience were so mysterious in their fuller meanings that the mind of religion was preoccupied with them rather than with the ordinary, everyday reality of man. There was mystery about God and about His ways with man, but little or none about man himself. At least there seemed to be no mystery comparable to that which surrounded God and His works.

Whatever the reasons for the omission of an affirmation of faith in man may have been in the past, they no longer apply. As intimated, controversy aplenty has raged and is raging about the nature and meaning of human life. The Church is confronted by the pressing necessity of making up her mind about her position and of presenting it to the day. While Martin Niemöller was still a prisoner he was asked whether he had lost faith in God. His reported answer was, "No, I have not lost faith in God but I have lost faith in man." Whether he actually said this I do not know, but it is clear that many of our contemporaries both believe it and would not hesitate to say it.

There is more profound skepticism and cynicism about man and his destiny abroad just now than at any other time in modern history. Everything man does seems to be infected from the very beginning with some fatal disease that eventually cripples and finally kills it. The rise of popular education is a great good and an incredible achievement. But literacy has rendered man susceptible to far-reaching effects of smooth propaganda techniques. The newspaper and radio, not to mention the movies, can be marvelous instruments for the dissemination of culture, but, actually, they have become ways of standardizing behavior and thought on an incredibly low level. The rapid development of science provided man with his last daydream about "the brave new world" in which the lot of man would be freed from so many of the scourges of the past. But, today, more people are affected by starvation than ever before, more people are stricken with diseases of one kind or another, and all of us live under the mushroom clouds of a doomed tomorrow. All this—the fair fruit of science!

Man needs to be reassured about himself, if this can be done honestly. If any cause has anything to say in his behalf, now is the time to speak up, and speak plainly, lest an increasing number of us succumb to the blight of despair that settled over the responsible leaders in the twilight of Greece and Rome.

It is significant that the most important work in Christian theology to be published in our time, Dr. Reinhold Niebuhr's Gifford Lectures, are on the theme *The Nature and Destiny of Man.* In fact, it seems to be one of the few major works on this theme written by a Christian theologian in the long history of our tradition. It opens with an instructive review of the three views of man which have been influential in the Western world. A brief look at each of these will serve to get our problem squarely before us.

The classical view of man is predominantly rationalistic. "Man is to be understood primarily from the standpoint of the uniqueness of his rational faculties."[1] The thinkers of Greece were confident that in the mind man possesses an instrument or ability which, if it did not set him on a par with the gods, did enable him to think their thoughts after them. There was nothing on earth or anywhere else that they were afraid to tackle under the guiding light of reason. But they knew that man was more than mind and reason. And so their thought was couched in the dualism between mind and body, thought and matter.

There seems to have been no thought among the Greeks that would correspond to the Christian notion of original sin. Man was essentially good. Despite the appetites and opinions which tried to play havoc with the reflections and knowledge of mind, life itself was good. Yet the Greeks, as Dr. Neibuhr points out, were not glowing optimists. The known facts of the brevity and mortality of life kept their estimates about the ultimate possibilities of human nature sober.

The essential rationalism of the classical view of man surged back into prominence during the Enlightenment, a period in modern history when European philosophy was willing to make reason central in life and the universe. The rise of modern psychology, opening up as it does the real depths of irrationality in life, has put the damper on all such enthusiasm now.

The historic Christian view is essentially Biblical in nature. According to it man is a created, finite being, dependent upon God both in mind and spirit. He is an individual, to be sure, but not a self-sufficient one. He, of the earth earthy, yet strangely luminous with the rays of spirit. This too is a dualism, the sharpness of which is blunted by the overarching fact of God the Creator of both earth and spirit.

The truly distinctive thing about the Christian view is its insistence that man is made in the image of God and can be truly understood from no other vantage point. This gives man the ability in a dim and feeble way *to see himself,* which, by any manner of reckoning, is a unique capacity among the creatures of God.

But man is a sinner; he is in open rebellion against God. He has taken full advantage of his freedom to follow his own undisciplined desires and prejudices. Consequently, all that he does is steeped in sin, i.e., savors of his rebellion against God. John Calvin gives this masterly statement of the sinfulness of man: "Let us hold this, then, as an undoubted truth, which no opposition can ever shake—that the mind of man is so completely alienated from the righteousness of God, that it conceives, desires, and undertakes everything that is impious, perverse, base, impure, and flagitious; that his heart is so thoroughly infected by the poison of sin, that it cannot produce anything but what is corrupt; and that if at any time men do any thing apparently good, yet the mind always remains involved in hypocrisy and fallacious obliquity and the heart enslaved by its inward perverseness."[2] Without the activity of the free grace of God man would be hopelessly lost in sin. Due to divine intervention man has a strictly limited opportunity to work the works of righteousness, but his good works never amount to much when set over against his evil nature. Thus both righteousness and humility could be set before man by the Christian gospel of salvation, according to the Biblical view of man.

The modern view of man, as outlined by Dr. Niebuhr, is partly classical, partly Christian, and partly distinctly modern in origin. Without attempting to single out each with a fine measure, the sum total is something like this: Man is a creature, but not therefore created in the image of God; man claims to be essentially good and that history is a steady movement in the direction of progress.

Needless to say any such view of man is having a hard time of it in the face of modern history. The claim that man is essentially good is seldom heard now, and few indeed believe that history exhibits an escalatorlike kind of progress. Even the claim that man is a creature has been exploited by the tragedy of modern life to mean that he is more animal than anything else. So, all in all, this modern view of man has few exponents in religious, educational, and political circles.

These various views of man make it clear that considerable thought has gone into the meaning of human nature even though no doctrine has found its way into the corpus of Christian belief.

What I propose that we do now is to examine what facts pour realistic content into the Christian faith in man. For there is an abundance of evidence that such facts do exist, and that they should be used by Christian theology. They can be summarized in a series of answers to the question: What is man?

III

Man is a creature. He is an individual item of existence, an instance of being, to use the philosophical term for existence. He is an organism that has developed, at least in part, through a long process of natural development from earlier forms of life. He is made of the same stuff that enters into the composition of other forms of being—elements in combination. This is true of a stone, a flower, a bird, or a man. The pattern of the combination is all-important, and it varies from one form of life to the other. In much of animate nature it varies from one individual to another.

While there are many "gaps" between various levels of development, so many in fact that there is little hope of ever filling them in, the over-all picture of development is quite clear and now commands the support of scientists the world over. The particular stream of development that issues in man begins with the ameba which seems to be capable of only the simplest forms of adjustment to its environment. But in man it reaches an incredibly comprehensive ability to adjust, due to the emergence of mind. Man has a power, unequaled in any other creature, to adjust to circumstances. But for this he would long since have passed from the cosmic scene.

To say that man is a creature of a well-defined creative process gives the lie to the superficial charges that man is either an accident or an incident in the cosmos. Man can be an accident or an incident only if the entire cosmos is either an accident or an incident. As we saw in our earlier study of belief in God, the men best fitted to discuss this possibility—the scientists themselves—attest not only the essential orderliness of the universe but go further and claim that such order can come only out of intelligence and purpose.

Yet all such attempts to "locate" man in the central stream of creative cosmic purpose must be prepared to meet the serious criticism which finds eloquent expression in this passage from the book of a thoughtful American writer:

> Edit and interpret the conclusions of modern science as tenderly as we like, it is still quite impossible for us to regard man as the child of God for whom the earth was created as a temporary habitation. Rather we must regard him as little more than a chance deposit on the surface of the world, carelessly thrown up between two ice ages by the same forces that rust iron and ripen corn, a sentient organism endowed by some happy or unhappy accident with intelligence indeed, but with an intelligence that is conditioned by the very forces that it seeks to understand and to control. The ultimate cause of this cosmic process of which man is a part, whether God or electricity or a "stress in the

ether," we know not. Whatever it may be, if indeed it be anything more than a necessary postulate of thought, it appears in its effects as neither benevolent nor malevolent, as neither kind nor unkind, but merely as indifferent to us. What is man that the electron should be mindful of him! Man is but a foundling in the cosmos, abandoned by the forces that created him. Unparented, unassisted and undirected by omniscient or benevolent authority, he must fend for himself, and with the aid of his own limited intelligence find his way about in an indifferent universe.[3]

Yet many of our greatest scientists would disagree with Professor Becker's conclusion. Sir James Jeans, Sir Arthur Eddington, Dr. Albert Einstein, Dr. Arthur Compton—to list a few of our noteworthy scientists—would dismiss his conclusion as being wholly dependent upon the now discarded mechanistic science of a half-century ago. Nor have they been merely passive friends of a profoundly theistic conception of the universe and cosmic purpose; they have actually contributed generously toward a clarification of its scientific rootage and meaning. They would have no hesitation whatever in saying that man is a creature of a great creative process in terms of which he lives and moves and both finds and has his being.

To call man a creature, to locate him among other products of a creative universe, is to make him deeply interdependent with the whole range of creation. He is interdependent with the air and earth, with plants and animals, with things past, things present, and things to come. We are not "strangers here within a foreign land." Our home is not "far away beyond a golden strand." This is our home. We are part and parcel of this universe of created things and creative spirit or power. There is neither reason why nor need for defining ourselves in opposition to it. In fact, to try to do so is a clear invitation to disaster. Henley's "Invictus" is supposed to symbolize man's independence. His cry:

> I am the master of my fate;
> I am the captain of my soul

is echoed by everyone who believes that self-expression consists in standing alone. But one thing is clear: Henley was no sailor or he would not have used a "captain" of a ship as a symbol of independence. Every captain knows that a safe voyage is dependent upon many factors: the tide, the current, the nature of the bottom over which he sails, the conditions of the boat, and the morale of his crew. To these he adds the factor of the course which he orders—but, obviously, the order itself cannot guarantee a safe voyage.

Any fair appraisal of the facts about man, then, begins with this acknowledgment of his creaturehood, his interdependence with all created things, and his kinship with the creative spirit or power or force throughout the entire reach of creation.

But man is readily distinguishable from other creatures by virtue of certain characteristics or endowments which are part and parcel of the nature of his life. A brief listing of these will constitute other important facts about him.

Man is a creature endowed with feeling. It might be more definite to say that he is a creature of impulse, desire, passion, and instinct. All these terms point to one of the undeniable characteristics of man. He shares this native endowment with many other forms of animal life. And when it is not under the guidance of reason and judgment we say that man is "just a brute"—which is a literal description of the way in which unleashed feelings can destroy life. But feelings are not therefore evil. They are essential to the recognition and achievement of great ideals and stable relationships. We speak of "loving the good," of committing ourselves "body and soul" to certain ends, of "losing our life in order to find it." The power to do these things, the actual drive which makes them possible, originates in the capacity for feeling which all men have.

It ought to be noted that feelings or the emotional equipment are probably an older part of our natural endowment than are, say, the rational faculties to which we are soon to refer. Not only are they prior in time but they express themselves in any given situation before our rational judgments are formed—at least so most of us would testify. We feel fear, shame, rage, or joy "like a flash," we say; and once they control our "seeing," reason has to work overtime to keep them in hand. Emerson was looking squarely at this emotional equipment of man and was appraising its unpredictable effect on human life when he wrote, "Every man is a divinity in disguise, a god playing the fool. It seems as if heaven had sent its insane angels into our world as to an asylum. And here they will break out into their native music, and utter at intervals the words they have heard in heaven; then the mad fit returns, and they mope and wallow like dogs."

Our mental institutions are full of people who need special care in the management of their emotional endowment. Certainly one of the permanent problems of ordinary human life is, and is going to continue to be, the control of the irrational by the rational faculties.

Man is a creature endowed with will. By *will,* we mean that man can gather himself into a responsible unit, as it were, and move in a definite direction. He can force himself to do things that he does not want to do, or thinks are wrong, or that may be dangerous if not fatal to him. During the war, men were cited for heroism and it was said of them that they had gone "beyond the call of duty." Likewise, the eight conscientious objectors who were subjected to extreme temperatures in order to determine what sorts of food were most nourishing under such circumstances had gone "beyond the call of duty." A vivid illustration of the activity of will was the tragic decision of an aged Negro who, when he discovered his house ablaze, ran out to get help in carrying his invalid wife to safety. But when he got back the house was a torch and no one could safely enter. The old man broke away from restraining hands, saying, "I've lived with her for forty years and we've always hoped to die together." Then he walked into the house. When Socrates' friends came to him with the proposition that he escape prison and go into exile in order to avoid death, he refused to do so. By an act of will, guided by reason and judgment, he gave the lie to the current aphorism that "self-preservation is the first law of life."

Obviously, then, in the will, man has been given a precious quality and capacity—one upon which religion has called and will continue to call for the kind of living it believes to be right and good. For if man did not have the ability to live sacrificially—and die if necessary—religion would long since have passed from the human scene.

Man is a creature endowed with reason. In the rational faculty we have what most men would agree is one of the greatest differentials, if not the greatest, between man and other forms of life. To describe it in functional terms, it is the capacity to study a problem, to plan for its solution, to consider alternatives, to choose one, and to evaluate the wisdom of the choice in the light of experience. Nothing forces us to meet a problem this way. We can—and frequently do—react in a frantic manner, flinging ourselves at one possible answer after another, all the time growing more hysterical. We can, as Hitler once boasted, "think with our blood" instead of our head. But we need not. The way of rational reflection and investigation is open to us.

As Augustine studied the mind, he concluded that in it "man has a mirror of the Trinity." He, a creature of time and space, can transcend time and space. He can do three things at once: learn from the past, study the present and plan for the future in and through the activities of his mind. In this multiple yet unitary activity, we have the general seat of man's imagination, his art, his inventiveness, his science, his judgment, and his ethics. In mind, man has the ability to single out as worthy of living the great goals for life: truth, beauty, goodness, and love. Whether he will single them out, and to what extent he will live for them—these are other, though related, questions.

Man is a creature endowed with conscience. By conscience we mean the capacity for feeling guilt, remorse, and shame. Like reason, this is another great differential between man and other creatures. It is not a learned ability so far as we can discover. For man, to live is to have conscience. Professor Nicolai Hartmann, one of the outstanding students of ethics of our day, believes that all moral and ethical activity and thought root in the capacity for feeling guilt and remorse. Though there be ever so wide a variation in what makes men feel guilty or remorseful, the capacity for it and the certainty of its operation are a part of the natural endowment of man.

When we betray the confidence of the others, or great ideals, or worthy causes, a sense of guilt and shame will break through the thickest kind of mat of rationalization by which we seek to ward off or soften the stroke of conscience. When we, having seen "first things," seek to settle down and be content with "lesser things," our conscience moves into action. Strictly speaking, conscience does not wait to be summoned by reason. It acts swiftly and almost without mercy, specializing as it seems to do, mysteriously enough, in the nay-saying side of life. It seems to be our standard of value as a whole, appraising or reacting to any given proposition or deed. If the standard of value is inadequate or wrong, conscience will act on it just the same. Conscience is ultimate in the sense that it is always present but its deliverances and judgments are never ultimate, being always relative to the experiences out of which they grew.

IV

These, then, are some of the most important answers that must be made to the question, What is man? He is a creature endowed with feeling, will, reason, and conscience. These, says the personalist in philosophy, constitute a person, giving him dignity and worth both in his own sight and in that of the universe itself. Be that as it may, every philosophy must include such facts in its appraisal of man. They are the firm facts which the Christian has in mind when he says that he believes in man. As the Christian thinker tries to interpret these facts in the light of other beliefs, what may he say?

Some may want to go farther than others in their answer, but all will agree with Pascal that it is our duty to tell the truth about man: "It is of dangerous consequence to represent to man how near he is to the level of beasts without showing him at the same time his greatness. It is more dangerous yet to leave him ignorant of either, but very beneficial that he should be made sensible of both." Yet to tell this kind of truth about man is not easy. It is much easier either to tell one half of it (no matter which half) or to echo Byron's sneer about man: "Half dust, half deity, alike unfit to sink or soar."

As I see it, we not only can but we must say of man that *he is a child of God.* The parable of creation in Genesis carries an eternal truth. As a phase (we men think the climax) of His creative activity: "The Lord God formed man of the dust of the ground, and breathed into his nostrils the breath of life; and man became a living soul." Man is a creature of the creative process, power or purpose which underlies all life. He is a creature whose endowments enable him to see truly, to feel deeply, and to struggle tirelessly for the best that he knows. He is a creature who can betray his own best interests, his dearest relationships, his highest ideals. He can sin against God and brother man—and does so, some men more than others perhaps, but the difference between us is always one of degree, not of kind. Man can so relate his life to the creative will or purpose of God that he can find forgiveness for his sins and the strength to rebuild his shattered life. He is always conscious of "the God beyond who is within"; he is, therefore, a creature driven by a restlessness that seeks complete conformity with—obedience to—the will of God. That, better than anything else, explains why he keeps hurling himself at those barriers which separate him from his fellow men. For to be separated from them is to be separated from the deepest and most effective way of experiencing God.

The second conclusion which Christian thinkers draw from these indubitable facts about men is this: *We are brothers one of another.* In thc profound sense that we are fashioned by the same creative act, sustained by the same moral order, redeemed by the same spiritual sacrifice we are brothers one of another. We are bound together in one bundle of life. We cannot even try to live alone, let alone learn to like it. It follows, then, that we ought to bend every effort to bring to complete and clear expression in our common life—our laws, institutions, conventions—our deep and divinely ordained interdependence with one another. We are brothers one of another—and though we may obscure that fact from much of our conscious living in periods of conflict we never remove it. We can sin against our divinely ordained togetherness, but we cannot finally deny it. We can even try to destroy it in the indefensible inhumanities of war, yet we will fail. We will find it easier to destroy ourselves individually and collectively than to destroy the bond which makes us brothers one of another.

The Rockefeller Foundation Report for 1942, written at the height of World War II, spells out man's interdependence with man:

> An American soldier wounded on a battlefield in the Far East owes his life to the Japanese scientist, Kitasato, who isolated the bacillus of tetanus. A Russian soldier saved by a blood transfusion is indebted to Landsteiner, an Austrian. A German is shielded from typhoid fever with the help of a Russian, Metchnikoff. A Dutch marine in the East Indies is protected from malaria because of the experiments of an Italian, Grassi; while a British aviator in North Africa escapes death from surgical infection because a Frenchman, Pasteur, and a German, Koch, elaborated a new technique.
>
> In peace as in war we are beneficiaries of knowledge contributed by every nation in the world. Our children are protected from diphtheria by what a Japanese and a German did; they are protected from smallpox by the work of an Englishman; they are saved from rabies because of a Frenchman; they are cured of pellagra through the researches of an Austrian. From birth to death they are surrounded by an invisible host—the spirits of men who never thought in terms of flags or boundary lines and who never served a lesser loyalty than the welfare of mankind.

That is one way of illustrating what we mean when we say we are brothers one of another, and that this is one of the incontrovertible facts upon which we build our Christian faith and seek to build a Christian world.

The third conclusion which faith finds deep within the indubitable facts is this: *Together we can build a new world.* And I mean TOGETHER—since there is no other way to build a *new* world. We can raise enough food, produce enough of the essentials of life to guarantee them to every human being on the face of the earth and, God willing, we can by a renewal of religious faith find the will to share these necessities with one another. But the time has gone when one part of the human family could live at the expense of the rest. Run over the great ends we seek—

or say we seek—so frantically these days: freedom, security, peace, justice—these cannot be corralled in small areas and enjoyed by a few of us; they are the property of all of us or none of us. They, like liberty, are indivisible in nature and universal in scope. To have secure rootage anywhere they must be encouraged to spread everywhere.

Although these great ends are denied us so long as we maintain our independence of one another, they are guaranteed us when we take seriously our interdependence with one another. This, says the Christian faith, is the plain outline of God's will for human life.

We believe in man: Man—the Child of God; Man—the brother of all his fellows; Man—to whom in his collective unity with all men a new world has been promised.

GOD FORGIVES SIN

GOD forgives sin merely out of grace for Christ's sake; . . . now it is also needful we testify in our works that we have received the forgiveness of sins, by each forgiving the faults of his brother. . . . And although we deserve nothing by our forgiving, yet we must forgive that thereby we may prove and give testimony that we from God have received forgiveness of our sins.

—MARTIN LUTHER, *Table-Talks*

VIII

We Believe in THE FORGIVENESS OF SIN

I

No statement in the creeds of Christendom lets us in for a more immediate and more heated challenge than this: "I believe in the forgiveness of sin." To begin with, both the meaning of the assertion and the manner in which it is to be implemented in terms of religious practices have been the subjects of some of the sharpest controversies within Christianity itself. Both Catholic and Protestant traditions profess to believe in it most devoutly. Yet each is certain that the manner in which the other seeks to carry out its meaning is wrong or ineffective. Many exponents of Roman Catholicism are fond of pointing out that Protestants claim to believe in the forgiveness of sin yet have no way of bringing it to pass in human consciousness and life. On the other hand, Protestants are fond of charging that in Catholicism "the priest forgives sin."

As a matter of fact, both sets of charges are distortions. Both traditions agree that "God alone can forgive sin." Both traditions have developed very effective ways of mediating the experience of forgiveness to man. Roman Catholicism has developed the traditional media of the confessional, priestly absolution, and participation in the sacraments as ways of creating a consciousness of a fellowship with the Church and with God that is of the essence of forgiveness. Protestantism, through private prayer, group prayer, the experience of conversion, sharing in the sacraments, and in the privacy of personal counseling, has developed equally effective ways of mediating the meaning and the experience of forgiveness. Strictly speaking, the quarrels between the Catholic and Protestant traditions on this score have to do more with the efficacious means of making forgiveness real in the life and consciousness of a person. Yet I would not minimize the sharpness of the disagreement between the two traditions on this matter. While it is impossible to foresee any early and completely satisfactory solution, the first step in that direction is to cease misrepresenting each other and try to understand the affirmative meanings of both positions.

Then, as if we did not have enough trouble with this particular dispute over the meaning of the forgiveness of sin, the Christian conception is sharply challenged by many ethical and moral thinkers of our day. In fact, it is not too much to say that it is the target of some of their deadliest shafts.

At first glance, the Christian conception of forgiveness does look like a moral scandal. How else can you interpret the claim that a man has simply been forgiven by God or by some other man for some very real sin or evil that he has been guilty of? No one, I take it, will minimize the seriousness of the inconsistency into which we seem to slide on this matter.

On the one hand, we say that one of the essential elements in a Christian morality is that a man shall feel fully responsible to God and man for what he does and says. We say we want people to treat life, possessions, and relationships as social trusts. We say we are to work out our own salvation with fear and trembling

—but we are to work it out. We teach as one of the greatest of New Testament parables the parable of talents which, assuredly, is a strong statement of the reality of personal responsibility. We study the Sermon on the Mount with its ominous warning about the road that leads to destruction and the house built on sand—all of which stresses the simple fact that a man must bear full moral responsibility for the evil choices he makes and the evil that he does in his own life and in the lives of others.

Yet, on the other hand, we in the Christian tradition say that the forgiveness of sin is to be expected from God, and, because this is true, it ought to characterize our dealings with one another. How, aroused moralists want to know, can both these affirmations be true? Are they not mutually inconsistent? First, we say we want men to react responsibly and warn them that sanctions will be exacted of them if they do not do so; then we tell them that they are to be forgiven the very offenses because of which they should be punished.

Keen moralists are not slow to point out that the Hebrew word usually used for pardoning sin means literally, to "overlook" it! They might, if they were so inclined, go through other metaphorical expressions used in the Bible to describe God's dealings with man's sin and find an imposing array of evidence to support their charge that religion is a dodge around ethical responsibility. For, according to the various scriptural meanings of the Hebrew phrases, God "heals them," He "removes them or puts them far away"; He "puts them behind his back"; He "conceals or covers them"; He "lifts or takes them away"; He "wipes them away or blots them out."[1] In fact, He seems intent on doing everything but forcing man to face his sin, if these scriptural definitions or descriptions are to be taken seriously!

The moralist concludes, and not without some justification, that all this points to two serious conclusions. First, it is a *de facto* if not a *de jure* condonation of evil. Clearly, man is not held fully responsible for the evil he has consciously done. In effect, the Christian religion says or seems to say with the German poet Heine, "Don't worry about your sins! God will forgive . . . That is his business." Second, it argues or seems to argue for the complete separation of religion and morality. Religion seems not to hold a man responsible for his life and deeds, while any stable morality must confront every man with a clear statement of what it expects of him and what will happen if he fails to live up to that expectation. There is no other way in which you can build a stable human relationship or a stable social order, the moralist argues. Religion is or seems to be turning the clock back to the time when the Protestant reformers contrasted the great experiences of grace with "the filthy rags of righteousness," to the obvious disadvantage of the latter. Hence, the issue between Christian theologians and sincere moralists has been and continues to be sharply drawn on this matter of the moral implications of the idea of the forgiveness of sin.

As I study this dilemma, I think I understand how Mark Twain felt in his story *The Terrible, Terrible Medieval Tragedy*. You may recall the outline of his plot. He had developed a situation to the point where every single character in the story was going to be destroyed as a result of any conceivable move which would be made by the principal agents. Having done this, Mark Twain closes the story with some such parenthetical remark as this: "I have these characters in such a fix I cannot get them out. Anyone who thinks he can is welcome to try!" I am not at all certain I can get religion and morality out of the "fix" they are in on this matter, but I am sure we must try. And the best place to begin is with a careful appraisal of the Christian idea of forgiveness.

II

Notwithstanding the implied taunt of Heine and the expressed disapproval of more orthodox moralists it is a profound conviction of great religion that God can, will, and does forgive the sins men commit against Him. The forgiveness of sin, then, is one of the cardinal affirmations of faith and no examination of fundamental beliefs could possibly ignore it. It is the gateway to the "peace that passeth all understanding" that lies at the far end of the Via Dolorosa over which all men must travel, not once but repeatedly. Whereas Dante saw above the portals of Hell the fearful inscription, "Abandon all hope ye who enter here," this gateway is differently marked: "Come unto me all ye that labor and are heavy laden, and I will give you rest."

An essentially pagan and secular generation like our own may appear to reject this affirmation along with the rest of the creeds of Christendom, but, if we may judge by its actions, it has not thereby freed itself from either the need of having its sins forgiven or from the hope that somehow this can be accomplished by other than religious resources. The phenomenal popularity of all forms of psychiatry and personal counseling illustrates this fact. The feeling of guilt, the sense of shame, the fear of inadequacy and failure—these and a multitude of other real and tragic ailments of the human spirit require a healing experience akin to and, finally, inseparable from the religious experience of forgiveness of sin. Though we can renounce the traditional religious doctrine itself, we can neither renounce nor escape from the need of the experience which underlies it, and to which it appeals for validation. A growing number of psychiatrists would subscribe to this sentiment without hesitation.

Turning now to the factual content of the experience of forgiveness and asking what actually goes on in it, we may find ourselves in the predicament of being able to use electricity in many marvelous ways without knowing too much about its actual nature. Yet we both continue to use it with confidence and continue to seek a truer understanding of its nature. Even so, certain facts about the experience of forgiveness deserve careful attention.

We begin with the empirical fact that given a God whose essential nature is best described by the word "Love" and is most clearly revealed in the life and teachings of Jesus Christ, the divine forgiveness of sin is a legitimate expectation. Qualify either of the prior convictions, and you necessarily qualify the expectation. But as long as there is reason to believe the basic convictions, the expectation comes clothed with the assurance that it is not so much a possibility as a certainty—if men are willing to come to terms with it.

Concretely, then, when we seek the experience of divine forgiveness of sin we are but taking our faith in God as we see Him in Jesus Christ at something like its face value. This we do with added confidence gathered from the fact that men have been doing this for nearly two thousand years now, and testify that, like Christian the Pilgrim, the weight of sin drops from their life and they stand humbly erect once more through the grace of God. After making liberal allowance for overstatements, stereotyped experiences due to autosuggestion, and so forth, there remains a solid body of experience both past and present underlying the creedal affirmation that we believe in the forgiveness of sin.

An adequate description of what occurs in the experience of forgiveness is difficult if not impossible. We have no way of knowing *all* that does go on, yet certain things are reported and felt with such frequency and regularity as to demand attention in any description of the experience. They may not tell the whole story, but they are real clues to its essential nature.

One such can be described as the reality and the concern of God in the life of the sinner. The realization that God is not something outside but One within and concerned about the life of the one in need is, for some, the decisive fact in the event. Johannes Weiss is of the opinion that this was true in the critical religious experience of Paul. "This coming of God to meet men by the sending and the sacrifice of his beloved Son . . . this was the unexpected thing . . . The vital point was the discovery that the prerequisites of salvation were no longer to be painfully secured by human striving, but that God had already freely offered them. That is the kernel of the Apostle's new outlook on life."[2] Indeed, how could it be otherwise if Jesus' parables of the lost coin, the lost sheep, and the lost son are reliable indications of God's will toward men? Many generations of Christians gladly bear witness to the fact that both the insight of Jesus and the experience of Paul are valid revelations of the fact that God is on the "inside" of every human experience of need and every desire to find forgiveness of sin that men know.

When the realization that the God of the universe is *within* the troubled life, seeking to bring peace through new union with Him, that He seeks not the punishment but the redemption of life, that, in Christ, we have His supreme effort toward this end —when these powerful ideas take hold of a person's thinking and feeling, more than a new situation has been created, a new person is in process of creation. The sense of aloneness, of being cut off from all that really matters, of being an outcast from self and others vanishes if not at once then as surely as the morning mist gives way to the rising sun.

Thomas Chalmers once preached on the theme, "The Expulsive Power of a New Affection." Although he dealt with the broad range of religious experience his insight is particularly illuminating in interpreting the experience of forgiveness, for the discovery that God is an integral and saving Fact in even the most desperate situation evokes the response of love for Him. As this love for God broadens and deepens it literally becomes the dominant factor in life, expelling doubts, fears, and the sense of guilt. There is nothing automatic about this process; it requires the constant attention of the person seeking peace, and he may need the help of both counselor and sympathetic group in order to keep alive the sense of reality and the "inwardness" of God's love. The familiar "relapses" into sin do but illustrate the long, costly struggle necessary to the redemption of sin in human life. Difficult as it is to get a new center for life, it is equally difficult to make and keep it central. Habits, impulses, conventions, ideas, and most relationships are almost demonic in their reluctance to accept the discipline of the new loyalty, and frequently win telling victories in their resistance. Our father's phrase, "fell from grace," was coined from such experiences of defeat.

Though the struggle to find the peace of divine forgiveness is a difficult one, great religious spirits have known that it was worth all it costs; have known, too, that it can be won because God is with them in their effort. This was the realization that prompted Paul to proclaim, "We are more than conquerors through him who loved us."

The experience of forgiveness, then, begins with the realization that the most powerful force on earth, the love of God, is seeking a radical transformation of life. It proceeds with acceptance of this fact as the real source of hope, courage, and new direction for living. It yields a sense of gratitude to, dependence upon, and love for God that can and, eventually, will take possession of one's life, thus becoming the new center of motives, ideas, ideals, and actions. Carried anywhere near fulfillment, the experience of forgiveness actually remakes the personality in which it occurs. It is, thus, a profoundly personal experience of salvation, and as movingly social because it affects the entire life.

To the skeptic who asks whether this can happen, the answer must be made, "It has happened; it is happening; it will continue to happen so long as needy persons find new life in and through this experience of the love of God."

III

There is no way we can separate the experience of divine forgiveness of sins against God from the necessity of our trying to forgive the sins which other men commit against us.

For a long time religion tried to separate the two but finally, with terrifying logic, the Christian faith has discovered that these are basically not two problems but one. It is safe to say that the Christian idea of forgiveness is one of the most startling if not staggering aspects of the Christian faith. It is Christianity coming to grips with the problem of the proper personal reaction to evil and sin. We are simply playing at the business of being Christians until we accept and seek to live by the Christian conception of forgiveness—this much is clear.

The Hebrew-Christian tradition, as recorded in the Bible, furnishes us with a most vivid account of the development of the idea of forgiveness. The lofty sentiments of the New Testament have a long heritage in Hebrew thought and life.

One of the oldest problems man has had to face is this: What is the proper reaction to someone who has injured you? Within the span of human experience recorded in the Bible four major answers have emerged.

The first is unlimited vengeance. I know of no better statement of this answer than that found in Lamech's warning to his hearers: "I kill a man for wounding me, and a boy for striking me. If Cain is to be avenged sevenfold, then Lamech seventy and sevenfold."[3] This, obviously, is the ethical credo of barbarism. It recognizes no limit to the vengeance which you can wreak upon someone who has injured you. You are entitled to take his life, the life of his family and tribe, his possessions, his burial ground, his god, his sacred places, and erase them from life and the face of the earth.

Unlimited vengeance is not merely the belief of the historic stage of civilization called "barbarism"; it is the belief of the barbarian in every man, even sophisticated modern men. It is the sentiment which writes this poem which comes from the heart of the suffering people—the Jews of central Europe suffering as they have seldom suffered in their long and tragic history:

> This time we shall not forgive—
> This time we shall not stretch our hand
> And offer "peace" to our foes.
> This time we shall build a raging fire
> Unquenchable
> Eternal
> Upon the altar of our heart!
> This time we shall not forget![4]

The next answer to the problem of how you deal with injury and injustice is considerably higher in the scale of morality than unlimited vengeance and might be called *limited vengeance*. This is the virtue extolled in the Book of Deuteronomy—a later and more humane edition of early Hebrew law. Its clearest and best known statement is "an eye for an eye and a tooth for a tooth." It stresses equal vengeance—retaliation in kind and in similar measure. If your enemy injures you, you are entitled to injure him in the same way and measure. You are not entitled to do more to him than he has done to you. By any manner of reckoning it represents a distinct advance over the earlier and more barbaric conception of unlimited vengeance. Here, again, it is far from being the convictions of only primitive men. We find it echoed widely among our own contemporaries. For example, a young Englishman, Mr. John Gordon, wrote this stirring paragraph to the *Sunday Express* in 1942:

> One thing Japan has certainly done for us. She has taught us to hate, to hate implacably and furiously. We scream for vengeance. Now, I am all for vengeance. And in a war against enemies such as we are fighting now I have no particular scruples as to how I exact it. The only thing I would make certain of is that I did exact it. I hope to live to see the day when the sacred carcass of the Mikado will be dragged out of his palace and bayonetted at the door by British soldiers as his soldiers bayonetted our people. I would like to see him and all his responsible generals and politicians dealt with on the "eye for an eye and tooth for a tooth" principle. For I think there are times when for the greater good of humanity we should put aside our squeamishness and civilized rules for a moment and deal out retribution with ruthless horror as a deterrent and an example.

This is limited vengeance brought up to date. But not all of us were even as civilized as Mr. Gordon in his sentiments. Many of us, when one of our cities was destroyed, wanted to destroy at least ten of the enemy's cities. In fact, we went so far as to warn our foes that this was our policy. By any manner of reckoning, this is a regression far back into barbarism—the barbarism which can so easily break through all forms of civilization.

The third rung in the ladder of the evolution of Biblical thought on the proper mode of dealing with someone who has injured you is *limited forgiveness*—a relatively late arrival on the religious scene. Peter knew that forgiveness was a virtue, but he wanted to know how long he had to be governed by it. Consequently he became the spokesman for the best statement we have of limited forgiveness when he asked Jesus, "If a man sin against me, how often shall I forgive him, seven times seven?" Peter was taking the common sense position that there is a point beyond which it is not necessary to follow the ideal of forgiveness. Enough is enough! he would say. It is all right to be generous and forgiving up to a certain point, and then you have a right to defend yourself and exact your own justice and vengeance in order to bring the other fellow to his senses. As you study the feelings clearly implicit in Peter's argument, you get the distinct impression that when Peter had reached the limit of forgiveness, he was then going to do what he had been wanting to do all the time! Before we pass too severe a judgment upon Peter for his shortsightedness we ought to ask whether we would be willing to go even as far as he indicated a willingness to consider going. Not that Peter ever honestly thought he would forgive someone forty-nine times! The phrase seven times seven is simply a scriptural way of indicating a very long period of time. Most of us do well if we restrain our natural and normal desire to retaliate through one or more repetitions of an offense against us. Usually, we do not have even that much fortitude.

Towering high above the ideal of limited forgiveness is the full Christian conception of *unlimited forgiveness*—the ideal and the goal of Christian ethics. It is to be found in Jesus' answer to Peter in the very incident we have been considering: "You are not to forgive someone seven times seven but seventy times seven"—the scriptural device for indicating infinity. Nor is this an isolated statement of the principle. It underlies his admonition that we are to turn the other cheek, go the second mile, give our cloak if the coat is asked for. And, let it be noted by those who think no one ever tried to live this way, that he himself practiced what he preached when, on the road to the cross, he prayed that most difficult of all prayers, "Father, forgive them, for they know not what they do."

Leonard Hodgson, a British writer, is well within the truth when he says that "Jesus [places] over against the principle of mere limitation of retribution a new idea, namely, the principle of undeviating forgiveness."[5]

IV

You—and every other member of the human race—are asking, "How can you explain, much less justify, the idea of unlimited forgiveness?" If you say, "It's not natural," I must agree. General George Oglethorpe was much more "natural" when, after hearing John Wesley preach a sermon on forgiveness he said, "I never forgive." John Wesley was true to the deepest insights of the Christian faith when he replied to the arrogant General, "Then, Sir, I hope you never sin."

I would not minimize the fact that the idea of unlimited forgiveness represents a literal revolution in ethical thought. There is a qualitative difference between the idea of unlimited vengeance and unlimited forgiveness. They represent antithetical answers to the question of how you deal with someone who has injured you. If you ask why and how this tremendous evolution amounting to a revolution in ethical insight came about, the only adequate answer is to indicate the deep relationship between ethical insights and religious beliefs. Here and there humanists may arise to claim that the evolution of ethics on this point indicates a growing humaneness among men, a desire on the part of man to be kind to his brother man. But the facts lead to another conclusion. The evolution which we have been studying was fought at every stage by men and all their works. A way for its development literally had to be blasted in consciousness and convention step by step. And the agent in the blasting was prophetic religious insight over the centuries.

The facts as we know them permit only one answer to the question as to how this evolution in the idea of forgiveness came about. It came about because man's idea of God and of God's will for human life and history was on the march from barbarism to Christianity. And ethical ideas are profoundly influenced by all changes in basic spiritual conceptions. Ethical ideals always derive their form and content from religious beliefs about the nature and the destiny of human life and history. Men believed in a parochial, provincial, barbaric god when they espoused the unsheathed barbarism of unlimited vengeance in ethics. Gilbert Keith Chesterton has written of such men:

> Their gods were sadder than the sea,
> Gods of a wandering will,
> Who cried for blood like beasts at night,
> Sadly from hill to hill.[6]

When man held a sharply legalistic conception of God as a Judge intent on strict justice for man, the only ethical conception permitted was that of limited vengeance. For, if God measures man point by point in all things and holds him accountable, then that is what man ought to do with his fellow man. When man believed, as Hosea did, in a God of mercy who has real concern for His children, he will be led farther up the scale of leniency in his dealings with those who injure him, and may be led, as Peter was, to the vision of limited forgiveness. But when men believe or profess to believe that God is love, they have no alternative to the ethical insight of unlimited forgiveness.

The matter can be put this way: "The Christian idea of forgiveness does not stand alone. It grows out of the Christian conceptions of God, Christ, and man. We say we believe that the nature of God is love; we say we believe that Christ is our clearest revelation of the will of God; we say we believe that all men are brothers; we say we believe that the Kingdom of God is to be a kingdom of love; we say we want to have our life controlled and transformed by these beliefs." In the Pauline phrase, we do well when we say these things, but in saying them we must realize that they are bound together by a fine integrity which does not permit us to select and choose among them.

It is impossible to exaggerate the difficulty of accepting the consequences of these beliefs. They point to so totally different a form of life individually and collectively from anything we have ever known that they seem utterly visionary. And they are so regarded by the rank and file of men today. As we confront the ethical ladder up which the idea of forgiveness has toiled slowly and tragically over the centuries—receiving its fulfillment in the life and teachings of Jesus Christ—and ask ourselves where on this ladder we find ourselves or where civilization finds itself the answer is most discouraging. Some of us, like General Oglethorpe, never forgive; others of us would like to forgive but feel that it is unjust to do so; still others of us would like to forgive but cannot find the spiritual strength to do it—our hatred, our enmity, our sense of injustice and wrong are so deep. All in all, most of us would like to do something other or less than accept the Christian conception of forgiveness as binding on us. Yet we ought to know what we are doing when we reject it—we are, thereby, placing ourselves entirely outside the whole corpus of Christian thought and life.

A discerning German scholar, Professor Beyshlag, has written, "He who would belong to the Kingdom of Love as a recipient must belong to it as an agent." This is an abstruse way of saying that the merciful alone can obtain mercy or rightly use it when it is granted them, that the forgiving spirit alone can obtain forgiveness or rightly use it when it is granted it.

Jesus saw all this when, as an integral part of the Lord's

Prayer, he included the phrase "forgive us our trespasses as we forgive those who trespass against us." For him, there is no such thing as a purely human relationship. All our relationships have a divine dimension to them, and we are never dealing merely with one another. In every dealing with one another, we are also dealing with God. Consequently, we cannot refuse to accept the Christian conception of forgiveness without placing ourselves beyond the pale of being forgiven by God himself. It is impossible, Jesus says, for a man who refuses to forgive his brother to be forgiven by God. He makes this dramatically plain when he says, "If you are offering your gift at the altar, and there remember that your brother has something against you, leave your gift there before the altar and go; first be reconciled to your brother, and then come and offer your gift."[7] This points up the deep inner logic of the prayer "forgive us our trespasses as we forgive those who trespass against us."

It could not be otherwise. God—not even God—neither can nor will insert His nature of love into the life of one—anyone—who is not willing to be *transformed* by it. Only as we are forgiving can we be forgiven. Only as the forgiving spirit becomes our spirit can the consciousness of being forgiven by God become a living reality in our lives. That is why Jesus insisted that men who would find peace with God must be willing to seek peace with their brothers.

There is no denying the fact that we draw back from the ideal of unlimited forgiveness as outlined in the teachings of Jesus. We are like King Arthur who says to Guinevere when she has begged his forgiveness:

> "Lo, I forgive thee as Eternal God
> Forgives."

But he continues:

> "I cannot take thy hand; that, too, is flesh;
> And in the flesh thou hast sinned: and mine own flesh
> Here looking down on thine polluted, cried
> 'I loathe thee!' "

A critic has observed that, "If that be how Eternal God forgives, our case would be desperate, indeed!"

Yet, unless we are willing to accept the responsibility of believing and living according to the Christian ideal of forgiveness, it is hard to see what new hope the Christian religion brings to the contemporary world. If we have no weapon but hate with which to face the hatred of the day in which we live, then failure is the last word in life.

But we do have other resources and a unique contribution to make to a generation like our own. Yet we cannot make it and ought not make the effort unless we are prepared to face the fact that we are trying to change the rules of the game. We are not trying to perpetuate life as it is and civilization as it is; we are trying to find a better way of life and a truer form of civilization than we have ever known. Obviously, we cannot do this merely by abiding by the old rules.

The Christian idea of forgiveness amounts to an astounding change in rules of ordinary human relations—a fact brought out in an incident in Dostoevsky's novel *The Brothers Karamazov.* A young man on the field of honor interrupted the duel in order to beg the forgiveness of his opponent. He had been wrong in some ways and his opponent in others, and he wanted to be sure his opponent had forgiven him for the mistakes that he himself had made. Yet his appeal to the opponent for forgiveness burst like a bombshell in the accepted social pattern. As Dostoevsky relates the story, "The seconds, especially mine, were shouting, too: 'Can you disgrace the regiment like this, facing your antagonist and begging his forgiveness; if I had only known this!' I stood facing them all, not laughing now. 'Gentlemen,' I said, 'is it really so wonderful in these days to find a man who can repent of his stupidity and publicly confess his wrong doing?' 'But not in a duel,' cried my second again." And, of course, the second was right! You cannot have duels if you are going to go around begging forgiveness of your opponent. As Robert Russell Wicks has pointed out in a recent book, "Mutual forgiveness never caused a war." When we confront evil, injury, and injustice as realistic facts, and say that the ideal of forgiveness is the way in which they are to be met, we are changing the rules of the game—the moralists are right in this.

V

This furnishes us our clue to an answer to the moralists who have been challenging the idea of forgiveness. We say to them that we are not trying to make the Christian idea of forgiveness fit any known form of morality. Rather, we are trying to make a morality that will give expression to the Christian idea of love. The love of which we speak and the fulfillment of which we seek is no irresponsible emotion: it is a realistic relationship fully charged with responsibility. Gertrude Atherton in her novel *The Mansion* illustrates this point. The unfaithful husband comes home and lays bare his disloyalty to his wife. He knows he deserves nothing from her but the severest kind of recrimination and separation. He expects nothing beyond these things but feels that he must make confession because of the violation of their love. After he had made his full confession, the wife with wet eyes and breaking heart turns to him and says, "I do not see yet how it will be best to do it, but—you and I must work this out together." This is forgiveness in the true and enduring sense of the term. It is an identification of life with life, a reaffirmation of a great relationship and of confidence in its ability to surmount challenge; it is the determination not to let hatred and anger have the last word when love alone can speak a final word that will save a relationship. But, above all, it is the identification of life with life, the merging of strength with weakness, in the conviction that in no other way is it possible to salvage and redeem a breaking if not broken relationship. It is our most serious attempt to "step inside," as it were, the experience of guilt, the sinful situation in which another—any other person—finds himself.

This incident illustrates the fallacy in the argument that forgiveness must be preceded by repentance on the part of the other. Although this was the case in the incident, it is not a prerequisite in the Christian conception of forgiveness. While there can be no fully redeemed relationship until both parties are willing to lose themselves in it, the one who sees this is obligated to go as far as it is humanly possible for him to go; he is obliged to cultivate a forgiving spirit whether the other repents of the sin or not; he is obliged to be willing to resume the relationship at a deeper level of understanding whether the other wills it or not—and he must make his willingness known to the other!

To the doubter who says that forgiveness is impossible and reconciliation a delusion, the answer can and must be made: Both are possible; both have been and can be done if we are willing to accept what Mr. Milton Mayer has called ". . . the dreadful circularity of the Christian commitment, namely, that the only way to try to be a Christian is to be one."[8] The question as to who has done it is referred for answer to incident after incident cited in that amazing book, *Above All Nations*,[9] which is a collection of "dramatic records of men and women who have found above nationalism a brotherhood that includes all mankind." Consider this event:

When 21 new church-wardens met at Gona, in the diocese of New Guinea, to plan their work under the chairmanship of their parish priest, Father John Benson, who was a prisoner of the Japanese for three years, one of the church-wardens said: "I think God would be happy if we sent half the balance of our offerings to Japan and used half for our own school. Then we shall be replacing our things and helping those people who despoiled our country to be better people, so that they will be helping ones, not spoiling ones. That is what I think God wants us to do, because we are His children."

To which the Assembly replied: "These are good words, and we shall do so."

These are the people whose teachers were killed and whose churches and schools were demolished by the Japanese.[10]

As long as Christian thinking and living like this is possible, the Kingdom of God is not impossible for men who have the courage of their convictions.

Bishop Hazen Werner once pointed out the therapeutic value of forgiveness to the one who is able to rise to the full level of its meaning. In answer to a letter from someone seeking advice he said, "You have been holding back forgiveness but see what it has done to you. The really bad thing about being an unforgiving person is the kind of a person you become. The debris of ill will, resentment, bitterness clutter up the conscience. What an accumulation! . . . There is a therapy in forgiveness. It is cleansing. It is peace after war. It is like fresh rain after an insufferably humid day. It is like coming home again after strange places and faces, where no one knew the language of the heart. Forgiveness brings peace."

It brings peace with man and peace with God. For he who seeks to belong to the Kingdom of Love as recipient, i.e., he who would be an honest participant in the love of God which shines forth through Jesus Christ, must belong to it as agent, i.e., he must be a source of shedding this illumination abroad in the dark crannies of all his relationships and of the relationships of the people whom he meets.

This is the Christian gospel and the Christian mission in a world where there is so much darkness and so little light. It is our business to change the rules of the game from vengeance and retaliation to forgiveness and love. The change must first be brought about in our own heart and life; only then will we be empowered to bring it about wherever our influence goes. It is a judgment and renovation which must begin within the heart but which cannot be contained there.

When we say we believe in the forgiveness of sin we are renewing our faith in the reality of God's love for us and for all men; we are reaffirming our conviction that there is strength and power for the redemption of human life and history in this love and that, upon it, we can rebuild life and society.

THE SECOND MILE

THERE IS no terminus, no finite stopping place, where one can halt and read his pedometer, and say: "Now I have arrived." Jesus, with infinite wisdom, said: "Blessed are they who hunger and thirst for goodness"—not blessed are they who are already good, righteous or perfect. It is the attitude of spirit, the high resolve, the passion, the insatiable hunger and thirst for it that count, not the attainment. The perfection which He calls for is nothing less than that of being "perfect as our Father in Heaven is perfect. . . ."

—Rufus M. Jones

IX

We Believe in RECONCILIATION

I

Literalists will be quick to point out that there is no such affirmation in any of the ancient creeds and might be inclined to draw the conclusion that a careful study of the idea of reconciliation is out of place in a survey of the fundamentals of our faith. Both as an answer to him and as a useful introduction to the Christian conception of reconciliation I should like to quote at length from Paul's letters to the Corinthians.

> From now on, therefore, we regard no one from a human point of view; even though we once regarded Christ from a human point of view, we regard him thus no longer. Therefore, if anyone is in Christ, he is a new creation; the old has passed away, behold, the new has come. All this is from God, who through Christ reconciled us to himself and gave us the ministry of reconciliation; that is, God was in Christ reconciling the world to himself, not counting their trespasses against them, and entrusting to us the message of reconciliation. So we are ambassadors for Christ, God making his appeal through us. We beseech you on behalf of Christ, be reconciled to God. For our sake he made him to be sin who knew no sin, so that in him we might become the righteousness of God. Working together with him, then, we entreat you not to accept the grace of God in vain.[1]

If we give this passage the study it deserves, we will never again treat the idea of reconciliation either lightly or as a recent innovation in Christian ethics. We will accept it forthwith as one of the most important ideas in the whole corpus of Christian thought. Paul is of the opinion that it, better than any other idea, expresses three very important truths of the Christian gospel: (1) The true meaning of God's activity and intention in Jesus Christ; (2) The true nature of the Christian gospel; (3) The meaning of the Christian ministry.

The entire passage is so pertinent that we will find it our best introduction to the problem of the meaning of reconciliation. Paul is writing of God as not only the creator of man in Adam but also the re-creator of man in Jesus Christ. He makes it quite clear that the Christian is one who has been re-created by the activity of God in Jesus Christ: "Therefore, if any man be in Christ, he is a new creature: old things are passed away; behold, all things are become new. And all things are of God, who hath reconciled us to himself by Jesus Christ, and hath given to us the ministry of reconciliation." Lest there be any misunderstanding this momentous fact, Paul repeats it: "God was in Christ, reconciling the world unto himself, not imputing their trespasses unto them; and hath committed unto us the word of reconciliation." He does not hesitate to draw the glory of this ministry in the most resplendent colors: "Now then we are ambassadors for Christ, as though God did beseech you by us: We pray you in Christ's stead, be ye reconciled to God." The whole purpose of God in Jesus Christ, Paul continues, is this: "For he hath made him to be sin for us, who knew no sin; that we might be made the righteousness of God in him." He closes with this earnest exhortation: "We, then, as workers together with him, beseech you also that ye receive not the grace of God in vain."

Reflections like these enable us to proceed with our survey of the meaning of reconciliation without being deterred by the frequently heard sneer that whoever tries to do what Jesus did is trying to be a "little Jesus." As I read this passage from Paul, that is precisely what we are supposed to try to be—co-workers together with Christ in the creation of a new world. In order to be his co-workers we must seek to be as near like him as we can, even though the achievement of this goal is difficult to the point of being obviously impossible.

Paul was as aware of the difficulty of trying to do as Jesus would have us do as any contemporary Christian could conceivably be. Yet he recognized the responsibility of attempting just that. What Paul felt to be fundamental not many of us will treat as optional. The stress he lays upon the idea of reconciliation, relating it as he does to the whole range of Christian thought, should provide all the incentive we need for the prosecution of our study.

Even as the miracle of creation is essential to life so the miracle of re-creation is essential to the Christian life and ministry—thus runs the thought of Paul. Most of us are glad enough to accept the miracle of creation with eager fingers for it brings the gift of life with all of the goodness and blessings thereof. But we shrink back from the miracle of re-creation not so much because we fear what God will do to us in it but because we are honestly frightened at the prospect of what God seeks to do through us by it. Like Paul, we stand in wonder before these twin miracles of creation and re-creation. Like Paul we realize that one makes us the child of God; the other the colleague of God. Like Paul, we are so overwhelmed by this activity of God that, though we shrink from the prospect, we can ask no less than have some part in furthering it.

The whole idea of reconciliation, then, grows, not out of the prudential judgments of men, but out of the profound religious experience of having found God's will and purpose for life in

Jesus Christ. We must always remember that reconciliation originates in the activity of divine love, not in the reasoned and prudential judgments of men. If we separate it from its proper source, it will wither away into a set of futile compromises. If we keep it in touch with that source, it will persist until men are actually reconciled with God.

II

In order to clarify the meaning of reconciliation let us proceed now to consider a series of factual statements about it.

The idea of reconciliation is integrally related to the whole system of ideas that constitute the Christian view of life. Like the idea of forgiveness, the idea of reconciliation rests upon the deeper and broader beliefs in the nature of God as we see it in Jesus Christ, in the activity of the Holy Spirit, in man, the Church, and the Kingdom of God, as these are visualized by Christian thought. All these great ideas and others lie like mighty layers of solid bedrock under many ethical peaks of which the forgiveness of sin and reconciliation are but two. Yet we need to be clear on this: These ideas are attempts to interpret, understand, and share an experience. The experience always precedes the idea and any idea which seeks to interpret an experience is always answerable to the experience itself for its adequacy. Hence, the idea of reconciliation grows out of the experience of reconciliation. But once men had the experience of reconciliation, as Paul did, they were bound to think about it and to try to understand and share it with others. Reconciliation, then, is an idea, a religious idea and belief, an integral aspect of the whole range of Christian thought. It gains its content both from the experience of having found God in Christ, and from the total Christian view of life, particularly the idea of the Kingdom of God. Reconciliation outlines a gospel to be preached, a mission to be performed whenever there is division and conflict in human life, whether individual or collective. Reconciliation, like every other great Christian concept, demands incarnation, else its real meaning will be missed. We must feel toward it as a great pianist did toward the instrument he was about to play, "It is sometimes as if I were shut up in there and had to play myself out." We must feel "shut up" in the Christian faith and through the discipline of reconciliation "play ourselves out."

Reconciliation is a strategy as well as an idea; rather it is an idea with a way of life clearly implicit within it. The end and aim of this strategy is to achieve peace and further community in human life and relations. As we study the meaning of the way of reconciliation we will be struck by the difference between conciliation on the one hand and Christian conciliation on the other. Whereas the conciliator may feel that he has done his job if he brings about peace between conflicting parties by finding the lowest common denominator upon which they can agree, the Christian conciliator will realize that he has not done his duty until he has lifted both disputants to a higher level of understanding of the rights of each other than either had before. Difficult as it is to be a good conciliator (and everyone who has tried to play that role in labor disputes will say Amen!) it is infinitely more difficult to try to be a Christian conciliator in the areas of human conflict. Yet the Christian is not left entirely on his own resources as he seeks to follow the high calling of conciliation in the name of Christ. There is a strategy in Christian conciliation which involves four movements or steps.

The first movement is toward God and a rededication of life to the Kingdom of God. This movement is made by the man who seeks to be a Christian conciliator. He will acknowledge the fact of God in human life in general and in his own life in particular. He will accept the meaning of God as love as being the true meaning of the activity of God and will renew his loyalty to it. He will worship the reality of the love of God, believing it to be the only fundamental and truly eternal fact in the world. He will seek God's will and God's way for not only his own life but for the dispute into which he is about to enter as a conciliator.

Having renewed and deepened his relationship with God the Christian conciliator will then be ready for the second movement or step, which is to be completely sensitive to both sides in the dispute or conflict. For there are always two sides, notwithstanding the obvious fact that neither side would agree to this statement. Effective reconciliation requires that the values of both sides be known and preserved as far as it is humanly possible to do this. There may be a place for the partisan frame of mind in life, but it has no part in the process of Christian reconciliation. Whoever enters into a conflict situation in a partisan frame of mind is sure to miss on this point. The Christian conciliator will not be an advocate of either side. He will seek to understand both sides.

The third movement is to be carefully and sympathetically critical of the vices and virtues of the contesting claims. We who seek to be ministers of reconciliation after the fashion of Paul are not simply "yes-men." We are not called upon to beat whatever drums are thrust in our hands in a moment of social crisis. We are called upon to be critically objective about the claims being advanced in any conflict which is threatening or raging. For, as we believe in God, we must try to bring His judgments to bear upon life, we must seek to be "the righteousness of God," in the processes of history.

The fourth movement in the strategy is this: The minister of reconciliation must be in the battle yet above it. The only effective person in the process of reconciliation is one who both "belongs" to both parties yet who is not limited to or by either.

Almost from the beginning Christians have realized that we are supposed to be in the world yet not of the world. A Christian conciliator will never forget that his interdependence with, yet his independence of, both parties are made possible by his loyalty to God. It is his task to try to lift both parties to a higher level of understanding of the values involved in the dispute. I confess that I am deeply impressed by the fact that when Gandhi wanted to quell the riots in India he took up his residence at the heart of the most turbulent area—first Calcutta then New Delhi—before he began his final fast. I cannot forget how Jesus went to stormy Jerusalem against the almost tearful entreaties of his disciples to stay in a safer place.

The Society of Friends, through recent centuries, have richly deserved their reputation as lovers of peace throughout the world. Because of this hard-earned reputation, they have been able, through two world wars, to function almost uninterruptedly on both sides of the major battle lines of the world. It simply has not occurred to any government, however narrow and bigoted, that these Quakers are partisans in a dispute. Small wonder they received a portion of the Nobel Prize in recognition of their work in behalf of world peace in 1948. They are rich exemplars of the statement that the place of the minister of reconciliation is in the battle yet above it. For they have accepted as their own the problem of the meeting of human need wherever it has arisen and come to their attention.

The minister of Christian conciliation will not be an outsider looking in on the conflict; he will be sharing it to the fullest possible extent, particularly at those points where it is tending to destroy the great values of life. It is at that point and for that reason that he must take issue with the disintegrating forces which always predominate in conflict situations.

We need to remind ourselves of the purpose of the strategy of reconciliation. It is to make possible the healing work of God's love in human life. We do not heal—God does that, God alone can do that. But we can help men turn toward God. The strategy of reconciliation has not been fully realized when we "get the idea across." The full realization of its intention comes about when a new relationship has actually been built; when a new structure of life has been introduced into human relations; when there is a new pattern of personality or social relationships actually in existence. For reconciliation is not an idea to be bandied about in odd and idle moments; it is a way of healing conflicts and building peace—great peace, where there is tension, fear, and war. Yet the idea of reconciliation must not only be preached, if it is to be fully effective; it must be exemplified in the thought and life of men neither better nor wiser than Christian ministers and laymen.

III

There is some comfort for us in the realization that from the very beginning of the Christian tradition men have had their difficulty being exemplars of the strategy of reconciliation. Fortunately, there are many instances of its dynamic work in human life to encourage us to keep at the task of being exponents of it. Since the idea could easily be lost in a maze of abstractions, I should like to cite a number of instances of reconciliation in the various areas where it is most needed and most useful.

Consider the ministry of reconciliation in a man's personal relations with God. The rich young ruler had kept the law as well as he knew how and better than most men yet he continued to feel separated from God. The great teacher pointed out to him that one thing only blocked the true functioning of the process of reconciliation between him and God and that was the fact of "great possessions" which loomed so large in his life. Instead of saying to him that everything would come out all right, Jesus told him that there was one thing he must do if he would know the peace of a true union with God and that was to divest himself at once and utterly of his material possessions. The advice continues to be good even though the original recipient of it refused to be guided by it and "went away sorrowing."

Paul himself furnishes an excellent illustration of how a man can be estranged from God and his own religious heritage and be in need of an experience of reconciliation with the God who is worshiped in all religious traditions. It is not necessary to relate here the harrowing experiences of Paul as he fought his way through one species of false reconciliation after another until, finally, the Christian strategy reached out for him and gave him the strength he needed. His was an experience of genuine renewal of life through a new pattern. He was a new creature, as he himself said; his life had a new pattern and a new meaning.

Every minister could supply not one but many illustrations from his own pastoral experience of how it is possible to assist someone whose life is being destroyed in conflict into a new and deeper relationship with God by virtue of which peace and a sense of usefulness come to the person. The old evangelical phrase "When I found Christ" continues to carry a meaning that we would be much the poorer for forgetting: When a man finds the will of God in Jesus Christ he is actually taken possession of by the new power and insight of that discovery and he is eager to broadcast it to the world.

There is reason to rejoice over the new birth of interest in churches in personal and pastoral counseling. For, through these efforts, an increasing number of counselors are being trained to deal helpfully with ordinary problems and find at hand in communities specialists to whom they can direct the really serious personality disorders. Consequently, many a person who would have been written off as queer or a crank a few years ago is now led carefully and definitely into a new kind of usefulness through the efforts of men and women who are trying to bring about a healing of a serious inner conflict in their life.

To the best of my knowledge, there has been no serious criticism of the Church's interest in this ministry of personal reconciliation, or, more accurately, the resolution of conflict within the person. But when the Church has tried to play the role of Christian conciliator in social conflict a different story has been written. A significant number of churchmen—ministerial as well as lay—have objected that this kind of interest and effort lies outside the province of religion. Yet, increasingly, this objection is being renounced and overborne within the Church itself. We are beginning to see that if our Christian gospel of reconciliation gives us a place in the resolution of personal conflict then, by the same token, it gives us a place and a responsibility in the resolution of social conflict. Any struggle which disrupts and threatens to destroy either the life of a person or the sense of community in a group is the legitimate object of careful Christian attention. Nor is this a recent concern of the Christian fellowship. We recall with humility the role played by our Master in the incident of the woman taken in adultery. This was an extremely critical social situation. Not only the Mosaic law but also the conventions of society had been invoked to justify punishment of the wrongdoer. It took a man of courageous conviction to call a halt to the proceedings when they had reached the point of stoning the offender—yet Jesus did just that. There is no need to recapitulate here the way in which he punctured the bubble of self-righteousness which characterized the thinking of the ones who surrounded the hapless woman, or to recall the way in which he strove to rebuild her confidence in herself as a person before he sent her on her way. But the effect of his effort, clearly, was to help a considerable number of people out of an acute social conflict and, we may hope, to a permanently higher level of understanding of human values.

Instances of the way in which Christian leaders are being called upon or are offering themselves as mediators in social conflicts are multiplying with each passing month. This is all to the good. Wherever men are at loggerheads with one another, wherever conflict is reaching the point of severing creative human relationships, wherever groups are girding for battle with one another—there is the place for the Christian conciliator who takes seriously his ministry of reconciliation. These words, spoken by one of the great preachers of our day to his congregation before going to the general convention of his church, come out of the great tradition of our faith:

> I hope to keep in my mind, and I hope that other delegates will in their own way keep in their minds, something that I might put in language like this: the church is in the world to do one thing, and one thing only, to reconcile men with each other and with their God. Everything else that the church does must be judged as it contributes to that, and therefore, when we are thinking about matters of organization and policies of discipline within or without the church and its worship, there must be one question and one only in the minds of the voters, and that is, does this move help the church to be more effective as a reconciler among human beings who know not which way to go, who are at sword's point with each other, and only on the most distant terms of relationship with God. If so, vote for it; if not, against it. A church so motivated will be prepared to proclaim, interpret and apply the Christian answer to the world's major problem.[2]

We may as well confess that not all—even not many—of our Church pronouncements have lived up to the high standard set by this conscientious minister. Many of them have me wondering how interested the Church is in the ministry of reconciliation in these dark and difficult days. We see races estranged from one another and the Church shrinking away from a definite pronouncement condemning this separation. Rather we see many churchmen searching frantically for some kind of pious justification for the segregation of races within the Christian Church. This is an old habit that does not grow more palatable with the passing of the years. Rather, it brings the Church under the judgment of preaching a gospel which it is afraid to put into practice and, because it is afraid to do it, is unable to speak with conviction to a world which is split into warring minority groups. Ever since the close of World War II the gap between Soviet Russia and her allies on the one hand and the Western powers and their allies on the other has been steadily widening. Unless the rift can be both arrested and healed, war will inevitably result. In the face of this calamity, you would expect that the Church would be working steadily at the process of reconciliation. Yet, as a matter of fact, there has been a noticeable reluctance on the part of churches and churchmen to assume the role of Christian conciliation in this matter. For to assume such a role would mean that we would seek to be in the battle yet above it, that we would seek to be sensitive to the values involved in both sides of the dispute, and that we would try desperately not to be partisan in our approach to and analysis of the conflict. Just now churches and churchmen generally seem quite willing to leave this dangerous rift which may lead to war to the ministrations of political leaders, rather than claim it for their own. The idea is gaining currency among church leaders that they should see to it that churches "preach democracy" as over against communism, that it is quite proper to criticize communism severely on any count and improper to praise it even mildly for any reason, that they may properly criticize communism as an economy but must not lift a word of criticism against capitalism. If these are straws in the wind then we may be sure that the Church is not fulfilling the high role of Christian conciliation in the presence of this conflict. If she were, her strategy would be quite different.

In the first place, she would point out that the popular charge that Russia is threatening the United Nations by the frequent use of the veto is, at best, a vicious half-truth. She would put the prior question before the consciousness of men as to who wrote the veto into the Charter of the United Nations, and she would give the answer properly: the United States as well as Russia! For, when the Dumbarton Oaks Agreement—precursor of the United Nations' Charter—was reached, the foreign relations committee of the United States Senate made it plain that unless the right of absolute veto were vested in the United States representative on the Security Council that there was no hope for congressional approval of the Charter. In the face of this threat, the veto was written into the Charter at the request of the delegate from the United States—and, obviously, with the consent of the delegate from the Soviet Union.

Having established this point afresh, the Church would then proceed to explain that the United States had been almost as guilty as Russia of undercutting the efficiency of the United Nations. She has done this by unilateral action as regards the control of disputed areas in the South Pacific, Palestine, Greece, and Turkey, not to mention a number of minor matters. When the Church points out failings like these, there are always those who are ready to rise up and say that she is favoring communism. Nothing could be farther from the truth. She is trying to bring both the United States and Soviet Russia under the condemnation of the same standard of values—of saying one thing and doing another. There can be no conciliation between these great powers so long as the citizens in each one are permitted to indulge in the conceit that their country is right and the other is wrong on all fundamental matters. There are significant reasons for believing that there is a good deal of discussion if not disunity about Soviet policy within Russia herself these days and there is every reason to believe that there is room for a most careful kind of discussion of our own policy as regards the United Nations and the world in general. It is the proper business of the Christian Church to see to it that conflict situations are brought out into the open, the values involved in them thoroughly aired, alternative solutions to them carefully explored, and the Christian conviction in regard to the situation clearly articulated all along the line.

IV

The simple fact that there are six hundred million nominal Christians throughout the world belonging to every race, nation, and minority group—excepting only religious minorities—makes us aware of the tremendous influence for reconciliation which the Christian fellowship can have if we take seriously our plain duty in the matter. As the last war was drawing to its conclusion one of the political leaders of this country, speaking to a group of churchmen, said, "How I envy you men when this war is over! You will be able to go across any battle line on the face of the earth with hand outstretched and the word brother on your lips and you will meet someone coming across in the same spirit from the other side. That is the real foundation for world peace." His insight into the peculiar advantage of the Christian faith should effectively rebuke the feeling on the part of churchmen that they must react first as citizens and second as Christians. To step within the Christian fold is to assume the primacy of the Christian gospel. And that is the gospel of reconciliation.

As we set ourselves to the tremendous tasks laid upon us by this ministry, there is real strength in the knowledge that we are but instruments in the love of God as He seeks to work His perfect work in the world. What we try to do is not done simply and solely in our own wisdom and strength, for we are taking our course of life and effort from the will of God as we see it in Jesus Christ. We have no alternative in this matter. As Emile Cammaerts saw, "Christianity is the story of the redemption of man, through the love of God, or it is nothing." If we are not willing to assume the ministry of reconciliation, we have no Christian ministry, however useful a purpose we may seem to serve in the promotion of racial, class, and national interests. Once we take seriously this searching and revolutionary character of the ministry of reconciliation we are in a position to appreciate the candid reaction of the person who was just quoted. He recalls that his mother, a free thinker, was helping him "unravel the skein of Dante's symbolism, one day when she suddenly exclaimed: 'I don't believe a word of all this, but if I did I should walk straight into a convent or start a revolution.' " Since the luxury of forsaking the world is no longer permitted any of us, the only alternative is that of trying to inaugurate a revolution—the Christian revolution, in the face of the conflict which now exists in personal and social living. It is a sobering thought that whatever hope there is for the future lies in our ability to do this with a measure of success. Yet, as God lives and is a God of love, this is what we should expect to be true.

In reply to the direct question "Should the Christian Church advocate policies of reconciliation in terms of specific social conflict?" two answers may be made: *First,* "No! The Church should not advocate these policies if she does not believe in the policy of reconciliation itself, or if she believes it to be inapplicable in historical events, or if there seems to be a better way of promoting the Kingdom of God in the lives of men"; *Second,* "Yes! The Church should advocate such policies if she believes reconciliation to be God's way of overcoming enmity, if she acknowledges that she herself has profited by it—being a forgiven sinner—and if she is prepared to lead out, to show the way, to level down the hills and fill up the valleys of difficulties, prejudices, and inequities which exist." Yet we always come back to the fact that if we are not willing to accept the ministry of reconciliation as the supreme work of the love of God in and through our life individually and collectively, it is a serious question as to whether we have any distinctively Christian ministry at all. This sobering fact will cause all of us to reappraise ourselves in the light of this responsibility.

THE KINGDOM OF GOD

UNTO WHAT is the kingdom of God like? And whereunto shall I liken it? It is like unto leaven, which a woman took and hid in three measures of meal, till it was all leavened. It is like a grain of mustard seed, which, when it is sown upon the earth, though it be less than all the seeds that are upon the earth, yet when it is sown, groweth up, and becometh greater than all the herbs, and putteth out great branches: so that the birds of the heaven can lodge under the shadow thereof.

Again, the kingdom of heaven is like unto a treasure hidden in the field: which a man found, and hid: and in his joy he goeth and selleth all that he hath, and buyeth that field.

If any man hath ears to hear, let him hear.

—Jesus of Nazareth

X

We Believe in THE KINGDOM OF GOD

I

For a long time now the contemporary world has believed and acted on the assumption, made famous by the Jesuits in the days of the Inquisition, that "the end justifies the means." Despite New Testament warnings that men cannot gather figs from thistles or good fruit from an evil tree, we have kept on thinking that evil means can be made to serve good ends. One verse of Scripture has done yeoman service to such Christian leaders as led out in these endeavors: "Surely the wrath of men shall praise Thee." A careful comparative study of Scripture would have revealed two things: The admonition in James that "the wrath of man worketh not the righteousness of God," and the notably different meaning given to the verse itself by Dr. J. M. P. Smith who calls attention to the fact that it is part of a total vision of the Day when the Reign of God will come on earth: "Surely the most violent of men will give thanks unto Thee; the most persistently violent will put on sackcloth." So, not even in the almost limitless variety of ethical admonitions found in Scripture can men find comfort for the grim illusion that the end justifies the means. Emerson drove to the heart of the matter, scripturally as well as ethically, when he said,

"The end is prefigured in the means." So to think moves us into a radically different ethical and moral world, a world where ideals and goals become desperately relevant to the complex problems men face every day. Nor has this role of the ideal been wholly lost on even so secular a thinker as Dr. John Dewey: "Every ideal is preceded by an actuality: but the ideal is more than a repetition in inner image of the actual. It projects in securer and wider and fuller form some goal which has been previously experienced in a precarious, accidental, fleeting way."[1] Miss Georgia Harkness directs our attention to still another way in which the ideal is rooted in reality: "An ideal is an idea that has gathered sufficient emotional and volitional momentum to control conduct."[2] Strangely enough, the eccentric yet many-sided Danish philosopher, Søren Kierkegaard, has done some of his straightest thinking on this matter: "There is only one end—the genuine Good . . . [only one approach] to be willing to use those means which are genuinely good."[3]

You cannot study the Christian faith without discovering that the Supreme End not only of the Christian effort but of God's will in history is the achievement of the Kingdom of God. It is the ideal, the goal, the end for Christian thought and practice. It is the end and the only end plainly prefigured in the means of forgiveness and reconciliation which we have been studying. Now we must approach it in a direct manner and ask, and answer as concretely as possible, the query, "What is the Kingdom of God?"

The earlier creeds of our faith make no direct reference to the Kingdom of God, though it is referred to in both in an indirect manner. The Nicene formula concludes its statement about Jesus Christ with this phrase ". . . whose kingdom shall have no end." The Apostles' Creed states belief in "the communion of saints" which is, as we shall see, one of the characteristics of the Kingdom of God as conceived in the early Church.

The later statements of faith deal more specifically with the reality and character of the Kingdom:

> We believe that this faith [in God, Christ, and Holy Spirit] should manifest itself in the service of love as set forth in the example of our blessed Lord, to the end that the Kingdom of God may come upon the earth.
>
> We believe in the Kingdom of God as the divine rule in human society, and in the brotherhood of man under the fatherhood of God.

It is easy to talk too glibly about the Kingdom of God. A sure cure for this habit is to undergo the experience of trying to determine exactly what is meant by it in our Gospels, coupled with the sobering experience of trying to determine precisely what it means to men and women involved in the confused problems of ordinary living. Since this points the way to an understanding of an affirmation of faith in the Kingdom of God let us attempt both in the suggested order.

II

The notion of the Kingdom of God in the Gospels is intimately related to the Messianic hope of Israel. Certain observations will refresh our memory about this hope. To begin with, it is ancient, going back to the prophets of Israel. Almost all of these men expected the Lord to intervene in human affairs at some particular time and as judge of men. Amos speaks of the "Day of the Lord" but does not develop it beyond the point of stark judgment. Hosea, Isaiah, Jeremiah, and Ezekiel regard it as inevitable that God will judge men and punish and reward them according to their deeds. During the Exile, Isaiah conceived of the Jewish people as "the suffering servant" whose purity and loyalty to God would redeem the world and draw all men to God. In short, the Messiah was the whole people. Prior to the Exile the Messianic Age was pictured as the triumph of Israel, as a people, over her foes. Only the probing minds of the prophets discerned in it the implication that the individual as well as society must confront God for punishment or reward.

But in post-Exilic days the belief that the Messiah would be an individual rather than the race grew rapidly. Undoubtedly it was stimulated by the troubled eras of Persian and Greek occupation of Palestine during which both the statehood and the rights of the Jews were ruthlessly trampled underfoot. The notion of a heaven-sent Deliverer became prevalent, and not a few of the scribes and rabbis read this interpretation back into the records of their people, giving it a historical rootage now denied by modern scholars. But, at the time and on the spot, no one denied it; it was one of the passionate beliefs and hopes of a suffering people. "Messiah" originally meant "the anointed one"—a man distinguished from others by the purity and steadfastness of his faith and designated by God to usher in His Kingdom. In popular thought, this man would be a descendant of David and would restore the glories of the Davidic kingdom.

Still another and more bizarre notion came to the fore later when "Messiah" came to mean a spiritual being who together with his angels would descend from heaven for the specific purpose of inaugurating a new earthly order centering in Jerusalem with God as king. This entire notion was invested with the majesty and power of a transcendent God bent on caring for his own.

Against this background the Kingdom of God had several meanings, two of which were prevalent in Jewish life and thought in New Testament times.

The first indicated a kingdom which would be based upon religious and ethical considerations alone. It was to be both heavenly and earthly in nature with men on earth and the angels in heaven bowing in perfect obedience before God. The earthly phase of it, while not bounded geographically, would have its center in Jerusalem. Power in earthly matters would rest with the Jews because they alone acknowledged the sovereignty of God; they continued to be the "Chosen People." The Kingdom would be ushered into human affairs when "the present age, by an Act of God, comes to an end." At that time all righteous Jews, dead or living, would form a community to enjoy its blessings in a special way.

The second meaning of the Kingdom of God is usually referred to in eschatological terms. "Here the Kingdom, the speedy advent of which was looked for, lay in the future, in the 'last times'; it would be heralded by natural phenomena of a terrifying kind, and by manifold horrors among men; this is all described as 'the birth pangs of the Messiah,' since the coming Kingdom was also to be the 'Messianic Age.' "[4] During the last century B.C. and the first century A.D. the rank and file of Jews looked for this kind of kingdom. It meant that their servitude to alien masters would be ended, with the masters coming under their rule; adversity would be at an end and prosperity would reign.

Both John the Baptist and Jesus of Nazareth began their public life with the announcement of the imminence of the Kingdom of God. There was real confusion among their hearers as to what they meant because of the different conceptions of the Kingdom abroad at the time. Consequently, the Gospels spend considerable time trying to clarify the meaning of the Kingdom. It would be pleasant to report that they succeeded, but the truth is far different. There is no one conception of the meaning of the Kingdom in the Gospels. In fact, the *Dictionary of Christ and the Gospels* concludes its careful survey of the variety of meanings of the Kingdom of God in the New Testament with these words: "From this survey it is readily seen that the term 'Kingdom of God (or Heaven)' in the usage of Jesus is not easy to be defined; that it appears to be an elastic poetic symbol rather than the vehicle of a single sharply-founded conception."[5] Against the background of this warning the writer of the survey hazards the judgment that the fundamental thought of the term, Kingdom of God, is something like this: "Where the will of God is done, there the Kingdom of God has come . . . accordingly . . . the fundamental idea of the Kingdom of Heaven is the rule of God." As you work your way through the various studies of the meaning of the Kingdom of God in the New Testament you come to the conclusion that among the rich variety of ideas and suggestions about its nature, these three stand out:

1. *The Kingdom is a future material reality.* It will be an earthly Kingdom established by God through a decisive victory over Satan. It will be for those whose lives have undergone moral transformation. Jesus is preparing men for entrance into the Kingdom when God inaugurates it. But man can only be prepared for it. He can neither force it nor know when it will come. Like the wise and foolish virgins he will either be ready for it when it comes and enter in or not.

2. *The Kingdom is an existing spiritual reality.* "It consists entirely of the triumph of Righteousness, of the love of God and of our neighbor, and of divine peace in the heart of man."[6] It is always at hand in the exact sense of being a permanent possibility in human life. Man can always step over the threshold if he is willing to become a fit citizen of the new order. Naturally, it will spread from person to person until finally it becomes a new social order, one in which love and community are basic. This means that its growth in human affairs will be slow; that it will be like the growth of a mustard tree, or the leaven in the lump. It is to be the earthly beginning of a condition of life that will be perfected in heaven. Jesus is setting men's feet on this pathway by

uniting them with God and man in such a way that their lives will be transformed.

3. *The Kingdom is fundamentally eschatological in character.* It has to do with the "final things"; it will happen in the future, at the end of time and history; it will be the complete transformation of all earthly things. The good news of the gospel is the assurance that the Kingdom is at hand and, also to give men a foretaste of what it will mean by exhorting them to become fit citizens of it. "Although principally the work of God it is, in so far as it is a present thing, the work of Christ, for its perfect achievement will only be realized if certain conditions of a moral order are fulfilled."[7]

It has even been suggested by some students that Jesus' own conception of the Kingdom grew with his experience; that he began by regarding it as an imminent earthly Kingdom, later feeling it to be a spiritual reality, and finally accepting the eschatological notion of it. Be that as it may, the plain truth is that a variety of meanings clusters around the concept in the Gospels. The most eloquent testimonial to this simple fact is the way in which eminent scholars sum up their understanding of the general meanings of the Kingdom of God as used by Jesus.

A French scholar, M. Guignebert, sums up his conclusions this way:

1. [The kingdom is to be the] gift of divine grace, to be established by the miraculous interposition of the divine will.

2. Jesus did not believe that this Kingdom would be set up on earth as the result of his preaching, but that his preaching, by announcing the Kingdom, was preparing the way for it, and by immediately preceding it served as an introduction to it. Hence he believed that in this case there was a close link between his own present activity and the future interposition of God, but he never confused the two.

3. He conceived of the setting up of the Kingdom as the result of

a miraculous act, but did not think that it would be preceded by all of the fantastic portents and disturbances which Jewish eschatology associated with the appearance of the Messiah.

Dr. C. H. Dodd, an eminent British scholar, submits these conclusions to his study of the usage of the Kingdom of God in the New Testament:

1. The common idea . . . underlying all uses of the term "the Kingdom of God" is that of the manifest and effective assertion of the divine sovereignty against all the evil of the world.[8]

2. The Absolute enters history. . . . But Jesus declared that this ultimate, the Kingdom of God has come into history, and He takes upon Himself the "eschatological" role of "Son of Man." The Absolute, the "Wholly other" has entered into time and space. And as the Kingdom of God has come and the Son of Man has come, so also judgment and blessedness have come into human experience.[9]

3. The early Church, which preserved the tradition of the teachings of Jesus, long kept the vivid sense of living in a new age which is implied in His declaration, "The Kingdom of God has come upon you." Beginning with the apostolic preaching, as we can recover it fragmentarily from the Acts of the Apostles, through the epistles of Paul and the Epistle to the Hebrews, onto the Fourth Gospel, the testimony of the Church is unanimous, that it is living in the age of fulfilment, God has acted decisively in history, and the world is a new world.[10]

With so much diversity in both Jewish and early Christian interpretations of the meaning of the Kingdom of God, we shall not be surprised to learn that succeeding Christians have made use of no one of the meanings. There can be little doubt that the usage most persistently clung to during the entire history of the Church regards the Kingdom as a world of perfection lying wholly outside, if not beyond the reach of, this world. Heaven has been a synonym for it in everyday thought and speech. The Kingdom is to be the New Jerusalem outlined so graphically in the Book of Revelation. Its appearance in God's own time will herald the end of the world and the return of the Lord Jesus to judge the quick and the dead. When this is done and the wicked condemned to their punishment, the millennium of peace, when God's will is done on earth, will occur.

A relatively recent conception of the Kingdom pictures it as an ideal world to be fashioned by divinely inspired men out of the materials of this life and world. When men speak of "building the Kingdom" some such image as this invariably and rightly flashes across our mind. This conception is neither mean nor prideful as so many critics have pictured it. It need not be a glorification of man; in fact, it is a glorification of the power of God which recreates life both personally and socially. The reality of God is as central in this idea of the Kingdom as in the more prevalent one. The reality of man as a responsible creature of God is much more in evidence in the latter notion than in the former.

Much of the discussion about the meaning of the Kingdom of God revolves around the where, when, and how of its nature and coming. There is no use pretending that we have conclusive information on such points. So far as the Bible and Christian history are concerned we plainly do not. This, however, does not mean that we are completely in the dark as to the meaning of the Kingdom for human thought and life. As a matter of fact, it is important enough to deserve a prominent place in any formulation of our faith. Consider, now, some of the indisputable and immeasurably important meanings of the Kingdom.

III

It is God's Kingdom. It is not Caesar's, not even man's; it outranks these in every way. No man will dominate it with his will. The leaders will be men whose wills are moved by God's will and purpose. To use two clumsy but exact words, the Kingdom of God is both theocentric (centered in God) and theocratic (ruled by God). Humility and obedience alone can open the doors for one to enter the Kingdom. That is why the penitent publican of Jesus' parable "went down to his house justified," while his proud companion stood outside and alone. Jesus' own humility in the presence of God's will is instructive. For obedience to the will of God is the North Star of his life. That is why he taught unnumbered millions to pray "Thy kingdom come, thy will be done on earth as it is in heaven." Dr. William Manson is persuaded that the fundamental meaning of the Kingdom of God lies in this area: "A supernatural would arise in which usurping evil would be judged and removed, and God would be visibly revealed as Saviour of His people. In short, it would be *the perfect rule of God.*"[11]

The Kingdom of God—the reality indicated by the idea—is the condition in life when God's will is understood and fulfilled. At once we confront the tragic fact that this condition has never been achieved by anyone, individually or collectively, excepting always Jesus Christ. Yet his prayer in the Garden indicates that even he found it difficult to be perfectly obedient. The reason for our failure is not hard to state. God made us men and not machines. If we obey Him it is because we choose to do so. If we disobey Him, it is usually for the same reason. Springing out of the depths of the mystery of creation is the strong fact that God made man a "free agent," as earlier theologians were wont to say. We not only have the power to disregard the admonitions of God's will, but we exercise it freely and frequently. Yet it is not an unconditioned, an unlimited freedom. As Jonathan Edwards saw, we are "bound yet free." We are limited by the simple fact that at the moment of choice we never have an infinite number of alternatives. We may have two, or two hundred, but in any case the number is limited, limited by the will of God in life and history. For example, we are never really free to choose to reverse history to any previous point in time. To try to do it is an immediate absurdity. Also, in the moment of choice we are not free to choose from the vantage point of any center of experience save our own. That, necessarily, is where we are in the providence of God at that particular time.

But our freedom consists in this: we can choose among the alternatives which are open, and more than one is always open in almost every case.

The Kingdom of God is that condition in which His perfect will for our good is seen, chosen, and realized. This, of course, exists only ideally at any given time short of its realization, much as docking at a port exists ideally until it is actually done. But this fulfillment is not forced upon us in spite of ourselves. If it is ever achieved, whether in personal or social living, it will be because we freely choose to seek and humbly choose to serve the will of God.

The idea of the Kingdom of God is the Christian vision of the true condition of life. It is a vision rather than a blueprint of the divine purpose implanted in human life. It is a mystical, ethical sketch of what God had in mind as the meaning and fulfillment of life. This notion is akin to the one Jesus seems to have had in mind when he likened the Kingdom of God to a seed that can and will grow to full stature if given the chance and the care. When he said, "The kingdom of God is within you" his thought was moving in this direction. If it were not possible to demonstrate the reality of purpose in life, i.e., if it were not possible to demonstrate the reality of God, then there would be no conception of divine purpose. But, given that basic idea for good and sufficient reason, then the acceptance of the Kingdom as a vision of the fulfillment of God's purpose for life is neither incredible nor unimportant. It is as reasonable as the idea of God and quite inseparable from it.

Keeping in mind this study of the historical meaning of the

phrase "Kingdom of God," one further matter remains to be discussed: How does belief in the Kingdom of God serve men? Has it been a creative influence in human life and history? Of what use is it in the total meaning of religion for life? Such queries cannot be answered by a single statement.

When the Kingdom of God is regarded as another worldly affair—something to be realized at the end of history—it comes close to being immoral rather than amoral because it denies enduring worth to anything man can plan for or achieve in history. Against this background men are encouraged to sing "I am a stranger here within a foreign land, my home is far away, beyond a golden strand," and one is led to concentrate on "spiritual things" rather than "earthly things." This is ethical nihilism, to say the least, because it places the stamp of unimportance across the energies, abilities, and achievements of men.

When the Kingdom of God is regarded as a condition to be achieved by an act, if not a specially created agent, of Divine intervention the consequences are scarcely less discouraging to man. Here, again, the onus of real responsibility for significant achievements is placed beyond the reach of man. All men can do is worry and work along at things that do not much matter while waiting for God to do the really important things. The evil in the world is thought to be too deep-seated, too malignant for man to manage, so he awaits an act of Divine Power which destroys evil and redeems the world by bringing human history to an end and ushering in the Kingdom.

This line of reasoning always emerges in an age of great trouble, and it is flourishing in Christendom again. It is world-denying, world-forsaking, either explicitly or implicitly, in all its forms. The premillenarian who waits around for God to intervene and the Kierkegaardians who both renounce and denounce man and all his works, counseling blind faith in the Christian revelation of

God are like "the Colonel's lady and Mrs. O'Grady"—"sisters under the skin."

It is no accident that the ethical nihilism of current French existentialism claims the same philosophic ancestor (Kierkegaard) as do some of the most powerful movements in Christian theology in Europe and America. Both finally declare that almost all that man can think or do is ultimately unimportant. Existentialism urges man to accept the fact that he is in an alien, unconcerned, unknowing, and actually hostile universe, that history is, literally, what men make it; it urges him to set up as goals whatever he desires, to use them as standards of right and wrong, to live by and for them, though knowing all the while that they are wholly arbitrary and ultimately unimportant.

Extreme Barthianism arrived at essentially the same ethical conclusion, though by a widely different sort of reasoning. This school urges man to accept the fact that he is a creature—a finite, proud, sinful creature—whose life in this world and in history is wholly at the mercy of God. In Jesus Christ we have a full, perfect, and final revelation of God's love for man. The only ultimately important thing a man can do is to accept this revelation by an act, not of knowledge, but of blind faith. As Dr. Karl Barth reminded the World Council of Churches, convened in Amsterdam in 1948, neither man nor the Church can do any good thing, save wait in faith for God to work His perfect work and will in history. This, too, is ethical and moral nihilism, and quite different in cast from the New Testament assumption that it is of supreme importance that men should see and do the will of God as revealed in the life and teachings of Jesus Christ.

Obviously, if belief in the Kingdom of God yields fruits like these, it is an evil thing, offering only discouragement and opposition to the effort to achieve either a good life or a good society defined in terms of human life and history.

But it is possible to mean something quite different from this when we say we believe in the Kingdom of God. We can mean (1) that God is real, (2) that He is at work in the world, (3) that His will provides man his only way to growth and permanence, (4) that the discovery of this will is or ought to be the major concern of our life, (5) that in the life and teachings of Jesus Christ we have our clearest revelation of the nature and meaning of God's will for life, (6) that we ought in all humility to seek to build our life and our society along the lines so clearly laid down by Jesus Christ.

IV

Dr. Frederick C. Grant, one of the ablest New Testament scholars of our day, makes the same point when he writes, "What is really needed in our distorted world is a complete submission of human motives to the will of God, a complete and radical renovation of human society, refashioning it upon the principle of faith in the righteousness of God and a determination to live in accordance with his revealed purposes. That was Jesus' program . . . for the tortured, distorted, chaotic world in which he lived; and it is still his proposal for ours."[12]

If this is what we mean when we say we believe in the Kingdom of God, then we are making a realistic statement about the nature of the world, the meaning of history, and the character of the good life. We are saying that life has a Purpose, not our purpose, but one in which we can find truly significant purposes. We are saying that living in and by that Purpose is both a way of life and strength for pursuing it with a whole heart and mind. We are saying that this Purpose is as truly concerned with the ordering or salvation of society as with individual life. For the Christian, then, the Kingdom of God is not a creation of his imagination; rather he seeks to be a creature of its ultimate and eternal meaning. To the extent that he is able to do this the Kingdom has come.

In brief, then, when we say we believe in the Kingdom of God we are putting in a single affirmation a series of the most important resolutions a person or a people can make.

For the Kingdom of God is a life to be lived, a work to be done, a destiny to be fulfilled. It is a new life—our present life redeemed and renewed by a humble and sincere appreciation of God's will for life as we see it in Jesus Christ. It is a work to be done—since the steadiest emphases in the teachings of Jesus are calls to action, to work, to duty. It is a destiny to be fulfilled because man's life can unfold because man can never know the meaning of the good, the abundant life except as he seeks to be a fit citizen of the Kingdom.

The Kingdom of God is the frame of reference for all our thinking and living when we think and live as Christians. And what a difference it does make! At a stroke, it delivers us from the grip of parochial concerns, provincial plans, and preoccupation with some fragment or other of human life. Race, nation, church, our "way of life"—all these nearer gods of human history become the half-gods they actually are when placed against the background of the Kingdom of God.

As the late William Temple was fond of saying, "The Kingdom of God is the sovereignty of love." This is a singularly acute way of stating an age-old conception of the Kingdom of God. Better than anything else, it drives home the fact that the Kingdom of God is not an other-worldly affair; it belongs to this world in the literal and exact sense that it serves as the ethical standard by which we measure our motives, plans, and deeds. By so doing it places upon man the unmistakable stamp of divine worth and eternal destiny, for God not only loves man with a love that outdistances our most far-ranging hopes, but He trusts man to hear and heed His will for life and history, and to become a coworker together with Him in the redemption of the world. This conception of the ultimate nature of the universe and human history is the firm foundation for Christian ethics—an ethics, let it be underscored, that aims at nothing less, and can be satisfied with nothing less, than new men, a new order of society, and a new direction for human history.

While convictions like these about the nature and the meaning of the Kingdom of God are not and cannot be presented as blueprints for specific and detailed changes to be made throughout society, they will, if and to a degree that they are taken seriously, keep Christian men everlastingly at the task of trying to discover the outline of such blueprints. Only two persons can seriously object to this effort: one who thinks the world cannot be improved, and one who thinks the Kingdom of God is either already here or was not meant to be relevant to human life and history. All other Christians will fall to the task of fulfilling the vision of the Kingdom of God in terms of themselves, their comrades, and human history.

In dark days like these, belief in the Kingdom of God so far from being wishful thinking is a straightforward factual statement that, as God lives, our peace lies in His will and nowhere else.

HE SHALL LIFT YOU UP

SUBMIT YOURSELVES therefore to God. Resist the devil, and he will flee from you.

Draw nigh to God, and he will draw nigh to you. Cleanse your hands, ye sinners; and purify your hearts, ye double minded.

Be afflicted, and mourn, and weep: let your laughter be turned to mourning, and your joy to heaviness.

Humble yourselves in the sight of the Lord, and he shall lift you up.

—JAMES 4:7-10

XI

We Believe in SALVATION

I

The jailer's question, "What must I do to be saved?" gives classic expression to one of the permanent needs of men. I say "permanent" advisedly. One of the wisest students of religion in our day gives it as his opinion, that "The notion of salvation is a very early and a very general one in the history of religion."[1] Professor A. E. Haydon, for many years professor of comparative religion at the University of Chicago, divides religions into two general categories: culture religions and religions of salvation. In the former, religion is so deeply interwoven with the total culture (language, customs, folklore) of a people as to be inseparable from it. Such a religion cannot move from one culture to another; its destiny is identified with that of one culture. Hence the name, culture religion. In contrast, a religion of salvation is both in yet not of any given culture. Its essential impulse (whether Christian, Islamic, or Buddhist) can blow, like seed, into the soil of another culture and there take root, flourish, and flower. Any religion that has become a world religion, i.e., involves many cultures, is basically a religion of salvation. This is another way of saying that the most vital, dynamic, and creative religions have been and are religions of salvation.

Nor is the quest for salvation merely a matter of interest to antiquarians. This memorable statement appeared in a daily newspaper early in 1949: "What must we do to be saved? In a thousand forms—and with a thousand answers—that is still man's leading and most tormenting soliloquy. Man wants the good life, the full life, and as much security as possible this side of paradise. No jesting Pilate, he will stay for all the answers that all the pilots can offer him in his wonderfully dogged pursuit of peace and happiness."[2]

It is important for us to bear in mind the fact that the idea of salvation is to be found so generally in religion because the need for salvation is felt so universally in human life. The interpretations and the techniques of salvation will and do differ from faith to faith, and from age to age within each faith, but the conviction that salvation is both needed and possible persists unchanged.

All religions, therefore, must be viewed as different answers to the same question, "What must we do to be saved?" As you would expect, there is much overlapping in the answers they give. In primitive religions, for example, the answers were phrased in terms of magic, charms, fetishes. Christianity and her parent Hebraism, in their early days, couched their essentially valid answers in a good deal of magic, miracle, and blind faith. Such answers are obviously up for modification or restatement today. The two-thousand-year-old heritage of philosophy and the four-hundred-year-old tradition of modern science stretch between us and the day in which they took form. There is no way we can and no reason for wanting to avoid the ways in which philosophy and science have influenced contemporary religious thought. The answers given by religion today to the jailer's question are, therefore, disciplined in an unprecedented way by fact, experience, and reason.

The fact that different religions are different answers to the same question has made collisions between them unavoidable. Nowhere is this more clearly seen than in those centuries when Christianity was getting under way. It is no exaggeration to say that the Christian Church was engaged in a literal struggle for survival for the first three hundred years of her existence. Christianity was not born in a religious vacuum. It began life when there were religions of every sort and kind in the Roman world.

There were the *state* religions; semipolitical cults with two deities—the god representing the Emperor and the goddess representing the Empire. An occasional act of worship at their shrine was considered a civic duty, a renewing of the oath of allegiance to Emperor and Empire. Then there were the *city* cults, since each city had a patron god or goddess. Paul and his comrades had an ugly encounter with a mob of Ephesians who were sure that this new faith was an affront to Diana of the Ephesians. Stemming from the rich intellectual heritage of Greece were the *philosophical religions* of Stoicism and Epicureanism which sought to outline a way of thinking about life which would issue in the assurance of salvation. Finally, there were the *mystery religions* —bizarre cults which guaranteed salvation to anyone who was properly initiated. Recent research has established the fact that early Christianity took full advantage of the centuries of labors of both philosophical and mystery religions in the Mediterranean world—a fact made possible because all three were essentially religions of salvation.

Reflecting on the polyglot character of the religious life into which Christianity was born, Johannes Weiss writes, "It is amazing that the apostles did not lose courage in view of such a multitude of fellow suitors for the people's souls, and it is a sign of the firmness and clearness of their conviction that they nevertheless dared to seek out the population of the chief cities, the very people who had been all but surfeited with intellectual and rhetorical display."[3]

We look back on all that now from the vantage point of the sweeping victory which Christianity won in this long, hard conflict. But it is small honor to the Christians who bore the brunt of that struggle simply to note the fact that they won it. Even if we are lacking in intellectual curiosity, a sense of honor born of indisputable indebtedness to them should prompt us to ask why it was they won. A keen historian of that period, George Foote Moore, phrases the reason this way: Christianity won because "it alone offered not merely a way of salvation but a philosophy of salvation."[4] There you have it! Christianity won not by default but because it *outthought* and therefore was able to *outlive* its rivals.

What we shall be doing for the remainder of this chapter is to study the factual content of the Christian belief in or philosophy of salvation. We shall be trying to give the Christian answer to the question, "What must we do to be saved?" not alone by grounding it as securely as we can in the past but by finding out what it has meant and continues to mean in the thought and experience of men.

II

The clearest, truest way of grounding the Christian philosophy of salvation in the past is to study its interdependence with the dominant Biblical ideas of salvation. As happens so frequently in Christian thought on all matters, what the Biblical writers thought and said proves to be "a lamp unto our feet" on this journey.

In the Old Testament, the predominant meaning of salvation

looks in two directions—it is deliverance from and preparation for something. It is never purely negative. It always ends in an affirmative expectation. It is both deliverance from danger, from defeat, from sin, from judgment, and preparation for a life of trust in God. After a meticulous study of the various shades of meaning of the idea of salvation, this is the judgment of a scholar, "Thus it appears that salvation in its specific religious sense is still viewed throughout the Bible as a deliverance from death and an introduction into the sphere of life."[5] "The word of salvation" means word of deliverance. "The joy of salvation" means the joy that attends the escaping of a great danger. "The rock of salvation" means a rock where you take refuge, finding safety and deliverance from an enemy. "The shield of salvation" means a buckler or defense that wards off harmful blows. Some such emphasis upon Divine deliverance runs throughout all the records, from the earliest to the latest, that we have of Israel's life and thought. Salvation faces both toward the past with its peril and the future with its promise. We find the idea in the Song of Deborah (Judges 5), which has been called the oldest extant monument of Hebrew literature.[6] When Deborah, the inspired prophetess, lifts her voice in song to celebrate the great victory which Israel has just won, she gives all credit to the fact that Yahweh marched before the Hebrew warriors, delivering them from the swords of the enemy and the enemy to their swords. This, however, did not end the matter! Far from it! The net result of this act of deliverance is Yahweh's expectation that Israel will be a truly faithful and obedient people—the clear implication being that she would regret it if she failed!

The Book of Micah contains the noblest insight of the Old Testament into the meaning of salvation. "He hath shewed thee, O man, what is good; and what doth the Lord require of thee, but to do justly, and to love mercy, and to walk humbly with thy

God?" This is a far cry from the savage chant of Deborah. It belongs in an entirely different ethical and religious world. But it is informative to note that it, too, stresses the fact that salvation is an act of God. "*He* hath shewed thee, O man, what is good." God has showed man how to be delivered from sin. Not by "rivers of oil" nor by the sacrifice of first-born sons, but by doing justly, loving mercy, and walking humbly with God. Salvation—deliverance from danger, preparation for a deep and enriching fellowship with God—this is the gift of God. For, as one of the students of the Old Testament has put it, "The religious importance of the conception [of salvation] in the Old Testament springs not so much from the nature of the evil removed, or from the nature of the blessedness bestowed, as rather from the fact that salvation, of whatever nature, is a work of Jehovah for his people, a Divine prerogative. . . ."[7]

The New Testament makes constant use of the idea of salvation. The word for it occurs half a hundred times or more. Its meaning continues to be that, essentially, of deliverance from and preparation for. Two kinds of perils are the special objects of the saving act of God: (1) deliverance from diseases or demonic possession; (2) deliverance from sin and death. It is of vast importance to understand that, for the New Testament writers, there are two kinds of death from which a man must be saved. One is the death of sin, which is a subjective, spiritual death but death nonetheless. The other is the grim fact of death as objective and eternal punishment meted out at the Last Judgment. Death, in either form, was fearful to contemplate yet almost impossible to escape. It hunted man down relentlessly, and only the grace of God could ward it off. To be delivered from death in both forms was to be prepared for an especial kind of fellowship with God.

Jesus' teachings are mainly concerned with salvation as deliverance from the death of sin. He sets himself against those attitudes and acts which cripple and kill the good life. "I have come to seek and to save that which was lost." "I am come that ye might have life and have it more abundantly." "Ye cannot serve God and mammon"—which is to say, "You cannot serve the kingdom of good and the kingdom of evil—between them you must choose, and I have come to show you the way."

Jesus nowhere seems to doubt three things: (1) that he was talking to persons who were "lost" in some sense or other of that term; (2) that they could be saved, or found; and (3) that they shared with God the responsibility for being saved. Study the parables that deal with the meaning of being lost (the parable of the lost sheep, the lost coin, and the lost son), and you understand the force of the conclusion, "A lost condition means estrangement from God, a missing of all the religious and moral relations man is designed to sustain toward his Maker. But this lost condition is further identified by Jesus with spiritual death, for the prodigal the father declared, 'This thy brother was dead and is alive again, was lost and is found.' Salvation of 'the lost' therefore is salvation from spiritual death. As such it includes both forgiveness of sin and moral-religious renewal."[8]

That Jesus thought of himself as one through whom the saving act of God became real to men is beyond the reach of reasonable doubt. By the amazing recital of the things he intended to attempt in his ministry (Luke 4:17-21), he not only places himself in the Messianic tradition, but he identifies himself thereby with human beings who need salvation. Yet he does not give the impression that salvation is easy of achievement. A man must accept, by faith, the outstretched hand of God. Faith, however, is more than belief, more than a conviction regarding the necessity and sufficiency of the Divine Power. It also involves trust, the reliance upon God's willingness and readiness to save.[9] Once man—any man—was able to establish this relationship with God, salvation was an accomplished fact, a present experience, even as it was for Zacchaeus.

Paul gathered the flaming faith of the early Christians into one brilliant utterance when he advised the jailer, "Believe on the Lord Jesus Christ and thou shalt be saved." This outlines cryptically at least the Christian philosophy of salvation which swept on to victory in the ancient world and which has kept moving outward until today it stands where the New Testament Christians believed by faith it would someday stand—in the uttermost parts of the earth.

But no one knew better than Paul that his answer, taken by itself, is too cryptic to have much meaning. It is no accident that he spent the rest of the night in the jailer's home both having his wounds dressed and explaining the fuller meaning of his advice. We are extremely fortunate in having Paul's priceless letters with their almost tropical profusion of phrases and figures describing as best he could what it means to believe on the Lord Jesus Christ and thus be saved. He himself never made the mistake which many self-styled "fundamentalists" and neo-orthodox theologians among us today make—that of supposing that you can safely separate belief in Christ from what Christ taught, or separate Jesus of Nazareth from the Christ of faith. To try to effect this sort of separation, to put it bluntly, is to make an excursion into the field of magic. Paul never lost his sense of immediate contact with the reality of Jesus Christ as a person. Hence his advice, "Let this mind be in you that was in Christ Jesus our Lord." No philosophy of salvation that ignores this admonition can claim for one moment to be a Christian philosophy of salvation.

Yet, in all candor, we must be prepared to face the fact that Paul did not formulate (and may never have tried to formulate) anything approaching a full-blown philosophy of salvation. In addition to urging his hearers to have the mind of Christ in them, he speaks of dying with Christ in order to rise with him; of being in Christ and of Christ being in him; of being led by the Spirit, yet never wholly free from the hindrances of the flesh; of being overcome by the world, yet in part being able to overcome the world. Paul is living witness to the reality of this sort of salvation. However difficult it may be to put an adequate explanation down in words, the towering fact of human transformation remains. Principal Sydney Cave summarizes Paul's thought on the meaning of salvation in this way: Salvation means deliverance from sin, the Law, the Wrath of God, and death; it means preparation for being a Son of God, a new life in Christ, and the experience of fellowship with the Spirit of God.[10] Another scholar, Adolph Deissmann, in his masterly study of Paul, gives the impression that our search for Paul's interpretation of the experience he himself had and was urging others to have will not make much progress beyond the vague category of his "Christ-mysticism," which, to put it in a sentence, is the mystical awareness of the power of the living Christ in life.

But Paul's colleagues and disciples did not let the matter rest with his explanation. They developed other answers of their own in response to the inescapable question: What, exactly, did Jesus do in order to save men? What actually happens to a man who is "saved by Jesus Christ"?

Neither the New Testament writers nor subsequent generations of Christians have been able to agree upon any one answer to this query. Yet the effort to do so has been and continues to be unrelenting. These answers usually come under the heading, *theories of the atonement,* since there is general agreement that, in some sense, Jesus actually makes possible a new and creative relationship between man and God, one which saves man. Such theories are, in effect, attempts to formulate the Christian philosophy of salvation and, before sketching the major ones, let it be remembered that they are the banners under which early generations of Christians not only found peace but marched to victory as a world religion. It is important, therefore, that any effort to discuss their diversity must not lose sight of their fundamental unity and ". . . in regard to the central content of the Christian message, there was no dispute . . . men interpreted the Christian message in accordance with their sense of need, but that message was for all alike a message of the risen Lord who had died for men."[11] Principal Cave finds different statements of this message in the Epistle to the Hebrews, I Peter, I John, the Gospel of John, and the Book of Revelation. Such diversity of interpretation is found throughout the first two centuries of our era. Under the careful, not to say skeptical, scrutiny of the Greco-Roman world, the explanations that satisfied the earlier and almost communal life and mind of the Christian group were amplified. Every major figure in the Church took his turn at trying to explain precisely what Jesus Christ did to save men. Some of their efforts are dignified, while others are incredibly crude. Irenaeus, illustrating the former, writes, "The Word of God was made flesh by the dispensation of the Virgin, to abolish death and make man live. For we were imprisoned by sin, being born in sinfulness and living under death. But God the Father was merciful; He sent his Creative Work . . . His Light appeared and made the darkness of the prison disappear and hallowed our birth and destroyed death, loosing those same fetters with which we were chained."[12]

Gregory of Nyssa introduced a metaphorical explanation that is crude in the extreme. God, in His desire to best the Devil and deliver the souls now in prison in hell, hit upon this stratagem. Clothing His Deity in mortal flesh, He (as Jesus Christ) appears to fall into the hands of the Devil, in that He died. The Devil, thinking his victim like any other man, takes Him to hell. After three days, the unconquerable power of Deity asserts itself, breaking open the gates of hell, and not only escaping Himself but releasing all subject spirits in hell. In this metaphor God is the great Deceiver as well as the great Deliverer! Yet it is amazing what persistence this explanation has had through the years. It is probably the crudest form of the "ransom" theory of the atonement.

In the main, the various theories of the atonement that have come up for consideration in the Christian tradition fall into three categories: the Patristic, the penal, and the moral. All three continue to have their champions today who say that they are satisfactory philosophies of salvation. Agreeing that history rightly divides with the advent of Christ, they advance different explanations for what he accomplished.

The Patristic theory holds that God in Christ was winning a victory over the powers of evil, one result of which was to deliver man from enslavement to them. The stratagem whereby the victory was won is distinctly of minor importance; the victory is the all-important fact. To "believe on the Lord Jesus Christ" according to this theory means to believe by faith that God in Christ actually broke whatever permanent hold the power or powers of evil may have on your life. Fortified by this faith and led by the Spirit of God, you are able to live as a son of God, i.e., sensitive to His will, grateful for His love, confident in His presence.

The penal theory holds that Christ, the Son of God, was moved to compassion by the separation of man from God through sin. Man in Adam had rebelled against God and was living in bondage to sin. Not only was man separated from God, but God's honor made it impossible for Him to initiate any effort to win man back to a happier relationship. Man had to make the first move, but, to make matters worse, sin had so corrupted man that he was unable to initiate any such move himself. Even if man should desire reconciliation, what offering could he bring that could conceivably satisfy the outraged honor of God? Could he, finite, sinful being, bring anything at all that might serve to reconcile him to the infinite, pure God? The answer, obviously, is negative, and the human plight as obviously hopeless.

But the love of God could not accept this separation as eternal; incarnate in Jesus of Nazareth the power of the love of God invades human nature and history, awakening man to the dire extremity of his plight and to the all-encompassing love of God. By his death on the cross he made the acceptable sacrifice, enabling the justice and honor of God to be guided by His love and once more extend His parental hand to man. To believe in Jesus Christ, according to the penal theory, means to accept him as the one who by the offering of himself transformed the just wrath of God toward us into love and to extend the hand of faith in filial trust, knowing that it will be clasped by the hand of God and we will be led in the way everlasting.

The moral theory holds that Christ is the perfect and final revelation of the love of God for man in and through which men are led to a new life of love for man and God. Here, too, is the keen awareness of man's estrangement from God through the activities of and indulgence in evil powers. Man, separated from God, is lost in sin, in the darkness of selfish passion and power, in the night of loneliness and despair, groping his way toward death and inevitable, eternal doom. God tried to reach man and speak to him through the Law and the Prophets, but these, divine though they were and are, did not turn man toward God. Finally, God in Christ inserted Himself in human life and history in order that He might speak, from within, to the human situation. Nor did He speak by marvelous precepts alone; He spoke by His life. He was the Word of God Incarnate—and when man heard this he heard, as if for the first time, the love of God directing him out of his predicament, telling him how to live with man and with God. Nor could even the fury of human sin which sought to silence the divine word on the cross, keep God's purpose from being fulfilled. The cross served to trumpet the word into every nook and cranny of human life, letting man know of the way, the truth, and the life. To accept Jesus Christ, according to the moral theory, means to follow, by faith, the clear meaning of the love of God which we find in him. So to live breaks the spell of sin and drives away the fear of death—for the love of God is eternal and all-powerful and all-merciful.

Thus the Christian tradition bears witness to its belief in salvation! Manifestly, any realistic attempt to interpret the Christian faith in terms of our thought and life today must inquire into the factual foundations of this belief in salvation and fashion, if possible, a philosophy of salvation.[13]

III

We begin with the simple fact that people can and do get "lost" in every important sense of that term. And, so long as this is true, there is room and need for a religion of salvation, providing, always, it is based upon a clearly articulated, profoundly held, and persuasively presented philosophy of salvation. As the first step in the direction of outlining the philosophy of salvation, we need to study the meaning or meanings of the idea of being "lost."

Admiral Richard Byrd had an experience, during his first stay on Little America, that few of us would care to endure. He was alone in the long night that had settled over the bottom of the world. Upon this particular occasion he had left his snow cave to look at some meteorological instruments, and to get some exercise. Since the danger of being lost was both real and guaranteed to be speedily fatal, he took the precaution of establishing a sort of lifeline of bamboo sticks set in the snow. He would walk back and forth beside the sticks. On this particular night he walked beyond the end of the line without realizing it. Suddenly he "came to" and went in the direction he thought he had traveled away from the sticks. He took one hundred paces but found no sticks. There came over him, he records, a "sinking, sickening sensation," and he whispered to himself, "Now, you're lost!" Fortunately he was able to devise an ingenious method of slowly broadening the scope of his explorations until he discovered the line of sticks and was on his way to safety.

It is only natural that we should be strangely drawn toward all such accounts of men being lost—and finding themselves again. It is in a strange way the human predicament, and it is especially true of our day and civilization, for we are, as one of our poets has put it, a "way-lost generation." Dr. Arthur Holt was speaking directly to us when he said, "A man is lost when he cannot define his present nor plan his future." When this happens to an individual, for whatever reason, several things automatically follow.

He falls into a kind of emotional and intellectual panic. He can no longer see himself or any suggestion or another person in proper perspective. Fear, anger, suspicion, or despair become the colored lenses through which he views everyone and everything. He both needs and knows he needs, yet hates himself for needing, outside help. He both seeks such help, yet, initially at least, he will spurn it, particularly if it contains the pointed suggestion of any criticism of himself. Instead of being able to think in a straight line from problem to alternate possible answers to one which upon trial actually brings freedom and movement into life, he seems locked in an ever-descending and ever-narrowing spiral of catastrophe down which he slides with a steady acceleration of speed. In a vague sort of way he is conscious of this and is both resigned to it, yet struggles feebly and futilely against it.

To say that such a person is mentally ill is to state but a part of the truth about him. He is just as truly personally and socially ill, and as religion would say, summing it all up, *he is spiritually ill.* He is lost in the exact sense that he is no longer able to define his present or to plan his future.

To select at random from among hundreds of such cases that are now available for study, here is a single illustration of the human meaning of a person being lost. A boy, Jim by name, grows up in a family of four sisters, a weak father, and a dominating mother. The mother and girls stand together against the father and the world in general. They shower every sort of affection upon the boy. He learns that any complaint he makes will be speedily and well received. His mother and sisters say, "Poor Jim," and take his side always and quite uncritically. When he gets to school age, he frequently runs home from the playground during recess or noon hour when he is rebuffed, denied, or hurt. He is greeted with "Poor Jim," and sometimes not sent back to school that day. The pattern unfolds in every new area of life: the church, work, and, finally, the army. In the last area of experience, Jim's skill at bookkeeping gets him the corporal's rank in the office of the captain. More and more work is shoved his way. He feels indignant about it; yet his mother is across the Atlantic Ocean and he cannot run to her. No one seems to notice him or to sympathize with him, so he gets into the captain's jeep and deliberately wrecks it, with only slight injury to himself. Had he not been practically indispensable in the office, there is some reason to think the army would not have said, "Poor Jim!"

But, as it was, the captain was almost as solicitous as he was outspokenly profane about the whole situation. In any event, Jim got some attention and considerable sympathy.

When the war was over, he began going with a girl in his home town. The relationship became serious, and she wanted to get married. Jim finally yielded to her insistence. He resented the marriage because it cut down on his "fun-money" and set him to paying rent and buying furniture. His wife, expecting him to be mature, had treated him as an adult. She did not say, or even seem to feel, "Poor Jim," when he complained. Perhaps unwisely she insisted on treating him as a mature person. Jim did not and could not "take it." The last straw was the discovery that they were to have a baby, and the realization that there would be a new center of attention and affection in the home, thus robbing him of what little he had received thus far. Jim left, breaking up the home and pretty thoroughly wrecking himself in the process. To say that Jim is a "lost soul" is to use words in a most exact manner. He is not able to define his present or to plan his future. He is a candidate for salvation, for that kind of redirection and reorientation of life that can give him a new perspective on himself, on other people, and on the proper relationship between himself and his world in general.

The fact that one marriage in every three now ends in divorce is evidence that great relationships in life, like individual persons, can get "lost." The normal creative unfolding of the shared life so radiantly expectant in the moment of marriage can be distorted, arrested, or wholly blocked by any one of a long series of events and developments. But, whatever the active cause, the result is the same—the promise of the shared life is blighted and the individual components of it go through the scarring process of separating themselves from each other and trying to start living a wholly different kind of life. When a marriage reaches that point, it is a "lost" relationship in a most exact sense, and the same sort of "lostness" can overtake any other great relationship in life, whether a partnership in business, or citizenship in a country, or membership in a race or a church.

It is now common knowledge that a very real and special kind of "lostness" has overtaken Western civilization. The famous historians, Oswald Spengler, and, in these latter days, Arnold Toynbee, have made that frightfully clear. One of the most striking descriptions of it comes from General Omar Bradley: "With the monstrous weapons man already has, humanity is in danger of being trapped in this world by its moral adolescents. Our knowledge of science has out-stripped our capacity to control it. We have too many men of science, too few men of God. We have grasped the mystery of the atom and rejected the Sermon on the Mount. Man is stumbling blindly through a spiritual darkness while toying with the precarious secrets of life and death. The world has achieved brilliance without wisdom, power without conscience. Ours is a world of nuclear giants and ethical infants."[14]

And as we build up momentum toward a third world war we, too—unless we are wholly insensitive to anything deeper than pride—have that sickening, sinking sensation which led Admiral Byrd to whisper to himself, "Now, you're lost!" The almost desperate fatalism of the current foreign policies of the major powers, including our own, deserves Lewis Mumford's ejaculation, "Gentlemen, you are mad!"

This multiple experience of being lost, in whatever form, is no stranger in the household of religious faith. In fact, it is the most persistent caller known there, and none is more welcome, for religion tries to take hold of a man (or a society) precisely at that point to help him find himself. It is not too much to say that all great religions are born in and through such experiences of desperation. No complacency, let alone smugness, is intended in the assertion that religion has met and mastered, in principle, at least, and in life, frequently, every known form of "lostness" which has beset mankind.

Take, for example, the sense of futility and despair which is rapidly paralyzing sensitive contemporary spirits. It is an old affliction, going back to Sophocles' lament, "Nothing and nothingness is the whole race of mortals." Or to the familiar dictum of Ecclesiastes: "What profit hath a man of all his labors which he has under the sun? I looked on all the works that my hands had wrought, and behold all was vanity and vexation of spirit . . . the dead know not anything, neither have they any more a reward; for the memory of them is forgotten." Tolstoi describes the plight from which religion rescued him: "I sought like a man who is lost and who seeks to save himself, and I found nothing. . . . The meaningless absurdity of life is the only incontestible knowledge accessible to man." And, from the tortured heart of contemporary Europe, Jean-Paul Sartre, writes *The Philosophy of the Absurd* and counsels men to reckon with the fact that "we are isolated [from everyone else]. We are conscious of our isolation. We make foolish and pathetic efforts to escape it . . . Man can do nothing unless he first understands that he must count on no one but himself, that he is alone, abandoned on earth in the midst of his infinite responsibilities, without help, with no other aims than the ones he sets for himself, with no other destiny than the one he forges for himself on this earth. . . . Life is absurd, love is impossible. . . . There is no way of knowing the true meaning of what we are doing; perhaps even our actions have no meaning."[15] We cannot help agreeing with William James that "the breath of the sepulchre" surrounds such sentiments as these.

Add to these experiences of "lostness" which either threaten or actually grip many of us, still another range of experiences deserving in every way the hard name of "sin," and you begin to realize the immeasurable importance of a gospel of salvation. Never did a generation stand more in need of it than we do today.

Saved from sin—what can that possibly mean today, you want to know. And the answer is not hard to find. Sin, as our fathers saw it, is personal hostility to the will of God. To be saved from sin may mean many things, but none are more important than these: to be saved from the spiritual death of sin; from sudden repudiation of or studied treason to our loyalty to God; from the temptation and the fact of having put first things in subordinate places; from the slow stripping of life of its sense of worth and value; from the weakening of great relationships through blindness to their meaning or unwillingness to assume the obligations or disciplines essential to them. Sin, so conceived, is not a matter primarily of biology (as our fathers tended to regard original sin), but it does deal with the defacement, the distortion of human personality. Sin, therefore, is not the creation of theologians, though it is the object of their undivided concern; it is rather an all-too-common and always tragic experience in human life.

I have known such sinners as these: people who know what they ought to do both for their own welfare and that of their loved ones, yet who will not do it; people who know what they ought to stand for and by (if they profess to be Christians), yet who will not do it; people who have the verbal forms of great religious convictions, yet who lack wholly the ethical courage to give them life and vitality; people who love the peace, serenity, and quietness of solemn worship services in churches, yet who insist that religion cannot concern itself in any direct manner with the evils which flourish in the market places of life. I say I have known people like this, and, God help me, I too frequently have been and too easily am tempted to be such a person myself.

Like Paul, "the good that I would I do not; the evil that I would not, that I do." This, I am sure, is another way of saying that *sin is real*—personal hostility to the will of God is real in the lives of all of us, from relative sinners to relative saints.

We are beginning to take with utmost seriousness another dimension in the meaning of sin. It means social, institutional, conventional hostility to the will of God as well. We can never be grateful enough for the heritage of good and honorable things our fathers have made possible for us. Yet we have inherited many things that are, ethically and tragically, evil.

Consider, for example, the vicious prejudices among races, religions, and cultures. Creatures of no one event or generation, yet, gathering momentum like an avalanche, they are threatening the annihilation of everyone today. Add to these the incredible blunders that, in the name of peace treaties, have burrowed their way deep in the emotions and spread their infamy on the maps of the world. Within the last two hundred years nationalism has become a new religion, demanding a fierce, unreasoning, blindly irrational loyalty to country. There is always that love of personal gain, by whatever means, that has drafted the principles of one kind of economic order after another—leading inevitably to misery, inequity, and injustice.

When we say that sin is real, that it means basically personal and social hostility to the will of God, and when we say that we have a gospel of salvation, we are not only talking directly to one of the greatest needs and hopes of our day, but we had better be prepared to talk facts with utmost clarity.

One of the finest contemporary descriptions of a lost soul and the meaning of salvation came from the pen of Dr. William Ernest Hocking.[16] Because of its incisiveness as well as comprehensiveness, I quote it in its entirety.

What Is a Lost Soul?

Our life is a process of conversation between ourselves and the whole of the world in which we live. It is possible for human beings to talk to one another with their lips and be remote from one another in their hearts. Falsehood and selfishness create chasms between man and man; and the professions of friendship have always to be tested by the inner facts of sincerity and love.

These principles of human intercourse are also valid for this continuous conversation between the individual and his world. A man may be at odds with his world and he may be in harmony with his world; but there is everything in human experience to give us, as we look at the facts of nature and at the facts of history, a sense of loneliness in the presence of the great unknown. There it is, in its immensity, operating according to natural laws, opaque, silent, inscrutable, frequently cruel, and apparently uninterested in the lot of us poor human beings.

Then, too, in the group which we call humanity, there is something massive, something immense, something in the preoccupation of individuals and of social wholes, which makes the individual person feel that he is alone and uncared for, and that his only possible policy is one of struggling with might and main to gain for himself by snatching from the whole what he can.

Now in so far as a person maintains this picture of the universe, he is a lost soul: he cannot look at the world with confidence. He cannot see beyond that horizon which closes his life in nothingness and means the ultimate wiping out of the race. He cannot see any meaning in his life beyond what he can enforce by dint of his own self-assertion. In so far as we feel in ourselves this absence of confidence, this absence of certainty, this fear of calamity and of death, this servitude to chance, this rebellion, this poor guesswork of questions thrown into the void and receiving no answers, we are lost.

The only thing which could come to us to make it possible for us to deal in full honor and trust with the world, and with each other, is some assurance *that these appearances are not true;* some assurance that out of the silence there is a voice which speaks, and in the callous machinery of the cosmos there is a heart which cares, and a purpose which plans. *Whatever brings this assurance comes as a savior.* The savior, to you, is that event, that person, that word, in which you can say, "The Universe speaks to me"; "God speaks to me."

I believe that Christianity has given the name of Christ to what we might call the voice of God to man; and I like to think of the word Christ as meaning what we might call the *human face of God.* The veil of reality has been broken, as though some being had come toward us out of the darkness; and we can say to the universe, not "*It* is there," but "*Thou* art there, and Thou carest for me."

It is this message which Christianity, I think, brings to men, and brings with an assurance and definiteness which we find in no other religion.

IV

What is the essential structure of the Christian philosophy of salvation? A generation better versed than ours in the whole range of theological vocabulary would expect and be given its answer in the form of a doctrine of soteriology, i.e., a philosophy of salvation cast in classical theological terms. What we shall be doing is to center attention upon the basic facts which must enter into the basic doctrine of philosophy.

In 1921 an English scholar named John Hutton wrote a book entitled *The Proposal of Jesus.* In it he gives the outline of the Christian philosophy of salvation. He says, "What our distracted world really needs is a complete submission of human motives to the will of God, a radical renovation of human society refashioning it upon the principle of faith in the righteousness of God . . ."[17] This he calls "the proposal of Jesus" as he came "to seek and to save that which was lost." Obviously, this proposal for the salvation of men and history is too probing to be reduced to and then dismissed as platitudes. It amounts to this: (1) To be saved, man must seek a new foundation for his life in the will of God; (2) to be saved, a society must seek a new foundation for its laws, conventions, and total life in the righteousness of God.

Such a proposal was laughed to scorn by the self-styled realists of Jesus' day—a fate which it has suffered almost uninterruptedly for nineteen centuries. And, more frequently than not, accredited leaders in the Christian churches have devised ways of tempering the high winds of his austere convictions to the shorn lambs of comfort-seeking Christians and outright pagans who want only to graze contentedly in the pastures of privilege. It took the combined efforts of a succession of great men in lay movements, both within and outside the orthodox churches, to keep the gospel of salvation alive and to take it as "the good news" to those who had not heard it.

This much can be said with certainty: while Jesus was an idealist in the best sense of that term, he was not an idealist isolated from the realities of life; he was a prophet peering intently into its depths, seeking to discern the movement and meaning of the will of God therein. He made his proposal to a world that was as tortured, distracted, and chaotic as ours today, and he made it in all seriousness, believing that it could and should be interpreted in terms of the great problem areas in human life and history. I know of no other way to account for the parable of the two foundations which concludes the Sermon on the Mount and the urgency of such ethical imperatives that sum up such parables as the Good Samaritan. It may ease our consciences a bit when some religious leaders tell us that he preached the gospel of perfection and, manifestly, the achievement of this is beyond the reach of men like us. Therefore, we are to accept his teachings *in principle* as being true of the world if it were the world of God's intention, but since it is a far different world due to human sin, we cannot take Jesus' teachings as our guides in actual practice. This line of reasoning finds its sufficient answer in the simple fact that not only do Jesus' teachings plainly intend to be taken seriously, but also his hearers knew it and were either repelled by them or led to try to put them into practice. Unless some such realistic acceptance of them as being relevant to moral problems is possible, then they must be set aside as ethically irrelevant. Yet, as we work our way into the meaning of Jesus' proposal for the world, we shall find it most relevant, bringing in fact, a new sense of values and a new sense of direction, both of which we need if we are ever to get out of the cultural, moral, and political impasse in which civilization now finds itself.

Three basic principles or affirmations recur steadily throughout the teachings of Jesus, constituting the outline of both his proposal and the Christian philosophy of salvation: (1) God is the supreme fact in life and in the world; (2) all men are His children; (3) life is a divine trust. These are not so much ideas to be weighed as paths to be followed. If we follow them to their end, we shall find ourselves in possession of a far different view of life and history than we now have, and, what is immeasurably more difficult, under the compulsion to be instruments of the redemptive will of God as He seeks to transform the world from what it is to what it ought to be.

When Jesus affirmed that God is the supreme fact in life and history, he was echoing the century-old faith of his forefathers. God is the creator, sustainer, and redeemer of the world. No absentee deity, His will for life is the deepest truth about it and should be sought with all diligence. His will is good; He can be trusted in all things both to sustain what is good, to rebuke and attempt to redeem what is evil. When man puts his trust in God and is able to keep it there, he becomes invulnerable to "the arrows of outrageous fortune," finding in God the strength he needs for living in adversity as well as in prosperity.

It follows, then, that all men are the children of God—rich and poor, good and evil, ill and well, joyful and sorrowful, white and colored—all are His children. This, I suppose, is one of the greatest needs of men—to know themselves to be the sons of God. This is the only effective answer to the fear so well put by one of Dostoevski's agents, "I am *X* in an indeterminate equation. I am a sort of phantom in life who has lost all beginning and end, and who has forgotten his own name."[18] There are many differentials in life, some more significant than others, to which we refer when we seek to "identify" ourselves. We may say we are "white," or a Methodist, or a Catholic, or an American, etc., and such statements do indicate areas of relative importance. Much if not most of the social tragedy of our times grows out of the assumption that differences like these which do set us apart from each other in some sort of identifiable way are more important than anything which might unite us. In this spirit, we (no matter which group we may be in) set out to try to transform the status quo until it reaches the point of our maximum advantage—and there we both try to freeze it and to damn if not destroy anyone who would change it! Once accept these differentials as being more important than any other fact about mankind, and the stage is set for a continuation of man's inhumanity to man. W. E. B. DuBois has described the true source of our trouble:

> Herein lies the tragedy of the age: not that men are poor—all men know something of poverty; not that men are wicked—who is good? Not that men are ignorant—what is truth? Nay, but that men know so little of men.[19]

And it is just this knowledge that Jesus' proposal calls to man's attention. For deeper than the things which separate us is this fact which binds us into an unbreakable unity: We are the children of God. Any purpose, plan, policy, convention, law, person, or institution which does not base itself upon this foundation is candidate for conversion by the gospel of salvation.

When man accepts himself and others as children of God, his

life acquires a new source of meaning, worth, and purpose. With this comes also a new sense of tolerance and understanding, for no man knows God perfectly and no man has lost Him completely. God is too great, too good, for the wisest and best of us to be able to say, "We know Him as He is!" He is too loving, too compassionate, to forsake even the worst of us, the difference between sinner and saint being always a matter of degree and never one of kind. God's rain and sunshine fall upon the just and the unjust alike. There is no room in this view for self-righteousness and pride—those twin distorters of a proper estimate of another. Nor is there any room for the depersonalization of man which has been so marked a characteristic of the economic and international policies of modern history. Napoleon is a fit symbol of this trend when, in defense of the French conscription law in 1805, he told Metternich, "I can use up twenty-five thousand men a month." He did; in fact, he used up two million six hundred and thirteen thousand men in the twelve years of the Napoleonic Wars. To depersonalize man in this fashion is more than a crime against man; it is a sin against God—if all men are the children of God.

Pascal was summing up the estimate of self and others as is nurtured by Jesus' proposal: "Let man know his value. Let him love himself, for there is in him a nature capable of good; but let him not, for this reason, love the vileness that is in him." When the Christian faith teaches man that he is the child of God, it is trying to teach him the true foundation for valuing himself and others. It saves modern man from the cry of desperation which produces confessions like this: "For all of us, from the most intelligent to the least intelligent, are weary of the materialist pummeling we have received during the last seventy or eighty years. . . ."[20] And unless man can be delivered from this sort of despair and lifted to a new plateau of understanding of himself, he is lost indeed. Yet the only answer to the materialist is, as it has always been, that of religious faith which proclaims the palpable inadequacy of materialism both as a valid interpretation of fact and as a guide to life, and, in addition, advances its own profound beliefs about the nature of reality and life and bids men refashion their thinking and living accordingly.

Implicit in the assertion that God is the supreme fact in life and history and that all men are the children of God is the claim that life is a divine trust. Life, everyday living, is a dealing with God. Life is our truest word to and from God. For Jesus, words, as words, did not carry much weight. *The deed*—that is the real revelation of a man's faith. "By their fruits ye shall know them," is Jesus' timeworn admonition. Our possessions and human relationships are sacred in the exact sense that they involve the divine intention as truly as our own. Property, food, clothing, security—all these are important providing they do not become ends in themselves but actually bring men closer to the Kingdom of God. But the Kingdom of God must come first in a man's thought and life if he would correctly appraise himself and his work. When a man sees in bigger granaries ease of soul, he has lost his soul. When a man's anxiety about tomorrow takes possession of him, he loses today as well as tomorrow. When a man worries so much about food and clothing that he forgets the purpose of life itself, he has not kept first things first.

Thus Jesus went through the great fears and worries of men pointing out the plain fact that faith in the fact and the reality of the will of God is the real and the only answer. Long before Dostoevski, he saw this truth: "For the secret of man's being is not only to live but to have something to live for. Without a stable conception of the object of life, man would not consent to go on living, and would rather destroy himself than remain on earth, though he had bread in abundance."[21] There are, of course, two other alternatives than those suggested by the Russian novelist. One, already mentioned, is the conclusion of the currently popular philosophical movement in Europe which holds that man makes up his own rules and is at liberty therefore to live for any end he chooses, be it mountain or molehill. The other is suggested by the beautifully phrased confession of one of the literary critics in a letter to a friend: "People like myself have got to take a direction finally, we can't go on forever being bright or smart or naughty young things."[22]

Salvation from the falsity and the futility of such alternatives is to be found in the will of God and nowhere else—of this Jesus was certain. From that day on men by the millions have found good reason to share his faith. They understood the Hindu who, upon reading the parable of the prodigal son for the first time, exclaimed, "This man must have known me. He has told my story."[23]

We are learning the hard way that unless life is treated as a divine trust, the human situation rapidly becomes intolerable. Treat other persons, or races, or nations as means to your end, as instruments in purposes that serve your own welfare, and you, to the extent that you are successful, have made revolution inevitable. Yet the illusions nourished by power, wealth, and position continue to darken our perception of this fact. Military power is such an impressive fact that in the day of confusion of uncertainty men turn to it as a kind of guarantor of security. We read the judgment of a military analyst: "We are the masters of our fate." We hear the judgment of a news commentator on world affairs: "History is what men make it. If we do not choose to get out and make it what we want, at whatever cost, it is going to be made for us by other men who are willing to work at it."[24]

Such counsels are more than futile, they are fatal. To say that history is what we make it is to utter a most dangerous half-truth; the full version of which is this: history is what God permits us to make it.[25] It is the scene of our dealings with God and His with us. It is true that we are free to try to build any kind of social order we choose; but the validity of our plan and the permanence of our building are determined by a Power entirely beyond our control. James Anthony Froude, after a lifetime spent in the study of history, bears this impressive witness: "One lesson and only one, history may be said to repeat with distinctness; that the world is built somehow on moral foundations; that in the long run it is well with the good; in the long run it is ill with the wicked."

These principles constitute the main movements in Jesus' proposal for the salvation of the world. No one knew better than he that they prefigured the complete transformation of the person or group which will take them as guides for living. When Zacchaeus began to walk in the new-found light of life, Jesus said, "This day has salvation come to this house." The austerity of his invitation to discipleship still leaves one speechless: "The foxes have holes, the birds of the air have nests, but the Son of Man has not where to lay his head," and "No man having put his hand to the plow and looking back is fit for the kingdom of God."

Douglas Clyde Macintosh writes thus of the social implications of Jesus' proposal: "He looked for a new order of things. The old order would be destroyed by his new gospel, as old wineskins are burst by new wine, or a very old garment has its rent made worse by the attempt to patch it. Jesus said 'farewell to reform' and announced nothing less than a social revolution—a revolution which was to be no whit less radical in its realization for its being spiritually inaugurated. . . ."[26]

Almost from the beginning of his ministry, Jesus sensed the costliness of such convictions. The transformation of life and history plainly implicit in them could not be accomplished by verbal proclamation of them; they had to "come alive," to become incarnate in the lives of men and in history before they could become the way of salvation. He made it clear that one could know the vocabulary of religion, could say, "Lord, Lord," yet not know or be known by its transforming power. Looking back upon the faith of Jesus as he went among his fellows and on the faith they meted out to him, Paul counseled his hearers to remember, "Ye are bought with a price." The Cross became the symbol not alone of the fate of Jesus but of the price which any man who follows him must be prepared to pay. Whether the gospel of salvation spreads slow or fast, every inch of advance is "bought with a price"—that is the unqualified testimony of nineteen hundred years of Christian history.

V

The gospel of salvation, so conceived, has always been a mediated salvation. Jesus himself is the great Mediator—one who reveals the will of God to the life of men in and through his own life and teachings. It is important to remember that he made this proposal for the world not to the world but to his disciples. He knew that they were to be the messengers of the coming of the Kingdom of God. Consequently, he exerted every effort to prepare them for their responsibility, outlining the nature of the Kingdom, stressing the unique character of citizenship in it, warning them that the wrath of men would break over their heads, yet counseling them to take courage from the fact that the power of the love of God would be with them always.

Fortunately for us, his confidence in them was, for the most part, well placed. Drawn to him by their deep affection for him, they were fertile seeds for the planting of the gospel of salvation. His proposal for the world strikes its strongest roots in those who love him. Seldom does it appear as important or even relevant to those who do not. But it is quite clear that it is not enough for men to respect Jesus as a "good man," or a "great teacher," or a "great prophet"—not enough, that is, if they are to become the effective witnesses for him. Men must be able to say with Thomas, "My Lord and my God," or with Clement of Alexandria, "He turned our sunsets into sunrises," or with Horace Bushnell, ". . . Jesus Christ, the Divine Word, coming out from God, to be incarnate with us, and be the vehicle of God and salvation to the race," or with Henry Sloane Coffin, "The Church declares that her Lord is with her followers always, that his spirit dwells and works unceasingly in and through the fellowship of believers, that her God is a 'very present help'" if they are to feel the compulsion that He has made them mediators of the gospel of salvation.

Sometimes the mediation comes through the worship services of the church; sometimes in the privacy of a personal conference with the counselor. It may find expression in the church school or the pastoral call; or it may grow out of the common life of the fellowship. In any and every event and activity the church should seek to be "the house of God" and its fellowship "the people of God" in the literal sense that, weighed down with human imperfections though they are, there is a deep and unshakable loyalty to the will of God as seen in Jesus Christ and a willingness to bear witness to it in the presence of human need.

Confronted by our frailty and fallibility, it is small wonder that we, like Jeremiah, shrink from the task of proclaiming by lip and in life a gospel which clearly intends to bring life and history under the redemptive judgment and activity of the God of the universe, as revealed in Jesus Christ. Yet that is the clear meaning of believing in salvation.

VI

In summary, then, when we say that we believe in salvation we are calling attention to a certain set of facts, among which these are prominent:

1. Men continue to get lost in their personal lives as well as their relationships with other people; they are lost in the precise sense of being unable "to understand their present or to plan their future."

2. The Christian understanding of life is based on certain principles which, when taken as guides for living, actually give men a new sense of direction and nourish the strength and hope to follow it with some degree of success and renewal of life.

3. The "gospel of salvation" becomes a power in human life in history when it was enunciated by and incarnate in the life and teachings of Jesus Christ. He became thereby God's saving work in human life and society.

4. The gospel of salvation continues to be a transforming power when the fellowship of Christian believers presents Jesus Christ as the Savior of the world and mediates his gospel in every efficient way to the needs of men and society.

5. As we profess our belief in the gospel of salvation and seek to use its basic principles as guides for our living we are not alone; the unconquerable power of the immeasurable love of God enters into our life and we partake in measure of its light and leading so long as we seek to be its instruments in the redemption of the world.

THE DEATHLESS VIRTUE

THE IMPERISHABLE thing in Hawthorne is not, as some have said, his prose. . . . His one deathless virtue is that rare thing in any literature, an utterly serious imagination. It was serious, and so it was loving; it was loving, and so it could laugh; it could laugh, and so it could endure the horror it saw in every human heart. But it saw the honor there along with the horror, the dignity by which in some eternity our pain is measured. Hawthorne was out of touch with his time, and he will be out of touch with any time. He thought man was immortal: a mistake made only by the greatest writers.

—MARK VAN DOREN, *Nathaniel Hawthorne*

XII

We Believe in IMMORTALITY

I

A discussion of this theme could not well have occurred earlier in our series of studies. This, notwithstanding the arresting fact that, in ordinary conversation about religious matters, the idea of immortality does not bide its time until all other basic conceptions have been discussed. Rather, it is one of the first to present itself for consideration because of its firm grip on human life and thought. It might well have been discussed in detail earlier in the book but for the fact that, more than any other single affirmation of faith, it depends for its meaning and validity upon the clarity and cogency of the other basic ideas here treated and with which it is plainly interwoven. If it is true that they demand it for their completion, it is equally true that it presupposes them for its foundation in fact and understanding. Hence the logical reason for postponing discussion of it to the end.

John Calvin was keenly aware of this necessity when he writes that he has deferred his discussion of immortality until ". . . the reader, after receiving Christ as the Author of complete salvation, may learn to soar higher, and may know that he is invested with heavenly glory and immortality, in order that the whole body may be conformed to the Head; as in his person the Holy Spirit frequently is an example of the resurrection."[1] Nor was Calvin unaware of the difficulty of the task he was undertaking: "To this subject [the doctrine of immortality], the most important of all, let us give an attention never to be wearied by length of time."[2]

All Christian creedal formulations, ancient and modern, affirm faith in immortality. The older ones link it with the idea of the resurrection of the body, the stately sentiment being, "I believe in 'the resurrection of the body, and the life everlasting.' " The Nicene Creed, with its usual explicitness, says, "And I look for the resurrection of the dead, and the life of the world to come." Even the casual reader will not miss the fact that there can be a significant difference between the phrases "resurrection of the body" and "resurrection of the dead"; also between "the life everlasting" and "the life of the world to come." The later creeds made little or no use of the specific idea of the resurrection of the body, though they unhesitatingly affirmed that in Jesus Christ we have "the promise of our deliverance from sin and death," and "in the final triumph of righteousness, and in the life everlasting."

It would be well, then, for us to begin our study by noting both these differences in detail and the fact that they do not mar fidelity to the idea of immortality. It is entirely possible for one to believe in the idea of immortality, yet entertain serious doubts about the resurrection of the body or even of the dead, though the traditional Christian position affirms some sort of definite connection between them. From Paul's day there have been significant differences of opinion over the meaning of the idea of the resurrection of the body, but never the slightest hesitation in affirming the validity of the hope of immortality.

Dr. Reinhold Niebuhr, one of our greatest contemporary

theologians, professes to find an irreplaceable meaning in the idea of the resurrection. "The hope of the resurrection . . . embodies the very genius of the Christian idea of the historical. On the one hand it implies that eternity will fulfill and not annul the richness and variety which the temporal process has elaborated. On the other, it implies that the condition of finiteness and freedom, which lies at the basis of historical existence, is a problem for which there is no solution by any human power. Only God can solve this problem."[3] Dr. Niebuhr develops this line of thought to the conclusion that the idea of the resurrection is more truly Christian than the idea of immortality, not alone because it implies the latter but more especially because it demands an act of faith, whereas the latter is actually born of "efforts of the human mind to master and to control the consummation of life." This conclusion will convince only those who will accept as valid the now-familiar and never fully explained antipathy in Dr. Niebuhr's writings to reason and the espousal of what amounts to blind faith. Suffice it to say at this point, that an imposing array of disciplined thinkers would and do disagree with both method and conclusion. Men like A. A. Bowman[4] feel it not only plausible but necessary to center attention upon the idea of immortality rather than the notion of the resurrection. And they do this with the humility characteristic of the great rationalists of the philosophical tradition of Christianity.

But whether we isolate the idea of immortality from its earlier comrades or try to treat them as inseparable parts of the Christian valuation of life and history, the plain fact remains that we confront a difficult task when we seek to set down in order the factual foundations of the belief or systems of belief in immortality.

II

There is no Christian doctrine harder to think clearly about than this doctrine of immortality. Several obvious reasons present themselves, and, when viewed together, go a long way toward explaining the nature of the difficulty. Memories of loved ones, now dead, come thronging in, bringing much more than a simple memory-image, bringing, in fact, an intense loneliness and longing for both the renewal and the fulfillment of the severed relationship. We must be on our guard, lest the wish become father to the thought in this most important matter.

Another reason is the prominence of certain naïve, if not actually crude, conceptions of the abodes of departed ones. Every religious tradition has sired a multitude of such bizarre conceptions, and, for the most part, they are so obviously the projections of arrested desires and anguished hopes that they are both confusing and quite undependable factors in any serious attempt to think clearly about the notion of immortality.

Add to these two reasons a third, namely, our inability to get much concrete evidence to think about, to base a careful judgment upon, and you understand why it is hard to think clearly in this area. In fact, these and other difficulties tower so high that many of us would forbear thinking about immortality altogether—*if we could.* But, "there's the rub" in this matter! We cannot let it alone because it will not let us alone. Whichever way we turn, there it is demanding recognition and consideration. Death—the foe we seek to conquer—is plainly implicit in the fact of life, beginning with birth itself. As one rustic philosopher put it, "The moment you're born, you're a goner!" Death waits, and not always quietly, at the end of the journey for every man. Yet the universality and inescapability of the experience of death has not bred in man a fatalistic acceptance of the fact that it has the final word on the ultimate meaning of life. That is precisely the point at issue in the idea of immortality, and it is one of the true glories of vital religion in all ages that it has raised the point persistently and kept at its various answers until they began to rise high in the scale of rationality.

Against this background there is no occasion to wonder at the result of a contest held in recent years to determine the most popular hymn in Christian churches. The easy winner begins with the familiar words:

> Abide with me: fast falls the eventide
> The darkness deepens; Lord, with me abide.

Lest the sophisticated mind dismiss this as evidence of popular credulity, we should recall what Alfred North Whitehead said when asked to state "the central problem of metaphysics." He answered, "Abide with me; fast falls the eventide." In this he is joined by the intellectual giants of the Western world from Socrates to most of our leading thinkers today. When ordinary mortals and the keenest minds ever to grace this or any other civilization agree on the paramount importance of some one idea, there is every reason to agree with them.

So think about the belief in immortality we must—if we would be at peace with it and have any sort of peace in its presence, let alone strength from it in hours of need. But where and how shall the process of thought begin?

To those who would advise a study of various definitions, the answer must be made that, as a rule, definitions of immortality are more negative than positive. Consider these: Immortality denotes "endlessness"; immortality is the "condition or quality of being exempt from death or annihilation." Not many avenues of development open out from such beginnings. Rather than try to launch the enterprise at the point of precise definition, more is to be gained from a brief biography of the idea of immortality; a study, if you please, of the various major meanings it has carried in the Hebrew-Christian tradition. This, at least, will lead us to the human heart of the meaning the idea has carried for men. It will explain why they have treasured it, and how they have sought to justify it.

III

To begin with, the idea of immortality is one of the oldest and most universally held of all religious ideas. What we know of his customs leads us to believe that prehistoric man believed in the continuation of life after death. Yet he seems not to have faced this fact with any discernible pleasure. "The fear of the dead" was one of the most oppressive fears in his life. His most potent charms were used to ward off intruders from the spirit-world who were believed to be capable of and bent on working incalculable harm to living persons. Sacrifices and offerings were universally relied upon to keep the dead content in their own sphere of activity in the abode of the spirits.

Ancestor worship is one outgrowth of this primitive conviction that death did not end the stream of life. The duties of the son to the father were continued at the latter's grave after his death. Early Hebrew religion reveals a strong strain of ancestor worship.[5] After death, the person continues somewhere, in some form. Sacrifices are made on the grave, serving the twin purpose of providing actual food for the deceased, and preserving his honor and dignity both in the memories of mortal men and his colleagues in the spirit world. Clearly, then, there was no sharp separation between this world and the spirit-world for early men. They seem to have been regarded as upper and lower areas of one world.

In our religious tradition, the idea of ancestor worship developed slowly from primitive rites, practices, and magical notions into the more carefully formulated idea of the immortality of the nation or race. Here, as with primitive man, the idea of continuity is all-pervasive and fundamental. Although the idea of the continuity of the individual was necessarily assumed, it did not receive the main emphasis. That fell on the notion of the eternality of Israel, or the Hebrew nation. For nearly a thousand years the form of the idea of immortality urged that so long as Israel, the people, lived, all Hebrews lived. They—the living and the dead—were knit together in a vital whole, not on the principle of individuality but of community. Each one was an unending thread in a mighty, chosen race which had been guaranteed perpetuity by God Himself.

It remained for some of the great prophets of Israel to bring the idea of individual immortality to the fore. It was natural that men like Jeremiah and Ezekiel should do this because they saw their nation actually disappear in the quicksands of historical events. Confronted by this fact, they began developing the principle of individuality rather than racial or national community as the true basis for life, religion, and history. One of the inescapable corollaries of their work was a restatement of the idea of immortality in terms of the individual.

Thus the idea of immortality proved to be stronger than the notions of national or racial perpetuity, and, in fact, actually began to separate from them. When history seemed to say that the Hebrew was going to have either individual immortality or no immortality at all, the latent strengh of the notion surged up in the new formulation. The prophets did not develop it clearly, but they did express it passionately: God will not let the faithful die; "the righteous live forever! The care of them is with the most High!"

Though the idea of the immortality of the Hebrew people as

a people had hard sledding in the calamitous period from 800 to 400 B.C., it did not die. Rather, in the expectation of the Messianic Kingdom, it took a new and firmer lease on life. While the full doctrine of Messianism is of tremendous importance on many counts (we have already called attention to it several times in the study of the development of various fundamentals of our faith), two aspects of it throw light on the developing notion of immortality in the life of the Hebrew people. First, it reaffirms the simple fact of the inseparable relationship between the individual and the community. If there is to be a future blessedness for the individual, it will be found in the context of the blessed community. Second, it demands some conception of the resurrection, for the faithful who died prior to the advent of the Kingdom will, as God lives and is just, be privileged to share in it—a fact which can be realized only if the dead are permitted and enabled to live again. This, we may be sure, is the deepest reason why, in our religious tradition, some notion of the resurrection is invariably associated with the idea of immortality.

The New Testament breathes a spirit of unquestioning confidence in the immortality of the individuals in the Blessed Community—the Kingdom of God. No mere continuation of life for the individual is asserted, but the continuation and the perfection of the fellowship found with one another in Christ. Thus the Christian faith, from the outset, draws together on a new level of spiritual insight and conviction, the two notions which had had an uneasy relationship with each other throughout most of Hebrew history—the immortality of the individual and that of the Chosen People. In effect, the Christian conception, as suggested in the Gospels, accepts and makes permanent the hard-won advances recorded in the latter stages of Messianic thought—notably the insight into the inseparability of the individual and the group—in the providence of God. But no passive acceptance of this idea is found in the early Christian community. For the Messianic idea provides the actual structure of the historical arguments and claims by and through which the evangelists presented their interpretation of the meaning of God in Jesus Christ. So far from being an addendum to Judaism (as is sometimes claimed), the Christian position is an authentic miracle in the spiritual transformation of an inherited idea.

One of the most significant New Testament scholars of the recent past, Johannes Weiss, devoted the major efforts of a lifetime to the study of the formation and the development of "primitive Christianity."[6] This means, in general, the fifty years immediately following the crucifixion of Jesus. One of the most rewarding sections of Weiss' great work deals with the rise of "the new doctrine."[7] Here we see, in amazing panorama, the ferment of ideas which agitated the early Christians. Although they are in complete (but not unquestioning) agreement on the fact that Jesus, though killed, continued to live, they appealed to at least three different bodies of evidence. These are found in the "narratives of [his] appearances," the "resurrection stories," and the "stories of the grave." Paul was acquainted with the first two, but, as Dr. Weiss says, "Paul . . . never even suggests the empty tomb."[8] I cite this as but one illustration of the way in which the early Christian community wrestled with such evidence as it had or thought it had for the reality of the idea that, in Jesus, there is an actual guarantee of immortality to the faithful.

What a warmly human idea of immortality actually radiates the New Testament! It is a condition or a place in which "God shall wipe away all tears"; where the injustices suffered in life will be rectified, where the true valuation of life is made clear, where you enter into the place prepared for you, where unswerving loyalty to God will be rewarded by His simple salutation to weary travelers, "Well done, good and faithful servant. Enter thou into thy rest." Deeper and more lasting than the various serious disputes which the New Testament records over details of immortality and the meaning and value of the resurrection of the body was the conviction that the truest statement of the work of Christ was this: "I am the resurrection and the life, saith the Lord, he that believeth on me, though he were dead yet shall he live!" Though the writers of the Gospel of John, the Epistle to the Hebrews, and the Epistle to the Corinthians start their interpretation of the work of Christ from different points on the spiritual compass, they move steadily until they reach the center of this common conviction that, in him, sin and death have found their ultimate answer, God's answer.

IV

When we are asked to give a reason for "the hope that is within us," what can we say? No man can speak for another in such a matter as this, yet each is obligated to study the thoughts and conclusions of others, to examine his own in the light of either common consent or incisive insight, and then witness to his own belief. I can only share my own reasons for believing that immortality is not only a hallowed but also an essentially true and immeasurably valuable religious idea. We do well to recall Renan's warning: "The day in which the belief in an after-life shall vanish from the earth will witness a terrific moral and spiritual decadence. Some of us perhaps might do without it, provided only the others hold fast. But there is no lever capable of raising an entire people if once they have lost their faith in the immortality of the soul."[9] I cite this as evidence of the importance, not of the validity, of the idea of immortality. And we need to remember always that much more than our own private interests are involved in the success or failure of the undertaking to state clearly and persuasively what we mean by and why we believe in immortality.

There are, it seems to me, three strong arguments for the validity of the idea of immortality: the argument from history, from logic, and from intuition.

Argument from History

I confess that I am increasingly impressed by the argument from history. To one who is tempted to dismiss it as "circumstantial evidence," I would call attention to the plain fact that neither in our law nor in any other area of life do we treat circumstantial evidence lightly. Even if there were no other form of evidence for immortality, the very strength of this kind would be persuasive, though not of itself conclusive for many of us.

But it is an impressive fact when put in a series of factually accurate statements:

Belief in immortality is coextensive with man in history.

Wherever the idea of immortality has emerged in a clear-cut, definite form in the latter stages of a religious tradition (as in Judaism, Buddhism), it has met so deep a need and has so successfully withstood the tests of time and questioning that it has not only never been discarded but has actually become one of the central convictions of their tradition.

The Hebrew-Christian tradition has developed and cherished (but never forsaken) the idea of immortality for nearly four thousand years. In the strength of this idea over six thousand generations of Christians have faced life with poise and death with peace.

Not only ordinary people but also the pivotal figures in the philosophical and religious traditions of the Western world have either openly affirmed or opened the way to a vigorous belief in the eternality of life.

The idea of immortality has been subjected to and modified by the severest questions man and human experience can devise; yet it has neither been made untenable thereby, nor have we found a way of making life tenable without it. The same critical intelligence that scotched the idea of witchcraft and demons, when turned on immortality, only purged it of many of its crudities and let its light shine with greater clarity and usefulness.

Although recognizing the limitations of such a summation of evidence, I recall Lincoln's dictum: "You may fool all the people some of the time; you can even fool some of the people all the time; but you can't fool all of the people all the time." It must be clear to all that the choice before us in this matter is this: either we dismiss, or try to dismiss, all history as a monstrous liar and cheat, or we accept as fair the assumption that there is something essentially true in the idea of immortality.

Argument from Logic

When I speak of the argument from logic, I do not mean to limit attention to the philosophical discipline of logic; rather, I want to study the clear logical implications of certain bodies of fact. A fuller and more accurate description of this procedure would be to label it "the argument from logical inference." Its purpose is to call attention to certain facts whose meanings carry significant implications for the idea of immortality.

The first and most important fact, obviously, is the reality of God. Without attempting to do more than to suggest the evidential basis of this idea as developed in an earlier study, it will be enough to say that the word "God" is a finger pointing at the observable and public facts of order, growth, and judgment in the world. These are the firm foundation upon which the idea of God rests, though, like Mount Everest, its towering pinnacles of meaning pierce the clouds of our ignorance and can be glimpsed only fleetingly by rare spirits for whom the clouds seem to lift. Take the fact of God at anything like face value, and we are in possession of one of the most powerful arguments for the reality of immortality.

Professor A. E. Taylor gives it as his opinion that the first and most important step toward establishing the idea of immortality is to establish the idea of God. He points out that in the Christian tradition this is almost an inescapable procedure, "Wherever we find a thinker who puts his human immortality in the first place, or tries to base his conviction of the reality and worth of the gift on any ground independent of the character of the Giver, we may be sure that we are dealing with one who is at best no more than half a Christian."[10]

Serious-minded Christians have always sensed this truth; without exception they use the fact of God (either assumed or demonstrated by some means or other) as the firm foundation upon which they rest all other affirmations of faith. John Calvin, for example, would not agree with some of our contemporaries that all we have to go on is "intimations of immortality." He would argue that while we have these, to be sure, we also have logical inferences from the facts of God and the revelations of His meaning in Jesus Christ. The contemporary British philosopher, A. A. Bowman, agrees in rooting his belief in or hope for immortality in the fact of God: ". . . the hope of immortality is part of our experience of God. . . ."[11]

God cannot be resolved into a fantasy of wishful thinking, as many contemporary critics have said. God is a fact—a fact whose nature and meaning are knowable and known (at least in part) through the investigations of science as well as in the fact of growth in human life. Since some of the most eminent scientists of our day have unhesitatingly affirmed their conviction that reality as known reveals a definite structure and pattern deserving the designation of purpose and intelligence, religion need not be either apologetic or hesitant about using the idea of God as the firm foundation on which to erect the superstructure of its total confession of faith.

As the first step, then, we note the simple fact that we live in a world which is essentially and reliably orderly. It is a cosmos, not a chaos. As Alfred North Whitehead once put it, "This world . . . responds to the demands of reason, and . . . what the mind sees to be true and necessary will be found to hold good in the natural order." This conviction clears away at a stroke both the ancient fear that man is but one among many incidents in a cosmos which itself seems to be incidental, and the contemporary suspicion that man is an accident (and a not too happy one!) in the blind surging of creative power in reality. Now we speak with a kind of humble confidence about Purpose in the universe, including human life and history, and we seek a fuller understanding of the meaning of that Purpose not in seance and trance, but by studying its activity *in life and in history.* To put it in the most general terms, the universe is not only not hostile to life but actually provides the conditions for its existence. What this can and does mean by way of logical inference for the idea of immortality is best seen by appraising the fact of growth in life.

The fact of growth, producing as it has the emergence and development of life, constituting as it does the process by which individual life and relationships mature and give life meaning, is a most significant approach to the notion of immortality. For it begins with the incontrovertible assertion that reality is essentially dynamic, purposeful, or, as religion has claimed, spiritual—that is, filled with Spirit. The whole life process is an essential part of reality as known and experienced; we are at home here; life as we know it and experience it is so dependable that it is as fundamental a clue to the nature of reality as can be obtained. Any view of reality which presumes to get at fundamental facts about the universe by either scaling down or canceling out the integral relationship between life as we know it and the essence of reality is a fraud on the face of it, because, as has been pointed out to materialists for two thousand years, life and knowledge must be assumed to be real in even any effort to deny them reality.

In human life, therefore, and in the process by which it came to its present stature and in which it finds its vital meanings, we have a fundamental insight into the nature, workings, and meanings of reality. Life, as we know it and experience it, is always dynamic, is streaming into the future, is seeking a more perfect fulfillment in terms of what is yet to be. Life is always incomplete in the sense that at any given moment it is both actual and potential. Every idea, relationship, and undertaking exhibits this dual nature because they are of the essence of life. Thus the creative process by which life came into being, through which human life reached its present stature, continues to be the very essence of human personality.

The French writer, Lecomte du Noüy, has put the matter this way: "Until man appeared, evolution strove only, from an observer's point of view, to manufacture an organ, the brain, in a body capable of assuring its protection. All the ancestors of man were but irresponsible actors playing an imposed part in a play which they did not understand, or try to understand. Man continues to play his part but wants to comprehend the play. . . . This transformation of man into an active, responsible individual is the new event which, more than any other, characterizes man."[12]

It is, then, this fact of human life which introduces a new dimension of meaning into our thought about reality. Just how different this dimension makes the total picture is seen not only in the further thinking of Lecomte du Noüy but also in that of another scientist, Sir Arthur Eddington. Du Noüy writes, "The religious spirit is in us. It preceded the religions, and their task as well as that of the prophets, of the initiated, consists in releasing, directing, and developing it. This mystical aspiration is an essentially human trait. It slumbers at the bottom of our souls awaiting the event, or the man, capable, in the manner of an enzyme, of transforming it into true mysticism, into faith."[13]

Sir Arthur Eddington agrees, "We all know that there are regions of the human spirit untrammeled by the world of physics. In the mystic sense of the creations around us, in the expression of art, in a yearning toward God, the soul grows upward and finds fulfillment of something implanted in its nature."[14]

Serious conclusions like these deliver us (let us hope forever) from the prevalent idea that man is either a ball rolling around on a cosmic billiard table, or "just an animal." He is not only an animal; he is a very special kind of animal, being a value-perceiving, value-serving, and value-incarnating animal. That sort of "animal" is man, and the clue to his humanity, to his personality, is to be found in his relationship to the value-structure of the universe.

To speak of a "value-structure" of the universe is not to speak in mysteries, though there are heights and depths of mystery in it that man will never measure. This awkward phrase designates the fact that the values by and through which we live are not our own creations. They are the laws of growth for life. Generations of men come and go, but these laws remain, as eternal as the heavens. The history of life, especially in its ethical and religious outreach, is the history of man's efforts to find and be guided by these values. In Christian thought they came to bear the great names, Truth, Beauty, Goodness, and Love. So far from being merely philosophical abstractions, these are certain kinds of concrete relationships between man and man, as well as between man and the universe. The good life, the abundant life, is one characterized by such relationships. They represent the only way life can truly "unfold," "realize itself," become creative. Every basic relationship and institution, every reliable moral and ethical standard, every useful convention and custom gathers its meaning from some one or all of these values. They are the laws of life, the conditions of survival as well as of progress and growth for mankind.

The seeker after evidence for the idea of immortality cannot help being arrested by this relationship between life and the value-structure of the universe, between man and God. Man is the one form of life that must see, at least dimly, and serve, at least in part, these values in order to live. The long and far-from-ended struggle away from barbarism toward some kind of humane, stable form of life is, in strict essence, a struggle to incorporate these great values in the common thought and life of mankind in a more effective manner. Of them can it be said, "If they be lifted up, they will draw all men unto them." As Nicolai Hartmann[15] has written, such values are never morally neutral; man sees them as the "ought-to-be" of life, and, having seen them, they become the "ought-to-do" of his own life. And as man follows their lead, not only is his life transformed, but he becomes an instrument in the transformation of the common life.

Man, then, is a creature of *eternal worth and values*. He has no recognizably human life apart from God, the value-structure of the universe. The driving force within his life is always this sense of incompleteness, the sense of being too far away from God, of knowing that God is seeking so to transform his life as to make him a worthy child of God. Saint Augustine would say, "Thou hast made us for thyself, and our souls are restless until they rest in thee."

It is a logically warranted inference to reason that there is a profound affinity between life and the value-structure of the universe, to conclude that life is in some essential way not so much akin to as inseparable from the values which are both within, yet always beyond, man at any given moment in his life. This being true, no sharp line can be drawn between the eternal nature of God and the temporal nature of man. Rather, man is a creature of eternal worth, is the child of an eternal destiny.

Argument from Intuition

It is far harder to present this argument in a clear and convincing manner than either of its predecessors. The main reason for the trouble is the fact that it is never possible to state an intuitive insight in a completely satisfactory way. Just as a "hunch" is not a reasoned conclusion, an intuitive insight is not a logical argument. The best way to illustrate both the argument from intuition and the difficulty of presenting it in any other manner than its own, is to cite some instances of it as it bears on the idea of immortality.

Paul was revealing an intuitive insight when he wrote: "I know and am persuaded that he is able to keep that which I have committed unto him against that day." Victor Hugo was not arguing like a rationalist when he wrote: "I feel in myself the future life. . . . The nearer I approach the end, the plainer I hear around me the immortal symphonies of the world which invite me. It is marvelous, yet simple. It is a fairy tale, and it is history. . . . The tomb is not a blind alley; it is a thoroughfare. It closes on the twilight, opens on the dawn."

Confronting the obvious incompleteness of the life of almost every great man, Dr. William Ernest Hocking feels therein the "intimations of immortality": ". . . To cease at the point of attainment is to lose the full meaning of that attainment. From the mere logic of meaning, there is no moment at which conscious existence could appropriately cease."[16]

Mr. Howard Spring, one of the foremost novelists of our own day, gives this as his testament: "I stand upon the brink of the unknown, utter and unplumbed. I have never seen as much as a ghost, or met anyone whose adventures in that direction have satisfied me of validity. All I can say of a surety is that I believe in the perpetual existence of the spiritual life. If we accept, as we must, the theory of the indestructibility of matter, no less must we accept the indestructibility of the spirit with which matter is informed. Having known something of the brightness with which that spirit may burn within its corporeal envelope, I cannot believe that it is lost and utterly cast away."[17]

I cannot think of a more incisive way of putting the argument than that used by Dr. Harry Emerson Fosdick in the funeral service of a close friend: "To be sure, the mystery of immortality is very great. Any way that one looks at it, this is a mysterious universe, but I beg of you get the mystery in the right place. It's not so much in the *survival* of spiritual life that is the mystery; it is the arrival of such a life in the first place, that it is here now in souls whom we have known and loved. There is the mystery—the arrival of a quality of living, essentially timeless and eternal. Would it not be a mystery if, having arrived, it did not survive?"

As might be expected, the poets, almost to a man, make use of this appeal to substantiate their belief in immortality. They do not fashion an argument for immortality; they announce the fact of immortality.

In Wordsworth's celebrated poem, "Intimations," it is quite clear that there is nothing tentative or vague about the "intimations of immortality"; they are as real and reliable as the experience of the present life, being inseparable from it. Tennyson struggled vainly for some sort of reasoned faith in immortality—even in God—in the long poem wrought out of his reactions to the death of a friend—"In Memoriam." Yet failure in this in no wise prevents him from assuming the posture of complete faith—the faith of a child in his father—in the certainty of the eternal character of life.

Goethe sums up both the general method and attitude of the poet in his truculent query: "Do you think a coffin can impose on me?"

Consider the probing confidence which characterizes the famous lines from the *Apocrypha:*

> The souls of the righteous are in the hand of God,
> And no torment shall touch them.
> In the eyes of the foolish they seem to have died;
> And their departure was accounted to be their hurt,
> And their journeying away from us to be their ruin;
> But they are in peace.

John Henry Newman knew neither uncertainty nor fear in the presence of death:

> So long thy power hath blessed me, sure it still
> Will lead me on,
> O'er moor and fen, o'er crag and torrent, till
> The night is gone;
> And with the morn those Angel faces smile,
> Which I have loved long since and lost a while.

Let Emily Dickinson conclude this summary of poetic intimations of immortality:

> This world is not conclusion;
> A sequel stands beyond
> Invisible, as music
> But positive, as sound.
> It beckons and it baffles;
> Philosophies don't know
> And though a riddle, at the last,
> Sagacity must go.

To guess it puzzles scholars,
To gain it men have shown
Contempt of generations
And crucifixions known.[18]

In every case the author of the argument both begins with some experience or phase of his experience and moves beyond it to the conclusion which he finds within it. This he does without attempting to defend logically the validity of the step, probably because it is impossible to do so—yet, this is the crux of the matter, he *feels* so deeply the force of the conclusion that state it he must in the most positive terms. A hundred other equally convincing testimonials about immortality could be added to the ones cited above, and in every case certitude and childlike trust frame the utterance. Such intuitionists seem to say, "Leave reasoned, tentative arguments to others; we bear witness to what we know to be true!"

While rationalists have their difficulty with this ultimatum, these witnesses cannot be brushed aside as irrelevant. Add their statement of faith to the other arguments for immortality, and it both fits in and adds to the impressiveness of the total faith in the eternality of life.

V

But does this sort of arguing point to anything beyond the fact of the simple continuity of life, the intensely social human spirit inquires? If not, it does not afford a clue to the ultimate fate of the relationships which mean everything to us—friendships and family. Confronting as we must a whole multitude of pointed and specific queries arising from this general area—queries for which we shall not be able to find as clear an answer as we might desire —there is some consolation in the fact that traditional and presumably less cautious notions of immortality seemed equally unable to provide really satisfactory answers. Here are some of the specific queries that the human spirit raises:

1. Will we know one another beyond death?
2. What of the ideas of reward and punishment, both as they apply to life now and to its continuation later?
3. Do not the moral judgments which mean so much now and which seem to come to the very heart of reality point to possible ultimate separations in circles of friends, even in our own family? Indeed, if this is not thoroughly implied, are we not overvaluing the importance of these judgments here?
4. Yet who could be happy or feel that any continuation of life beyond death was other than an eternal torture if some loved one were absent?

Simple continuation of individual life obviously is not enough for the spirit of man. Almost to a man we would say, "If immortality does not mean the continuity of the relationships of life in some essential way, if it means little beyond the eternal perdurance of individuality, I am not interested in it." Purge this attitude of such pride and petulance as may well infect it, and there still remains, nonetheless, a solid core of sound instinct and fact. Life as we know it is not a multitude of little individualities paralleling each other (whether close together or far apart). It is more like an organism which welds all of the parts that constitute it into a living unity. There is reason to believe, then, that the relationships through which life unfolds, through which it finds the meaning of its existence, are, in some profound sense, inseparable from it and an eternal aspect of it. To put the matter in minimal terms, if anything about life survives, these essential relationships will because they are the conditions through which we are born and mature and through which life finds its meaning.

To put it in the strongest terms permitted by the various arguments for immortality, "The God who chose fellowship as the matrix of life, who made us deeply interdependent with each other, is as concerned about our togetherness as our individuality, both here and hereafter."

It is against some such background as this that the Christian preacher can speak thus to the hearts of his people when death comes into their midst:

"The Christian faith comes to us in hours and experiences like these with certain great assurances; assurances that have driven their roots deep in human life and history; assurances that have stood the test of time, of human experience, and of man's soberest doubts and sharpest questions. Dealing as they do with the greatest, the most important questions known to man—the meaning of life and death—it is not to be expected that they can or will dispel the darkness from every corner of our minds, but they do throw the searchlight of understanding and faith far enough ahead on the roadway of our life to enable us to walk with confidence even in hours like these.

"The first great assurance of the Christian faith is this: birth and death are essential parts of God's plan for life. The meaning of life is to be found in both together, not in either separately. Each one is surrounded by a mystery we cannot penetrate. Yet this we know from our own experience, that the life which streams from one and into the other is or seems to be essentially good. It is this experience of the essential goodness of life that religion uses as its key for unlocking the twin mysteries of birth and death—and that key either fits both or it fits neither. It is the testimony of millions of men that the divinely intended goodness which comes welling up in new form with each birth continues through life and through death. Even as birth is natural, so death is natural. One opens the door for the entrance of life in this form we know; the other closes the door as life passes on to other realms.

"The second great assurance of the Christian faith is this: the true measure of life is to be found not in quantity of years or possessions, but in quality of character. Tennyson reminds us that living is more than breathing: 'As though to breathe were life!' he exclaims. Of course, the kind of life we deeply want for ourselves and honestly honor in others is worlds removed from any simple numerical succession of threescore years and ten. The life that excites our admiration, that causes us to say to ourselves if not to others, 'That is real living!' has a qualitative richness that is quite unrelated to length of years. Rather, the true measure of life is to be found in the integrity and humility of a man; in the warmth and depth of his relationships with his friends, his neighbors, his colleagues, and his loved ones; in the determination with which he addresses himself to some of the great problems of life; in the quiet, courageous way discouragements and defeats are faced and mastered. Some men live out seventy years, and when they die, you think, 'What a long life!' Others master its meaning in the few years they live, and their lives are so radiant with intimations of immortality that you find yourself exclaiming with Emerson, 'What is excellent, as God lives, is eternal.'

"The third assurance of the Christian faith is this: love and loss go hand in hand. To love is to lose—that much is tragically clear. Where there is no love there can be no real loss. The presence of love is what makes loss so devastatingly real, so tragically hard to bear. Love is the real clue to loss—and that because it lies at the very heart of life and death. For love, even the love of God, is the ultimate fact about this universe in which we live. We are neither strangers nor orphans nor strays in this world. This is our home, and the love which is the essence of our life is at home here. When we say with John, 'God is love,' when we sing, 'O Love that wilt not let me go,' when we echo the strong words, 'The Lord is the strength of my life: of whom shall I be afraid?'—we are but saying that love, the love of God, undergirds our love, our life, and our death. Death does not stand at the heart of life and love. Love stands at the heart of life and death.

"To say this, to be able to believe it with all our mind and heart and strength, is to be prepared, at least in some essential way, for moments like these. When we stand, as all of us must, at the side of a grave that is as wide as our world, life and love, the life and the love of Eternal God, speak from the depths of our suffering—and the words we hear are the words of life and love. Then our hearts find peace, poise, and strength not alone for today but also for all of the tomorrows that God in His wisdom may give us.

"Deeper than the sorrow that now engulfs us, stronger than the loneliness that will continue to tear at our heartstrings through the years ahead, more enduring than the desolation of shattered hopes and broken dreams is this great assurance: 'Yea, though I walk through the valley of the shadow of death, I will fear no evil: for thou art with me; thy rod and thy staff they comfort me. Surely goodness and mercy shall follow me all the days of my life, and I will dwell in the house of the Lord forever.' "

REFERENCES

Chapter I. WHY A CREED IN RELIGION?

1. *Christendom,* Winter Number, 1937.

2. William Cecil Dampier, *History of Science and Its Relations with Philosophy and Religion* (New York: The Macmillan Company, 1930), p. 70.

Chapter II. WE BELIEVE IN GOD

1. Lenker edition, vol. XXIV, p. 23.

2. Charles A. Hartshorne, *Man's Vision of God* (New York: Harper & Brothers, 1941), p. ix.

3. A. E. Taylor, *Plato: The Man and His Works* (New York: Dial Press, 1936), pp. 303-4.

4. The most acute study available of this fact is George Herbert Mead's *Mind, Self and Society* (Chicago: University of Chicago Press, 1934).

5. St. John of the Cross has thus described the mystical experience. I am using the phrase in a somewhat different setting.

6. Stated most succinctly by Thomas Hobbes in his *Leviathan.*

Chapter III. WE BELIEVE IN JESUS CHRIST

1. *The Gospel of Matthew* (New York: Harper & Brothers, 1921), pp. 68-9.

2. *Ibid.,* p. 59.

3. *Bees in Amber* (New York: American Tract Society, 1913; London: Methuen & Co., Ltd., and Miss Erica Oxenham).

4. A fuller discussion of this matter is reserved for Chapter VIII.

5. George Bernard Shaw, *Androcles and the Lion,* Preface.

Chapter IV. WE BELIEVE IN THE HOLY SPIRIT

1. *The Book of Worship for Church and Home* (Nashville: The Methodist Publishing House, 1944).

2. *An Outline of Christian Theology* (New York: Charles Scribner's Sons, 1917), p. 372.

3. C. K. Barrett, *The Holy Spirit and the Gospel Tradition* (New York: The Macmillan Company, 1947), p. 2.

4. *Ibid.*, p. 41.

5. *Summa Theologica,* Question 68, Article 2, p. 221.

6. Adolph Deissmann, *Paul* (New York: Doran, 1926), p. 3.

7. Elton Trueblood, *The Knowledge of God* (New York: Harper & Brothers, 1939), p. 11.

Chapter V. WE BELIEVE IN THE BIBLE

1. William Lyon Phelps, *Human Nature in the Bible* (New York: Charles Scribner's Sons, 1923), pp. ix-x.

2. Quoted in Arthur Holt, *Christian Roots of Democracy in America* (New York: Christian Education Movement, 1941), p. 71.

3. *Ibid.*, pp. 54-5.

Chapter VI. WE BELIEVE IN THE CHURCH

1. *The Book of Worship for Church and Home* (Nashville: The Methodist Publishing House, 1944), p. 251.

Chapter VII. WE BELIEVE IN MAN

1. Reinhold Niebuhr, *The Nature and Destiny of Man* (New York: Charles Scribner's Sons, 1941), vol. I, 6.

2. *Institutes,* II, v. 19.

3. Carl L. Becker, *The Heavenly City of the Eighteenth Century Philosophers* (New Haven: Yale University Press, 1932), pp. 14-15.

Chapter VIII. WE BELIEVE IN THE FORGIVENESS OF SIN

1. Millar Burrows, *An Outline of Biblical Theology* (Philadelphia: Westminster Press, 1946), pp. 178 ff.

2. Johannes Weiss, *The History of Primitive Christianity* (New York: Wilson-Erickson, 1937), vol. I, pp. 192-3.

3. Genesis 4:23 (American Translation).

4. Paul Etrick Eldridge, *Opinion,* 1946. Reprinted by permission.

5. Quoted in Kirby Page, *Living Abundantly* (New York: Farrar & Rinehart, 1944), p. 324.

6. Gilbert Keith Chesterton, *The Ballad of the White Horse* (New York: Dodd, Mead & Company, 1911; London: Methuen & Co., Ltd.). Reprinted by permission.

7. Matthew 5:23-24 (Revised Standard Version).

8. *Fellowship,* May, 1949, p. 17.

9. Devere Allen, editor, *Above All Nations* (New York: Harper & Brothers, 1949).

10. *Ibid.,* Australian Anglican News Letter, October, 1947.

Chapter IX. WE BELIEVE IN RECONCILIATION

1. II Corinthians 5:16-6:1.

2. From a sermon preached by The Reverend Theodore P. Ferris, Rector, Trinity Church, Boston, on Sunday, September 8, 1946.

Chapter X. WE BELIEVE IN THE KINGDOM OF GOD

1. John Dewey, *Human Nature and Conduct* (New York: Henry Holt & Co., 1922), p. 23.

2. Georgia Harkness, *The Recovery of Ideals* (New York: Charles Scribner's Sons, 1937), pp. 237 *passim.*

3. Alan Hunter, *Say Yes to the Light* (New York: Harper & Brothers, 1944), p. 89.

4. William O. E. Oesterley, *The Gospel Parables in the Light of Their Jewish Background* (New York: The Macmillan Company, 1936), p. 21.

5. James Hastings and J. A. Selbie, *Dictionary of Christ and Gospels* (New York: Charles Scribner's Sons, 1906), vol. I, pp. 932-33.

6. Charles A. H. Guignebert, *Christianity, Past and Present* (New York: The Macmillan Company, 1927), p. 328.

7. *Ibid.,* p. 327.

8. C. H. Dodd, *The Parables of the Kingdom* (London: Nisbet & Co., Ltd., 1941), p. 50.

9. *Ibid.,* p. 107.

10. *Ibid.,* p. 132.

11. William Manson, *Christ's View of the Kingdom of God* (New York: Doran, 1918), pp. 24-43, *passim.*

12. Frederick C. Grant, *The Gospel of the Kingdom* (New York: The Macmillan Company, 1940), p. 134.

Chapter XI. WE BELIEVE IN SALVATION

1. S. J. Case, *Evolution of Early Christianity* (Chicago: University of Chicago Press, 1914), p. 284.

2 Charles Poore, "Book of the Times," *New York Times*, February 24, 1949, in his review of Paul McGuire's book, *There's Freedom for the Brave* (New York: Morrow, 1949).

3. Johannes Weiss, *The History of Primitive Christianity*, I, pp. 235-6.

4. G. F. Moore, *The Birth and Growth of Religion* (New York: Charles Scribner's Sons, 1923), p. 178.

5. Hastings and Selbie, *Dictionary of Christ and the Gospels*, vol. II, p. 554.

6. *International Critical Commentary* (Charles Scribner's Sons), vol. I.

7. Hastings and Selbie, *op. cit.*, vol. II, p. 552.

8. *Ibid.*, p. 554.

9. *Ibid.*, p. 555.

10. Sydney Cave, *The Doctrine of the Person of Christ* (New York: Charles Scribner's Sons, 1925), pp. 47 ff.

11. *Ibid.*, p. 45.

12. *Ibid.*, p. 99.

13. Shailer Mathews' book, *The Atonement and the Social Process* (Grand Rapids: Zonderran, 1930), is required reading for anyone who wants to study the social factors which enter into the various ideas of the atonement.

14. From speech made November 11, 1948, at the Tomb of the Unknown Soldier.

15. Albert J. Guerard, "French and American Pessimism," *Harper's Magazine*, September, 1945.

16. Chicago Theological Seminary *Register*, March, 1933, Vol. XXIII, No. 2. Reprinted by permission.

17. F. C. Grant, *The Gospel of the Kingdom* (New York: The Macmillan Company, 1940), p. 134.

18. *The Brothers Karamazov*, p. 694.

19. W. E. DuBois, *The Souls of Black Folk* (1903).

20. From a book review by Henry James Forman, Book Review Section, *New York Times,* December 3, 1939, p. 16.

21. *The Brothers Karamazov,* p. 268.

22. Harry Emerson Fosdick, *The Secret of Victorious Living* (New York: Harper & Brothers, 1934), p. 143.

23. Karl Heim, *The Power of God* (Nashville: Abingdon-Cokesbury Press, 1937), p. 89.

24. Elmer Davis, *Saturday Review of Literature,* November 29, 1941, p. 20.

25. I have developed this point in further detail in *On Final Ground* (New York: Harper & Brothers, 1946), chap. I.

26. D. C. Macintosh, *Social Religion* (New York: Charles Scribner's Sons, 1939), p. 37.

Chapter XII. WE BELIEVE IN IMMORTALITY

1. Hugh T. Kerr, *Compend of Calvin's Institutes* (Philadelphia: Presbyterian Board of Christian Education, 1939), p. 142.

2. *Ibid.,* p. 141.

3. Reinhold Niebuhr, *The Nature and Destiny of Man,* vol. II, p. 295.

4. A. A. Bowman, *Studies in the Philosophy of Religion* (New York: The Macmillan Company, 1938), vol. II, chaps. XXIV and XXV.

5. R. H. Charles, *Eschatology* (London: Block and Co., 1913, 2nd ed.), chaps. I and III.

6. Johannes Weiss, *The History of Primitive Christianity.*

7. *Ibid.,* chap. IV.

8. *Ibid.,* p. 90.

9. *Encyclopaedia Britannica,* Sydney Castle Roberts edition, XIII, p. 113.

10. A. E. Taylor, *The Christian Hope of Immortality* (New York: The Macmillan Company, 1947), p. 9.

11. A. A. Bowman, *op. cit.,* vol. II, p. 382.

12. Lecomte du Noüy, *Human Destiny* (New York: Longmans Green & Company, 1947), p. 226.

13. *Ibid.,* p. 178.

14. A. S. Eddington, *The Nature of the Physical World* (New York: The Macmillan Company, 1928), p. 327

15. *Ethics* (New York: The Macmillan Company, 1932), I, *passim.*

16. W. E. Hocking, *Thoughts on Death and Life* (New York: Harper & Brothers, 1937), pp. 199-200.

17. Howard Spring, *And Another Thing* (New York: Harper & Brothers, 1946), p. 244.

18. Emily Dickinson, *The Poems of Emily Dickinson* (Boston: Little, Brown & Co., 1931), pp. 195-6. Copyright, 1914, by Martha Dickinson Bianchi. Reprinted by permission.

INDEX